The end of the communist power

This major new interpretation analyses the inte[rn] external pressures that led to communism's term[in] the first book to link systematically the history of E[u] Prague Spring to the momentous events of 1989 t[o 1991.]

Michael Waller focuses on the essential elements of the communist monopoly of power – autarky and the closed frontier, central command planning, the leading role of the party and the psychology of democratic centralism. He reveals the internal weakness of the monopoly and traces the long process of a decline in which the communist parties of both Eastern and Western Europe played an important part. The positions of the Italian Communist Party and the Czechoslovak reformers of the Prague Spring are presented as nodal points in a process that could not culminate until the monopoly in the Soviet Union itself faltered, at which point the monopoly's characteristic mechanisms rendered its final collapse inevitable. The author's extensive familiarity with the evaluation of communist parties across Europe qualifies him well for his task.

This is essential reading for students of politics and modern history, and anyone who seeks to understand the mainsprings of communism's demise.

Michael Waller is Senior Lecturer in Government at the University of Manchester.

The end of the communist power monopoly

Michael Waller

Manchester University Press

Manchester and New York

Distributed exclusively in the USA and Canada by St. Martin's Press

Copyright © Michael Waller 1993

Published by Manchester University Press
Oxford Road, Manchester M13 9PL, UK
and Room 400, 175 Fifth Avenue, New York, NY 10010, USA

Distributed exclusively in the USA and Canada
by St. Martin's Press, Inc. 175 Fifth Avenue, New York, NY 10010, USA

British Library Cataloguing-in-Publication Data
A catalogue record for this book is available from the British Library

Library of Congress Cataloging-in-Publication Data
Waller, Michael, 1934–
    The end of the communist power monopoly / Michael Waller
    p.   cm.
    ISBN 0–7190–3819–7 (cloth). — ISBN 0–7190–3820–0 (pbk.)
    1. Communism—Europe. Eastern—History. 2. Europe, Eastern—
Politics and government—1989– 3. Communism—Soviet Union—
History. 4. Soviet Union—Politics and government—1985–1991.
5. Power (Social sciences).   I. Title.
HX240.7.A6W25   1993
321.9'2'0947—dc20   93–9671
                                                                      CIP

ISBN 0 7190 3819 7 hardback
      0 7190 3820 0 paperback

Photoset in Linotron Sabon
by Northern Phototypesetting Co. Ltd, Bolton
Printed in Great Britain
by Biddles Ltd, Guildford and King's Lynn

Contents

List of figures and tables

Figures

Tables

Note on abbreviations

Abbreviations and acronyms have been avoided as far as possible in this text. Abbreviations have, however, been used at times for the names of communist parties. These are presented in their most familiar form, whether that is in the original language or in English. Thus the Communist Party of the Soviet Union is abbreviated to CPSU, whilst the French Communist Party (*Parti communiste français*) is abbreviated to PCF, since it is these forms that are most likely to be encountered in other English-language texts.

Acknowledgements

I am grateful to Christopher Binns, Manon Lallée and John Lockhart for reading drafts of this text, either fully or in part. The responsibility for any failings that it may still contain is mine alone.

Figure 5: This figure was first published in *Studies in Comparative Communism*, Vol. 7, No. 4, 1975, p. 40, and is reproduced here with the permission of Butterworth–Heinemann, Oxford, UK.
Table 4 © RFE/RL Research Institute.
Tables 6 and 7 © Jaroslav Krejci 1972.

Introduction

The communist power monopoly in Europe

In 1989 communist parties fell or were effectively driven from power in all the Soviet Union's client states in Europe. In the Soviet Union itself in the same year the holding of free and open elections was a major milestone in the dismantling of the communist party's monopolistic hold on power in that country. These events had been heralded by a deep crisis in the non-ruling communist parties of Western Europe, they were accompanied by the break-up of the Yugoslav League of Communists, and they were soon to be followed by the collapse of communist power in Albania. Within three years the Soviet Union had ceased to exist, whilst the Yugoslav federation had been broken apart in the only large-scale military conflict that Europe had seen since the end of the Second World War. These events constituted a cardinal turning point in the history of Europe, and of socialism.

Whatever forms of government are established on these various territories, and however authoritarian those forms of government are, it is in the highest degree unlikely that they will reproduce the characteristic features of the very particular form of rule that they are replacing, and that it is the task of this book to analyse and portray. Communism took its characteristic shape in the Soviet Union during Stalin's period in power – that is, from 1928 to 1953. But it can be regarded as having been born with the Russian revolution of 1917, and 1989 can be taken as the symbolic year of its death, at least as far as Europe is concerned. In dying, it has left a legacy which, in the case of certain countries and in certain areas of political and economic life, remains strong. It has, indeed, formed an important part of the history of the societies that once hosted it and, perhaps particularly in the Soviet Union, which was the womb from which it was born, traces of a communist past are certain to form part of a post-communist future.

The historian is therefore now presented with a phenomenon that has a beginning, a period of development followed by one of decline, and an end. Communism can now be examined in the round. The fact that it collapsed so abruptly, so speedily and so unexpectedly forces us to look at our own perceptions of communism also in the round. From the moment that the Soviet Union surged to dominance in the east of Europe after the turning of the tide in the Second World War in 1943, a communist 'threat' to a Western world was the chief preoccupation of Western chancelleries, but a source of anxiety so widely spread as to represent the norm in public opinion in Western Europe. In that diffuse threat, fear of communism and of the Soviet Union ran together – and quite justifiably, since it was the Communist Party of the Soviet Union (CPSU) that, during the quarter of a century of the Stalinist period, had forged the particular pattern of political thought and action that was given world-wide currency through the Communist International. In countries where communist parties came to power they added to this political pattern a mode of economic organisation which was again derivative of Soviet experience and became in turn an essential ingredient of communism. It is the creation, the development and the eventual collapse of that Soviet creation, in the Soviet Union itself, in communist Eastern Europe, and in a family of communist political parties in Western Europe, that is analysed in this book, at a time when communism is no longer perceived as a threat, and when the whole sweep of the movement that bears its name can be surveyed with a degree of detachment.

The distance separating Marx's reactions to early industrialism in the west of Europe in the middle of the nineteenth century from the Soviet Union's policies and structures after the crystallisation of the Stalinist system in 1928–32 is in every sense immense. The 'communism' that Marx claimed to be haunting Europe in 1848 was derived from an analysis of a novel historical predicament facing societies whose growing wealth was generating social dislocations. It was an analysis of a Western European predicament conducted within a Western European discourse. The predicament confronting the Stalinist CPSU, on the other hand, was that of a new élite having come to power in a society disadvantaged in relation to the West and faced with the problems of development. Whilst Marx was dealing –

if on behalf of the disadvantaged – with problems created by relative national wealth, the Stalinist Soviet Union was dealing with problems of relative national poverty.

Other new élites likewise coming to power in the twentieth century in far poorer parts of the world were often to identify with the Soviet experience, and in some notable cases to imitate Soviet policies. But these cases – perhaps particularly the Chinese – served to reveal the intermediate position that Russia, and then the Soviet Union, occupied in the story of the world against the West. This was a feature of Russia that had been stressed even in the nineteenth century by the Russian Herzen. Lenin, who was party to the debates among socialists in Western Europe, where he spent most of his adult life until 1917, was alluding to the same feature when he wrote that Russia represented capitalism's weakest link; though the role that the Soviet Union was to play after his death resembled more that of the developing world's strongest link, on the other side of that particular divide. There are indeed innumerable arguments available to support the view of Russia, the Russian revolution and Lenin himself as 'threshold' phenomena, situated squarely on historical, geopolitical and developmental boundaries.

The accumulation of economic and political power that the Bolsheviks (renamed the Communist Party of the Soviet Union in 1952) acquired in the Stalinist period, which will be presented in what follows as the communist power monopoly, reflected the non-Western aspects of these ambiguities. It was in many ways a product of relative underdevelopment and of a perceived weakness and disadvantage in relation to the West. It was presented in a celebrated analysis as a case of 'oriental despotism'.[1] But with the passing of time, and with steady social and economic advances (for which, whether we like it or not, the communist party must be given some credit) a dissonance developed between an increasingly complex industrial economy and a political and economic system designed for simpler developmental tasks – and that dissonance was to go on growing until it became itself a major factor in the collapse of the power monopoly.

Analysis of Soviet politics and of communist political systems in the broad, has attributed their specific nature to a wide range of sources. The totalitarian analysis assimilated it to a pair of regimes in Western Europe – Hitler's Germany and Mussolini's Italy – but lost its persuasiveness as those two regimes receded into history, leaving an expanded collection of communist regimes which seemed more amenable to other typological schemes.[2] The importance of the Russian cultural element in the Soviet system itself was given an important impulse by Robert Tucker's *The Soviet Political Mind* and later works.[3] It was not until surprisingly late that John Kautsky explicitly made the link between communist politics and the politics of development, his *Communism and the Politics of Development* being published in 1968.[4] These various analytical schemes evolved against a parallel exercise using Marxist categories. This was a discourse that was congenial to a discussion of communist, or Soviet, politics in terms of revolution, development and bureaucracy – although a Marxist preoccupation with class relations inside each society, together with a distinctive terminology and an element of *parti pris* which was an essential corollary of an ideologically divided Europe, erected barriers between Marxist and non-Marxist approaches.

Two other theoretical developments are worth noting. First, some of the most evocative and persuasive accounts of communist politics were concerned less with typology than with catching the essence of communism. Meyer's presentation in terms of bureaucracy in 'USSR Incorporated', Kassof's 'administered society', Rigby's 'mono-organisational societies' and Tucker's 'movement regimes' each contributed a nugget of understanding to the nature of communist rule.[5]

Secondly, in the debate about typologies, which followed the questioning of the totalitarian model, a strong view emerged that communist political systems were *sui generis*, and that there was little point in using the categories of Western political science (parties, pressure groups, participation) in analysing them, since the terms involved carried such conflicting meanings. It was the conviction of the present author throughout that there were dangers in this view.[6] Communist regimes were as *sui generis* as we wished to make them. They had characteristics that distinguished them from other political types, but they also had features specific to them. The danger came from not preserving a separation between the two. Yes, it was legitimate to analyse processes of group formation in the Soviet Union, but to talk of the articulation of interests required a constant attention to the use of terms, and to preserving necessary distinctions. Yes, elections were held in the Soviet Union, but they had no place in a discussion where elections involved choice and accountability.

The concept of monopoly occurred randomly in these various discussions. But with few exceptions, no attempt was made to use the term in discussion of the politics of communism in a rigorous analytical way. It has been chosen, however, as the organising concept of this treatment of the political and economic processes characteristic of communism, and obviously reasons must be given for this.

The first, and by far most important reason, derives from what was said above about our now being able to see communism in the round. When the deep changes that were taking place in the Soviet Union and Eastern Europe began to settle down, and new political and economic forms began to appear, certain features of the previous order acquired a particularly sharp outline in contradistinction to them. Marketisation in the economy was accompanied by the promotion of political forms that also displayed characteristics of the market. In particular it became clear that instituting choice in the economy had a close connection with allowing both voice and choice into political life *whilst they had been absent from both economic and political life before.* The market and the freely-printed word meant the expression of individual preferences which would, when aggregated, provide the raw stuff from which public decisions could be made, whilst the vote meant at least some accountability of those who would make the decisions. Etymology makes bad arguments in the social sciences, but it is of some terminological interest that a number of the movements that eased the communist parties out of their position of power in Eastern Europe called themselves 'forums' – Civic Forum, New Forum, Democratic Forum. The reference was to a forum in the sense of place where people met to discuss; but the Forum from which the term derives was, of course, the Roman market-place. It is not too bold a generalisation to say that circumstances that have favoured the circulation of goods have also favoured the circulation of ideas. That, at any rate, was the assumption of the new élites in the societies where communism had tumbled, and it was sufficient to throw a particular light on the absence of these things in the communist period.

What the newly instituted economic market was setting out to escape from was monopoly in the form of the system of central command planning. Yet if that economic monopoly is subjected to examination, it can be seen not only to have accompanied, but to have implied, a political monopoly. The clearest evidence of this is in the realm of ownership. In the Soviet Union – to take the formative and most extreme case – ownership was not vested entirely in the state. There was an area of collective ownership associated with a collectivised agriculture (though the land itself was nationalised), and the collective farmers disposed of a very small but not insignificant area of private property in the stock they kept on their household 'plots'. But neither collective farms nor the outlets to which collective farmers could take their produce escaped the control of the state. The state's political power was such as to make the question of ownership irrelevant – you could do little with it. The monopoly involved in central planning was, in fact, matched by a monopoly of political power in the hands – as we shall see – of the communist party in a close functional relationship with the state. Looking back over the phenomenon that was communism in Europe, monopoly stands out as one of its cardinal features.

Secondly, once the turn to change had been made, authoritative spokesmen in both Eastern Europe and the Soviet Union frequently said expressly that they wanted to be rid of monopoly both in economic and political life. In many cases, including that of Gorbachev himself, it seems likely that this constant reference to the evils of monopoly was an attempt to throw out ballast so as to preserve the communist party's authority in some reduced but revitalised form. But whatever the motive, the criticism was seriously meant, and by suggesting that monopoly was the villain of the piece it constituted an invitation to analyse communism in terms of that monopoly. It could indeed be claimed that earlier treatments of communist, and particularly Soviet, politics have paid insufficient attention to the element of monopoly, taking it largely for granted. That it should be so taken for granted is, of course, a good mark of its relevance, but the lack of attention occasionally had curious effects.

It will be recalled, for instance, that two of the six key characteristics of totalitarianism presented by Friedrich and Brzezinski made an explicit reference to monopoly – a 'technologically conditioned near-complete monopoly of control, in the hands of the party and its subservient cadres, of all means of effective communication, such as the press, radio and motion pictures' and 'a similarly technologically conditioned near-complete monopoly of control (in the same hands) of all means of effective armed combat'.[7] There was involved also, in their view, 'central control and direction of the entire economy'. That is, monopoly was taken seriously in this model, and much of the treatment of the six points that Friedrich and

Brzezinski presented illustrated the monopolistic nature of power in the Soviet Union and the other suggested cases. It is not, however, placed at the centre of attention. Had it been, the authors might have been more sensitive to the distinctions between the cases of monopoly that they do present. There are very few states that do not, in fact, hold a monopoly of weaponry, just as it is normal for states to hold a monopoly in taxation and the application of the judicial system. Moreover, where they talk simply of 'central control' in the economy, they were in fact dealing – at least as far as the Soviet Union was concerned – with a quite clear case of monopoly. In other words, there is little that is surprising in a state exercising a monopoly in this or that area. What was special about monopoly in the hands of the party-state in the Soviet Union was its sheer extent.

Thus, in order – very reasonably – to establish the primacy of *control* in the model that they presented, Friedrich and Brzezinski were led to make allowances for variation between the three cases on which the model rested, Hitler's Germany, Mussolini's Italy and Stalin's Soviet Union. These variations often concerned the degree of monopoly held by the party leadership. In Germany, Hitler not only left the ownership structure of business intact, but was 'obliged to compromise with big business and indeed to strengthen its position of monopolistic control in the German economy'. Likewise, Friedrich and Brzezinski note that in Mussolini's Italy it was the *army* that held 'a monopoly of the sword' and that relations between the Duce and the armed forces had the character of a *modus vivendi*. In the Stalinist Soviet Union, after the outright slaughter of a considerable part of the High Command during the purges of the 1930s, a specific mechanism subordinated the Soviet armed forces to the political leadership leaving, indeed, room for the expression of a rival interest, but going much further towards monopoly than was the case in Mussolini's Italy.[8]

But the totalitarian view, as it was applied to communism, provided invaluable insights, as did each of the other approaches listed above. None of them need eliminate the others: to use Lewis Carroll's expression, it is a caucus race where all must have prizes. Each casts light on one or another aspect of the communist reality. Similarly, no special claim is made in this book to impose monopoly as an exclusive organising concept for making sense of the economics and politics of communism. In that realm, happily, there is no monopoly; the approach is offered to the reader as one among others, to take or to leave. The author's voice invites the reader's choice.

There are, however, certain problems in applying a concept of monopoly to economic and political life across the board. In economics, the term has a reasonably precise meaning – the exclusive possession of the trade in some commodity. Even in its basic economic sense, however, as with the market itself, monopoly is rarely encountered in a pure form in an untidy world. There are ragged edges; it is often a matter of more or less. But the fact that it is dealing with partial or leaky monopolies does not prevent a Monopolies Commission from setting to work to identify cases of monopoly and making proposals concerning them. That there was a strong element of monopoly in Soviet central planning is readily accepted. The market was severely circumscribed, and the institutions and people that controlled the distribution of goods in the economy could be identified. It will be seen that this control was far from watertight, and that markets of black and many other hues not only existed, but enabled the central monopoly itself to survive. But no understanding of a Soviet-type economy is to be had without recording its monopolistic nature.

It is in the political sphere that the problems arise. Here it is possible to speak of monopoly only in a metaphorical sense, and the dangers of analogy in political discourse are well enough known. Here, however, Western political science, which seemed to many to have so little purchase in discussions of a communist world, can come to the rescue in a day when transitions from communism to the market add a particular salience to certain models and views set up to cater for Western market societies. Works such as those of Downs and Hirschman, for example, once so totally inapplicable to communist politics, now acquire a remarkable relevance as the societies in the east of Europe move to the market from something else. What that something else is was bound to acquire a new profile in relation to what is replacing it. Hirschman's *Exit, Voice and Loyalty*, published in 1970, is a particularly rich source of ideas, and of a terminology, for analysing the transition from a communist monopoly in economics and politics to a post-communist market-place in both goods and ideas.[9] Reference will be made to Hirschman's work in the present analysis of a form of economic and political organisation that worked in such a way as to reduce to a minimum both choice and voice in the economy and in political life. Interestingly, if choice is missing in Hirschman's title, it may be simply because his readers could assume its existence. Students of communist politics have had to assume its absence.

Works such as these have served essentially an heuristic purpose. The same, and no more, is claimed for the present treatment of the communist power monopoly. We can only be as precise – as Aristotle so obligingly put it – as the subject matter allows. In this case the subject matter is an interlocking economic and political system marked by a quite exceptional degree of centralisation, with a single definable political body arrogating to itself powers of decision-making or authoritative interference over a range of society's affairs which is so extreme as to be almost total. A powerful term is needed to portray this state of affairs. To call it monopoly does no injustice to that term, whilst permitting an essential aspect of communist rule to emerge in full clarity.

This book is both a story and an analysis. It contains the story of the circumstances in which the communist power monopoly was born and developed. It tells how it was transmitted to other countries from the Russia of its origin, and how in the end it came into crisis and, abruptly, collapsed. It is also an analysis of why it was that the communist power monopoly collapsed, based on an anatomy of it as it developed in the Stalinist days and on an examination of the weaknesses – systemic and non-systemic – from which it suffered and of the external pressures that hastened its demise. All the communist parties of Europe, from Moscow westwards, have their place in both the story and the analysis – necessarily so, since communism's crisis involved both the ruling and the non-ruling parties.

The story has sufficient drama in it to make it interesting, if the story-teller is up to the job. At the close of the 1960s, when Andrei Amalryk wrote his *Will the USSR Survive until 1984?* he was not taken too seriously by most commentators on Soviet politics. Indeed, one of his compatriots, Alexander Zinoviev, developed the argument that the Soviet system was capable of stewing in its own juice into an indefinite future. Meanwhile a number of assaults, in other communist countries, had been made on the communist power monopoly, to fall back beaten by the apparently invincible defences of the monopoly. The lie was given to Amalryk (who himself failed to survive until 1984) by a general secretary of the CPSU who, after assuming power in 1985, acknowledged many of the criticisms that the monopoly's enemies had been making. From that point on the drama was intense, and completely overshadowed the long, involved and in many ways more interesting story of the weakening of the power monopoly over time before Gorbachev provided the jolt that was to bring about its final downfall.

As regards the analysis, there are three places in this book in particular where theoretical aspects of the communist power monopoly are considered. The first is in the second chapter, where the formation of the monopoly is recounted. It is introduced there as having four components: autarky and the closed frontier, central command planning, the leading role of the party, and the psychology of democratic centralism. The first of these set physical parameters without which the monopoly could not have been exercised; the second was the key mechanism underpinning monopoly in the economy; the third was the practical expression of monopoly in the political realm; and the fourth was its psychological or ideological expression. Further theoretical considerations are treated in a later chapter that deals with the weaknesses inherent in the monopoly and the pressures to which it was subjected. Finally, the conclusion draws together certain particular theoretical threads.

As the account proceeds, a number of dominant themes will recur, and it would be as well to indicate at the outset some of those that are of especial relevance to the monopoly itself. Perhaps most importantly, frequent reference will be made to the wide discrepancies between the various societies in which the power monopoly was being exercised, and also between separate phases in the development of a single society. It is impossible to understand what was at issue in the Prague Spring without taking into account the differences between Czechoslovakia's social and economic development and those of the Soviet Union. Also, social and economic development inside the Soviet Union itself meant that a political system created to deal with certain tasks would fail when other, more sophisticated, tasks were on the agenda, and when changes in the social structure had thrown up new social forces with new demands and new competences. In general, the story of the communist power monopoly is a dynamic one, very much concerned with change. As such, it provides plenty of good arguments for a functional view of politics which would emphasise the link, or match, between a political system's goals and its political forms, and consequent mismatches when development brings change in a system's goals and perceptions of itself. It was Alex Pravda who described the change in the Soviet

Union's political style at the end of the 1970s as 'from getting there, to being here'.[10]

Another theme concerns the relationship between economic and political reform. It has been difficult to state in clear terms what this relationship is, which makes it easy to question whether it exists at all. It will be seen also that the turning-points in the story of economic reform do not always coincide with the crises that proposals for political change usually engendered. Finally, the power monopoly tolerated quite wide variation in economic practice – a privatized agriculture in Poland, the Hungarian New Economic Mechanism from 1968, Yugoslav social self-management – but it was remarkably intolerant of challenges to its political norms. Yet few would dispute the fact that in communist political systems there is a far greater fusion of economic and political factors than in market societies. The argument of this book overall is that the communist power monopoly was an integrated system, the elements of which were interdependent. Beyond that it must be for the reader to judge.

There are other running themes in the book that might appear to be of lesser moment, but that enjoy a particular salience within the history of communism. It might seem a small matter whether a communist party's base organisations are located where members work or where they live. But in fact it has been of the greatest importance not only in fact, but in view of the symbolic power of this particular communist tradition. The 'cell' (the bodily metaphor was deliberate) was designed to bring together workers at the point of production, where a collective solidarity could easily be achieved and maintained. As the emancipatory atmosphere of the revolutionary days gave way to the manipulations of the Stalinist state the cell structure enabled the party leadership both to exploit the cell structure as a means of social control and to promote a sense of the exclusiveness of party membership. This structure was transmitted, with all the other mechanisms on which the power monopoly rested, to the Eastern European countries, whilst in the non-ruling parties of Western Europe, organisation in the workplace became an important part of the communist identity. It underpinned the militancy of those parties – at least until the Eurocommunist movement caused many of them to abandon this essential part of the communist tradition.

At the source of that tradition lay the Russian Bolsheviks. It is with

the ideas and organisation that they brought to the task of constructing the post-revolutionary society in the infant union of soviets that
this account of the communist power monopoly must begin.

Notes

1   K. Wittfogel, *Oriental Despotism: A Comparative Study of Total Power*
(New Haven, CT: Yale University Press, 1957).
2   The version to which reference is most generally made is Carl J.
Friedrich and Z. K. Bzrezinsky, *Totalitarian Dictatorship and Autocracy*
(Cambridge, MA: Harvard University Press, 1956). Leonard Schapiro,
Totalitarianism (London: Macmillan, 1972), contains an account of the
literature on totalitarianism.
3   Robert C. Tucker, *The Soviet Political Mind: Studies in Stalinism and
Post-Stalin Change* (New York: Praeger, 1963), and his edited work
Stalinism (New York: Norton, 1977).
4   John H. Kautsky, *Communism and the Politics of Development: Per-
sistent Myths and Changing Behavior* (New York: John Wiley, 1968); T. H.
Rigby, 'Stalinism and the Mono-organisational Society', in Robert C.
Tucker (ed.), *Stalinism – Essays in Historical Interpretation* (New York: W.
W. Norton, 1977).
5   Alfred G. Meyer, 'USSR Incorporated', *Slavic Review*, Vol. 20, No. 3
(1961); T. H. Rigby, 'Totalitarianism and Change in Communist Systems',
Comparative Politics, April 1972); Robert C. Tucker, 'Towards a Comparative Politics of Movement Regimes', *American Political Science Review*,
Vol. 55, No. 2 (1961).
6   Michael Waller, 'Problems of Comparative Communism', *Studies in
Comparative Communism*, Vol. 12, Nos 2 & 3 (1979), pp. 107–32.
7   Carl J. Friedrich and Z. K. Brzezinski, *Totalitarian Dictatorship and
Autocracy* (Cambridge MA: Harvard University Press, 1956), p. 10.
8   *Ibid.*, pp. 76, 199 and 276.
9   Albert O. Hirschman, *Exit, Voice and Loyalty: Responses to Decline in
Firms, Organizations and States* (Cambridge, MA: Harvard University
Press, 1970); Anthony Downs, *An Economic Theory of Democracy* (New
York: Harper and Brothers, 1956).
10 Alex Pravda, 'The Soviet Union: From Getting There to Being Here',
title of a review article in *Political Studies*, Vol. 30, No. 1 (1982), pp.
110–19.

Part I

The formation of the communist power monopoly

1

The legacy of the Russian revolution

The roots of the communist power monopoly lie in the Russian revolution. The chain of events can be traced, step by step, from the Bolshevik seizure of power in October 1917 to the full development of the Stalinist system in the Soviet Union in the 1930s, and on to the further regimes that were established on the Soviet model. So much is easily stated, but it raises some crucial questions which have exercised historians and political activists alike. One of them is how much weight to assign to policies and ideas, and how much to circumstances, in explaining how the monopoly came into being in its birthplace and took root there. The second concerns the distinctiveness of the Stalinist period, and therefore of the Leninist period which preceded it. These questions are obviously of the greatest importance to those who wish to apportion blame for the evils of Stalinism. Did Lenin have aspirations that were frustrated by the circumstances surrounding the revolutionary attempt to remodel society in which he and the Bolsheviks were engaged? To what extent was he responsible for what was to come later, and did he, in the celebrated phrase, 'open the door through which Stalin walked'?

The Bolshevik predicament

The Russian revolution was a major turning-point in a story that is, above all, Russian. The circumstances in which it took place were those of that particular society at that particular time, in relation to other societies which Russians saw, in one sense or another, as Russia's peers. The new society grew necessarily to some extent out of the national past, despite the revolutionary break and the attempt by a new élite to instil new values in the people. That attempt to implant new ideas in a Russian cultural soil, in the circumstances of the time – economic and political – created a particular predicament on which this account of the origins of the communist power monopoly must focus. It was a predicament that in many of its aspects has been common to all deep revolutionary processes throughout history. Others of its features were specific to Russian society at that particular stage of its development. But it is a predicament that happens also to have faced a number of other modernising élites that have come to power during the twentieth century in disadvantaged parts of the world – disadvantaged, that is, in relation to an industrialised West.

The ideas that the Bolsheviks espoused, and the policies and strategies on which they embarked, were necessarily, whatever their intellectual origin, moulded to a great extent by those circumstances and that predicament. It is not only in the Marxist ideas that the Bolsheviks brought to the revolutionary struggle that the roots of the communist power monopoly must be sought. They are located also in the nature of the tasks that the revolutionaries faced on taking and exercising power. To reveal and to understand the revolutionary predicament that the Bolsheviks confronted three aspects of the Russian revolution can usefully be examined, each of which has at various times been blamed for the rise of the communist power monopoly. The first is the process of revolution itself as it occurred in a Russian setting; the second is the ideology of the revolution; and the third is the cultural influence of the past.

The revolutionary process
Revolutions are not made in a day. Like the French revolution before it, and the Chinese after it, the Russian revolution grew out of a crisis of political power, and passed through long years of political upheaval and social change before achieving even the provisional stabilisation that Stalinism turned out to be. The abdication of the tsar in February 1917, and the storming of the Winter Palace in October of that year punctuate, it is true, the passing of an old and the advent of a new order. But those symbolic events – the second acquiring a much higher mythic status than the first with the passing of the years – constituted only the opening phase of the revolutionary process. They were to be followed by a period during which the revolutionary power of the Bolsheviks was consolidated, and that period was in turn followed by an entirely new phase during the

1920s when the power relations within the Bolshevik party itself were being clarified. This third period was also one of a search for a strategy of development for the future, and the fact that power rivalries within the party and the crucial debate about a post-revolutionary strategy ran together during the 1920s was of central importance in the formation of the Soviet political and economic systems.

This simple sequence – the revolutionary event itself, the consolidation of the power of a victorious revolutionary élite, and the settling into place of a new pattern of social development – is general enough to be common to all major revolutions. It is the variation in the detail that gives each of them its specific nature; nor can a true image of each be presented without due attention to all that detail. The broad outlines in the case of the Russian revolution, however, are by now clear enough. The fact that the accession to power by the Bolsheviks was a matter of insurrection and military organisation (the first revolutionary government, for just a few hours, was the Military Revolutionary Committee of the Petrograd soviet led by Leon Trotsky) was important. Even more important was the fact that the consolidation of Bolshevik power involved three years of civil war from 1918 to 1921. But if one single aspect of the Russian revolution is to be singled out for its salience to the way in which the communist power monopoly came to take shape, it is the economic and cultural circumstances of Russia at the point of revolution.

Raw statistics on the Russian economy before the revolution are not enough to illustrate the historical force of those circumstances, since they can serve to support a number of quite separate and distinct conclusions. It can be shown, for example, that Russia's industry was growing fast during the fifty years preceding the revolution (Table 1). But this growth took place from a starting-point well behind the major industrial nations of the world, and indeed was able to benefit to a great extent from their technical advances. Again, whilst for the Russian peasant life was often a struggle for survival, Bideleux has pointed out that if the number of horses that the peasantry disposed of is taken as a measure, the Russian peasant was somewhat better off than his counterpart in many countries that were, after all, less favoured.[1] Facts such as these have to be taken into account when assessing Russia's degree of development at the time of the revolution.

Table 1   *Industrial output in manufacturing and mining in Russia (1900 =*
100)

1860	13.9	1896	72.9	1905	98.2
1870	17.1	1897	77.8	1906	111.7
1880	28.2	1898	85.5	1907	116.9
1890	50.7	1899	95.3	1908	119.5
1891	53.4	1900	100.0	1909	122.5
1892	55.7	1901	103.1	1910	141.4
1893	63.3	1902	103.8	1911	149.7
1894	63.3	1903	106.5	1912	153.2
1895	70.4	1904	109.5	1913	163.6

But what counted in historical terms was Russia's position in
relation to the West, and in particular the perception of that position
held by the Russian intelligentsia. An awareness of Western
economic and above all military superiority formed the backdrop to
a good deal of Russian social thinking and state action from Peter the
Great onwards. This perception of relative weakness appears in the
division of the Russian intelligentsia in the nineteenth century into
'westerners' and 'slavophiles', the first basing hopes for Russian
progress on an endorsement of Western economic practice, the
second deploring the materialism of the West and seeking salvation
in the spiritual values of the 'Russian idea' – 'new, sane, and as yet
unheard.'[2] It appears also in the saying current at the time of the First
World War that it took ten Russian soldiers to fight one Western
soldier.

Passing from perceptions to economic facts, Russia's weakness in
relation to the West can be read in the amount of foreign capital
involved in the surge of economic development at the close of the
nineteenth century. True, this investment resulted in the construction of industrial plant and the training of Russian technical personnel, which offset its negative aspects. But the boundary between
colonial exploitation and economic aid for developing countries is
notoriously difficult to draw. It is defined often by the attitudes and
actions of the leadership of the nations involved, and for the
Bolsheviks the internal class war was heavily overlaid by a notion of
'imperialism'. This was to provide an ideology of anti-Westernism
and of a 'capitalist encirclement' during the Stalinist period, but it
was during the Leninist period that Western capital was sequestered
(rendering 'tsarist bonds' valuable only as material for making lamp-

shades) just as it was Lenin himself who provided communism's most celebrated theoretical treatment of imperialism.[3]

Lying behind Russia's relative economic weakness was a social structure marked by a low level of urbanisation (Table 2) and widespread illiteracy (Table 3) – again, in relation to the West. The growth of towns characteristic of Western European development had not taken place to the same extent in Russia, and in so far as an entrepreneurial class existed, it was predominantly composed of merchants, often of non-Russian origin and with a low social prestige.

Table 2 *Juvenile and adult illiteracy in Russia and selected European countries, c. 1900 (percentages)*

	Total	Male	Female
Russian Empire (1897)	72	61	83
France (1901)	17	14	19
Belgium (1900)	26	23	28
Austria (1900)	23	21	25
Spain (1900)	56	45	66
Italy (1901)	48	42	54

Table 3 *Rate of urban growth in Russia/USSR in the nineteenth and twentieth centuries compared with that of other countries*

	Russia/USSR		Japan	USA	France
	Urban population (%)	Urban housing (m² per inhabitant)	Urban population (%)	Urban population (%)	Urban population (%)
1860	9		26	20	26
1910	16	7.3	32	52	44
1940	33	6.5	46	57	57
1960	50	8.9	63	69	64
1975	60	12.2	76	74	73

It remains to say that the economic development of the end of the nineteenth century revealed in Table 1 was therefore brought about not so much by indigenous entrepreneurs as by foreign capital, foreign expertise, and an interventionist state. Bolshevik policies were to alienate foreign capital, but for their own process of economic development they were to continue to use the centralised state inherited from the tsarist past. Needless to say, it was a state that had little tradition of political limits on its power.

If, then, Russia's backwardness at the time of the revolution is to be presented as a factor in the emergence of Stalinism, and therefore of the communist power monopoly, it must be seen as backwardness in relation to the West; and it is equally important to stress that whatever the figures say about the economic, social and cultural circumstances of Russia at the time, those circumstances were *perceived* as putting Russia at a disadvantage in relation to the West. An armchair conclusion as to whether or not there really was a 'capitalist encirclement' of the infant Soviet Union is worth less than a simple recognition that the ruling party could base its power and its policies on that perception and mobilise society on that basis.

The force of this factor is revealed at very many different points in the story of the revolution and of its aftermath, so much so that it can be left to emerge as this account of the formation of the power monopoly unfolds. It is worth noting, however, one particular moment, in many ways the crucial turning-point in the history of the revolution, when this factor was determinant. That moment came in the mid-1920s, after Lenin's incapacitation and death, when rivalries within the Bolshevik party were being played out against the backdrop of a debate about a post-revolutionary strategy. It is of no little historical importance that this debate about how to move to socialism in circumstances of poverty took place while the party was going through a succession crisis. As a result, the subsequent evolution of the Soviet Union reflected not so much the strategy that had been adopted as the poor quality of the materials with which the Bolsheviks had to put that strategy into practice.

That moment is commonly conceived and discussed in terms of two individuals – Stalin and Trotsky – and of the two phrases that have come to be associated with their names: socialism in one country, and permanent revolution. But it was a struggle, in fact, that lasted throughout the 1920s, and was to be resolved only in 1928 when the policy of industrialisation at a forced pace announced the victory of Stalin and of the social forces that supported him – the myriad soldiers of the revolution, peasants and workers, or the children of peasants and workers, who had risen from among the people into positions of power over the people. It was they who provided the delegates to party congresses after the twelfth party congress in 1923, which was the last when any real debate took place. Thereafter a congress was an occasion to show solidarity with the leadership's line.

From 1928 the strategy that the revolutionary élite was to follow became clear, as did relationships within that élite. A Western European debate about the revolutionary growing over of capitalism into socialism gave place during the Stalin years to a drive for national economic construction in a semi-feudal country, and to the development of a political system suited to that task. The slogan of 'catching up and overtaking' encapsulated this, although it was many a long year before the full implications of the productive march of Soviet-style communism into ever more countries of the developing world became clear. When it did, it was possible to see how great a part anti-Westernism had played in the logic of the revolution itself and also in its consolidation.[4]

When the revolutionary process in Russia is viewed in this per-spective it can readily be seen that at all the crucial points – in the seizure of power itself, with its military and insurrectionary elements, in the consolidation of the revolution in a period of civil war, and finally in the post-revolutionary strategy of economic development at a forced pace – there was fertile soil for the develop-ment of an authoritarian pattern of politics. To make the point clearer, it would have been perfectly rational for whatever new élite that emerged in Russia in the power vacuum created by the fall of the tsar to do all that it could to maintain its power against its revolu-tionary rivals, and, in a situation of national weakness and relative backwardness, to gather into its own hands all the productive capacity of the nation in order to secure that nation's future and with it that of the revolution, and thereby to secure also the power of the new modernising élite itself. It would have been rational without reference to any Marxist ideas, even though, of course, in the event, the appeal to Marxist ideas did in fact play a crucial part in deter-mining the way in which these policy choices and political rivalries were conceived and presented.

The Bolshevik ideology
The revolutionary process therefore promises to be a profitable source of evidence from which to construct a profile of the

communist power monopoly. A second source is the revolution's ideology. If it can be claimed that the circumstances surrounding the Bolshevik consolidation of power explain the authoritarianism that emerged, and to an extent absolve Lenin of at least a part of the blame for what was to follow, he must surely be held responsible for the policy choices he made, and these choices can be held to have stemmed from the Marxist views to which he and his followers subscribed. Turning now to those views, and then to the actual policies of the Leninist years, we shall see that whilst there is much substance in this view, it is difficult to lay the blame for the formation of the communist power monopoly unequivocally at Lenin's, and much less Marx's, door.

The greatest care is needed in dealing with the ideology of ruling communist parties. Care, first, must be exercised in not ascribing any autonomous function to ideology: it is constructed and propagated by flesh-and-blood people who have a particular reason for talking in a certain way and getting people to listen. The apparatus that ruling communist parties have built up in order to generate doctrine and to transmit it to the population to the exclusion of rival doctrine is not, to say the least, politically neutral, despite its traditional emphasis on objective laws. Secondly, it is misleading to talk of that doctrine simply as Marxist. Marxist it has been, in a certain sense and to a certain extent. It uses the terminology of Marx, and it has been made to relate the policies of the party in question to the goals inherent in the Marxist canon. But the meanings assigned to the items of that terminology have been moulded by particular cultural contexts.

Nor is it sufficient to see the ideology as a Russian (or a Chinese or Cuban) Marxism, although that is already a useful step for making some necessary historical distinctions. The ideology of each communist party, like that of any other political party, contains many disparate elements. Their Marxism jostles with other items brought in from their particular experiences and perceptions. Thus 'catching up and overtaking the West' has been a much more active element in the CPSU's ideology than have notions of the end of alienation, whilst the vast bulk of ideas concerning political organisation – what is the right way of doing things and what the wrong, and what constitutes the normal, in relation to which political leaderships can call for 'normalisation' – stem directly from habits and practices that the party has itself generated over the years, investing them with the title of 'Leninist principles' which is not always strictly merited.

Finally, the ideology is yet another of the features of the lives of these parties that must be seen in terms of the revolutionary process, and it is this that has provided the essential link between the ideology and the power monopoly. Having come to power by thrusting aside an existing, if bankrupt, system of legitimacy, the revolutionary élite had to replace it with another, one that could not fully reflect the liberating element in revolution since it had to re-create order and summon up loyalty to that new order in circumstances of social flux. In fact the Bolsheviks had to address four tasks on achieving state power. They had to instil in people's minds the identity of the new order; they had to provide that new order with legitimacy; they had to reintegrate society after the upheavals of revolution and the Civil War; and they had to mobilise the masses for the daunting process of economic construction in circumstances of acute austerity.

The Bolsheviks, and other communist parties that have modelled their practices on those of the Bolsheviks, have taken this 'instrumental role of ideology' particularly seriously, and have built up widely ramified systems of control over the written and spoken word. By doing so they have no doubt protected the revolution against its enemies, but they have also protected their own position of power, first in the consolidation of the revolution, and then in an authoritarian and austere drive for national economic construction. Once again, it is not simply the revolutionary fact that is at work here. It is revolution in a certain context, in which a modernising leadership confronts, cajoles and to that extent leads the undifferentiated and untutored masses. Should those masses become more differentiated and no longer tolerate that tutelage the position would of course change, and much of the text that follows will document this evolution in the case of the Soviet Union and Eastern Europe – except that in certain Eastern European countries those circumstances never obtained at all. The implications of this, too, are matter for further discussion below.

It is against these considerations that the socialist component of the ideology of the Russian revolution must be viewed. From the time of the revolution the CPSU claimed to espouse long-term goals drawn from the Marxist canon, its political discourse was couched in the rhetoric of Marxism, many of its short- and medium-term policies went much further than those of Western European socialist parties in the direction of social welfare and of social equality. But the version of socialism that resulted leaned heavily towards centralisation in economic and political relations. As producers, as consumers and as citizens the masses were told what to produce, how much they might consume, and what policies they should support. Moreover, the prevailing view of the new order held by the Bolsheviks was that the class power of the proletariat would guarantee the 'revolutionary consciousness of right': constitutions, parliamentary 'talking shops' and all the paraphernalia of bourgeois democracy conflicted with the socialist goals as the Bolsheviks perceived them, and had no place in that new order. The ideology of the Russian revolution was indeed in good part Marxist and the revolutionaries espoused socialist goals. But when it comes to seeking the roots of the communist power monopoly what is most important is the very particular way in which those goals and the means necessary to attain them were conceived.

In the formation of the communist power monopoly, therefore, factors deriving from the turbulence of the revolutionary process itself were amplified by ideological factors which attended the revolutionary process.

The Russian cultural past
Rather less straightforward is a third source to which the roots of the communist power monopoly might be traced: the place within the revolutionary process in Russia that was played by the national cultural past. This issue is extremely contentious, but fortunately little weight need by placed on it here, since all that will be claimed is that the roots of the CPSU's power monopoly lay, at least to some extent, in the pre-revolutionary culture. It could hardly be otherwise. The new élite, for example, contained not only well-travelled and highly literate Marxist theoreticians, but also very many often totally unlettered cadres who were taking the decisions in the lower levels of administrative life and were having to put across new values and to explain the higher leadership's policies to the masses. No doubt those cadres were alive to the new ideas and receptive to some extent to new patterns of administrative behaviour that were being enjoined on them. But those new ideas and new expectations must at least to some extent have coexisted in their minds and actions with more familiar perceptions of authority, and were presumably all too often influenced by them. And one does not have to read far in the literature of pre-revolutionary Russia to realise how strong in the

traditional behaviour was an acceptance of leadership roles and a tendency to pass responsibility upwards.

In sum, the Russian revolution can be viewed from three different angles. Each of these perspectives highlights a different aspect of the revolution and of the predicament that the Bolsheviks faced. Each illumines in turn the origins of the monopoly of power that the Bolsheviks acquired and handed on to their Soviet successors and to other communist parties.

First, the revolution was socialist in its aspirations, in the rhetoric of the revolutionary élite and in many of the policies that were adopted; but it was a version of socialism that assigned an exaggerated role to a centralised state and thus to the élite that staffed that state.

Secondly, the revolution can be seen as part of the struggle of the world against the West, from which perspective the Bolsheviks partook of the situation of later fronts of national liberation even under Lenin, whilst under Stalin the Soviet Union developed a technique for economic development that was to appeal to more than one other revolutionary leadership faced with the same developmental predicament (in China, Vietnam and Cuba, for example).

Thirdly, the Russian revolution can be seen as an internal adjustment of Russia to changing circumstances. At the extreme in this perspective Stalin continues the tradition of Peter the Great, a tyrant whose historic role is to drag the Russian nation willy-nilly into modernity; on a more moderate view the absence of political and economic autonomy in the middle ranges of the old order was to live on to influence the shape of the new.

The communist power monopoly in embryo

The communist power monopoly, then, was born in particular circumstances. Those circumstances were shared by other, even poorer, countries in which communist parties were later to come to power — notably in Asia, in Cuba, and in certain exotic cases in Africa. It was most certainly not shared by many of the Eastern European countries in which communist parties came to power, and this description of the birth of the power monopoly must be borne in mind when the tale of its demise in Eastern Europe is recounted below.

Before that, however, the actual formation of the power monopoly in the post-revolutionary period in Russia must be examined.

The monopoly achieved its full flowering in the Stalin period, to which the next chapter will be devoted. But before moving from the revolutionary period in Russia into the formative Stalinist period, it is worth recording, if only in outline, the embryos from which the Stalinist system grew. The term 'embryos' is used here advisedly, in this minefield of dispute over the extent to which the Leninist period determined the shape of things to come. Other outcomes than that associated with Stalin were no doubt possible. Had Lenin lived longer things might have been otherwise. In the fascinating and wide-ranging debate about economic strategy in the 1920s were to be found more than one perfectly viable alternative to the course actually adopted. That is, there were other embryos that might have developed. But with the hindsight of history, it is not too difficult to see in the developments of the Leninist period the shape of things to come.

The policies of the early years
In the economic realm, both the idea that society's productive processes should be planned and that co-operation in agriculture would bring social and economic benefits were a part of the Bolsheviks' thinking at the time of the revolution, and steps were taken at an early stage to put those ideas into practice. The germ of future planning, for example, was contained in the establishment of a Supreme Council of the Economy (the *Vesenkha*) and in the celebrated scheme to electrify the country (the so-called GOELRO), the future central monopoly in the allocation of resources was prefigured in the Utilisation Commission, which co-ordinated the distribution network, whilst the Council of Labour and Defence, through which passed many of the early decisions to nationalise individual enterprises, created an organisational framework for an extension of state ownership. By the close of the Civil War at the end of 1920 the state was running most of industry and organising most of the supply network; private trade had been banned; and the peasantry was being required to make compulsory deliveries to the state.[5]

The rhythm at which nationalisation occurred, however, was not determined entirely by the Bolsheviks' choice. Carr points out that it 'was treated at the outset not as a desirable end in itself, but as a response to special conditions, usually some misdemeanour of the employers; and it was applied exclusively to individual factories, not to industries as a whole'.[6] But as tension mounted in 1918, the Bolsheviks were drawn, for one reason or another, into increasing the pace of nationalisation. In the disruption and doubt caused by the revolution, many factory owners emigrated. In other factories workers took matters into their own hands in the name of workers' control, selling their tools in a situation of desperate shortages.

In cases such as these the Bolsheviks were led to 'intervene' and thus had the pace of the process of nationalisation forced on them. The threat of civil war, and then its onset, brought more interventions. It might be noted, by way of comparison, that the revolutionary leadership in Yugoslavia in 1948, and in Cuba in 1968, were led similarly to 'intervene' in the economy at a moment of crisis, bringing into their control sections of the economy that the first revolutionary wave had spared. It is extremely difficult in all three cases to separate out the factors of doctrine and expediency, nor is it clear that they can be separated out at all.

The upshot, in the Soviet case, was that by the end of the Civil War the new revolutionary élite had acquired control, through the process of nationalisation, of the bulk of the industrial potential of the country.

In agriculture the decree on the land, announced at the moment of the seizure of power, nationalised the land, but gave the peasant use of it. The precise arrangement adopted – effectively municipalisation – owed much to the land policy of the Bolsheviks' revolutionary rivals, the Socialist Revolutionaries. But it gave the Bolsheviks control of the land, and control was to turn out to be the crucial factor. When, at a later date, the Stalinist leadership collectivised the peasantry, a novel legal charter was drawn up (in 1935) to spell out this concept. Apart from regulating the affairs of the collective farms, the 1935 charter gave collective peasants an entitlement to a small private plot of land, and a right to ownership of a certain number of animals. But the realities of that period make it quite clear that politics was in command. It is in the agricultural area that lie the best examples of the interaction between the political and the economic monopoly that the party has exercised in the Soviet Union. No form of ownership was to limit the prerogative of the state to dispose of the means of creating and appropriating wealth.

The New Economic Policy (NEP), which followed the Civil War and lasted from 1921 and 1928, brought a hiatus in this process. In this period the party's monopoly in the economy did indeed come into question. But the incremental gains made then by the peasantry in the countryside and by artisans and small entrepreneurs in the towns only temporarily checked the onward march of the communist power monopoly. What would have brought a real end to the party's retention of its monopoly of power would have been a final decision by the party itself to wager on the peasantry, and thus to allow the development of a market-based agriculture to determine the pace of growth. That, however, did not transpire. Instead, the process of nationalisation was completed with the policy of industrialisation at a forced pace and the adoption of the first five-year plan.

This mixture of early experimentation and desperate reaction to the exigencies of the Civil War period cannot, however, be seen as constituting the final entrenchment of the power monopoly in the economy. Alec Nove writes that whilst some of these early measures represented interesting pioneering efforts at thinking out means of developing Russian natural resources on a large scale, 'in the short run nothing whatever could have been done to make a reality of them'.[7] Yet they constituted an attempt, in the extraordinary circumstances of the war communism period, to find a substitute for the market, and they were to provide a reservoir of tested and partly tested ideas on which later decisions could draw.

The end of the Civil War and the introduction of the NEP brought a change of policy and a relaxation in the pace of revolutionary change, but the 'war communism' of 1918 to 1921 came to be endowed with a mythic status that was to gain ground as the money-making ethos of the NEP developed. Moreover, much of the thinking of the time, not only in the Soviet Union but outside it too, favoured the promotion of the state and grand public projects at the expense of the individual. This was the time when Le Corbusier was designing his *ville contemporaine* as an integrated habitat for three million people, and when ideas about social engineering, based on an optimistic assessment of the future benefits of technology, were widespread. It was also the time when Aleksei Gastev, who ran the Central Labour Institute under the All-Russian Central Council of Trade Unions, was talking of the psychology of the proletariat as a mechanised collectivism. 'Machines', he wrote in a graphic phrase, 'from being managed will become managers'.[8] It was Gastev's notions that inspired Zamyatin's novel *We*, which George Orwell was later to imitate for his *1984*. Ironically, the Soviet Union was at this time equipping itself with an educational and penal system based on the most enlightened thinking of the day at the same time as it was envisaging society and its productive processes as a single factory. The images of modernity that abounded in the revolutionary atmosphere were at times not too discriminating in terms of their political impact.

But despite the revolutionary mystique that war communism acquired, despite these induced interventions in the economy, and despite the early experiments with planning and collective agriculture, it was not until the rivalry within the leadership after Lenin's death had played itself out and the question of the future developmental strategy had been closed with the adoption of the first five-year plan and later the forced collectivisation of agriculture that the power monopoly settled into place in economic life – a moment that was symbolised by the removal of Bukharin, the most prominent advocate of the NEP, from his post in 1929. Until then the NEP allowed a market to function, with a fairly wide degree of private ownership even in industry, whilst peasants were free to market their grain and, after 1925, within limits, to hire labour and extend their holdings. The power monopoly in the economy thus took shape only gradually, from a fitful start in the war communism years and a partial move away from monopoly during the NEP, until its final consolidation during the first five-year plans from 1928.

Pre-echoes of the political monopoly
If the economic monopoly was slow to form, that in the political system proceeded at a much faster pace. Indeed, a power monopoly in the hands of the Bolshevik leadership took shape in the revolutionary events of 1917 itself. From the start the Bolsheviks refused, with one minor concession, to share power with rival revolutionary parties. Moreover, from an early stage power began to drain from the periphery of the party to the centre, a parallel process took place in the structures of the soviets – the 'councils' of workers', peasants' (and initially also soldiers') deputies that had given their name to the revolutionary state. Finally, the soviets soon found the party eating into the power with which the revolution had originally seemed to endow them.

These processes were all accelerated by the extenuating pressures of the Civil War. Before long oppositionists within the party were complaining of being turned into 'obedient gramophones' and were wondering whether the militarisation of society that the war had brought about could ever be undone once the war was over. It was during the Civil War years, too, that the electoral process succumbed to one of nomination as the party's staffing agency – *Uchraspred* – strove to assign as effectively as possible to responsible posts those who showed any signs of administrative competence whatsoever. This development in fact was to provide the foundations on which would rise the political institution that has lain at the heart of the power monopoly – the *nomenklatura* exercised by the party's apparatus.

Whilst the future is more clearly visible in the early political structures than it is in the economy, here too it was not until the period of the first five-year plan (1928–32) that the monopoly finally took shape. Yet it was in 1921, when victory in the Civil War appeared to be about to be cancelled out by peasant discontent and discord within the party, that a debate took place, and a decision was made, that were to give the politics of communism its most particular characteristic. At their tenth congress, the same congress when control of the economy was eased to the benefit of the peasant, the retailer and the artisan, the Bolsheviks debated the question of 'party unity'. At the heart of the debate was the question of how far internal differences within the party should be allowed to take organisational form. The group that was targeted at that particular moment was the 'Workers Opposition' which had formed around the figures of Alexander Shlyapnikov and Aleksandra Kollontai, and also the 'Democratic Centralists'. But the problem was more general, and was inherent in the contradiction between the liberating effects of revolution and the Bolshevik determination to dominate those effects.

At the end of a lengthy debate a motion was put that organised fractions should not be permitted to form within the party. The motion was carried, on an open vote, with only twenty-five delegates voting against it, and it was decided that provision would be made for the full airing of oppositional views in bulletins and broadsheets devoted to that end.

This self-denying ordinance within the party was to become, in the hands of the later Stalinist leadership, a tool that would in the future rule out free debate, free voting, and the freedom to publish dissenting views not only in the party but in the state as well. The ban on fractional activity was to become, in the words of Ralph Miliband, the 'sacred cow' of communist organisational practice.[9] It acquired a quasi-constitutional status, having in fact more constitutional force than many a provision of the formal constitution itself, and, once extended from party to state level, gave the power monopoly a semi-legal basis.

It remains to record one further feature of the Leninist period that was later, in the circumstances of the Stalinist Soviet Union, to contribute to the formation of the power monopoly. When Lenin spoke in the debate 'on party unity' at the tenth congress he used the analogy of bodily health and disorder to support his argument against fractional activity. There was in Bolshevism from its birth a particular way of thinking about the revolutionary party that saw the party as an organism, subject to good and bad health, and having a collective purpose in which individual members realised themselves.

There is, of course, nothing untoward in a political party's generating the cement that will give it cohesion and guarantee its continued existence, and to that extent there has been nothing special about the 'Leninist principle of democratic centralism'. But the uses to which the ban on fractional activity was later put in the Stalinist period, and even more fatefully the extension of the ban on the promotion of alternative policies from the party to the state as a whole, were to have a momentous effect on the formation and consolidation of the communist power monopoly. And the factors that produced this way of thinking of the party and of society as organisms, the health of which takes precedence over the preferences of its parts, were no doubt the same as those that led to the formation of the Stalinist system in its entirety – traditional Russian ways of thinking about the individual and society, notions of a socialist purpose, and the pressure of circumstances.

Notes
1   Robert Bideleux, *Communism and Development* (London: Methuen, 1985), pp. 14 and 254–5.
2   Fedor Dostoevsky, *The Diary of a Writer*, trans. Boris Brasol (London: Cassell, 1949), p. 780.
3   V. I. Lenin, 'Imperialism: the Highest Stage of Capitalism', in *Collected Works* (London: Lawrence and Wishart, 1964), Vol. 22, pp. 185–304.
4   Jaroslav Krejci, 'The Russian Revolution as a Response to Challenge from Without: An Appraisal with Hindsight', *The Journal of Communist Studies*, Vol. 4, No. 2 (1988).

5   Alec Nove, *An Economic History of the USSR* (Harmondsworth: Pelican, revised ed. 1982), pp. 70–4.
6   E. H. Carr, *A History of Socialist Russia. The Bolshevik Revolution, 1917–1923* (Macmillan, 1963), Vol. 2, p. 81.
7   Nove, *An Economic History of the USSR*, p. 70.
8   Kendall E. Bailes, 'Alexei Gastev and the Controversy over Taylorism in the Soviet Union, 1918–1924', *Soviet Studies*, Vol. XXIX, No. 3 (July 1977) p. 378.
9   Ralph Miliband, 'Moving On', in *Socialist Register 1976* (London: Merlin Press, 1976), p. 135.

Further reading

E. H. Carr, *The Russian Revolution: From Lenin to Stalin, 1917–1929* (London: Macmillan, 1979).

Marc Ferro, *October 1917: A Social History of the Russian Revolution* (London: Routledge and Kegan Paul, 1980).

Sheila Fitzpatrick, *The Russian Revolution* (Oxford: Oxford University Press, 1982).

Geoffrey Hosking, *A History of the Soviet Union* (London: Fontana, 1985).

Basile Kerblay, *Modern Soviet Society* (London: Methuen, 1983).

Moshe Lewin, *Russian Peasants and Soviet Power* (London: George Allen and Unwin, 1968).

David McLellan, *Marxism After Marx* (London: Macmillan, 1979).

Alfred G. Meyer, *Leninism* (Cambridge, MA: Harvard University Press, 1957).

Roger Pethybridge, *The Social Prelude to Stalinism* (London: Macmillan, 1974).

2

Democratic centralism and the patrimonial system

Whatever view is taken of Lenin's contribution to the Stalinist system, the date of birth of the communist power monopoly in its full form can be attributed to a series of remarkable decisions taken by the Bolshevik leadership at the end of the 1920s. Two decisions in particular were to have an epochal significance for the formation of the communist power monopoly.

The first was a decree issued by the Council of People's Commissars (that is, the Soviet government) on 8 June 1928, calling for

a united all-union plan which, being the expression of economic unity of the Soviet Union would facilitate the maximum development of economic regions on the basis of their specialisation, . . . and the maximum utilisation of their resources for the purpose of the industrialisation of the country.[1]

This decree was to lead to the launching of the first five-year plan in that year, and to the birth of a radical form of economic organisation that was to constitute one of the chief pillars of the power monopoly.

A second decision was taken not publicly, but as an administrative measure within the party in 1929. Individual peasants were required to combine their labour, their implements and their animals with those of others in collective farms. What collectivisation contributed to the power monopoly, despite a collective farm charter which from 1935 qualified the monopoly in purely formal terms, was *control* by the centre over the countryside, and in particular over the grain supply.

These two decisions ushered in what has come to be known historically as a 'revolution from above'. They mark the beginning of the Stalinist period proper. The years of the first five-year plan, from 1928 to 1932, were a major turning-point in the history of the Soviet

Union, and therefore of communism. It saw the consolidation of the communist power monopoly which it is the task of this chapter to present and to analyse. Its chief characteristics were the virtual elimination of choice in the economy, the reduction of voice in politics to that of the party, the enjoining on all members of society of loyalty to the party, and controls on the entry and exit of goods and people into and out of the territory of the system.[2]

The power monopoly

The communist power monopoly must now be defined. It may usefully be seen as comprising four interconnected components:

1 economic autarky and the closed frontier;
2 central command planning;
3 the 'leading role of the party';
4 the idea of democratic centralism.

It is hard to overemphasise the importance of the linkages between these components. It was discovered time and again in the history of the various attempts to reform the Stalinist system that it was impossible to modify one part of it without modifying the rest. At times (notably in Yugoslavia after 1948 and in Hungary after 1968) a communist party claimed to have instituted a partial reform; but those reforms turned out, in the long run, to have left the core of the monopoly in place. The communist power monopoly has constituted a system, each part of which has contributed to maintaining the whole in being.

Autarky and the closed frontier
How much of the blame for the infant Soviet Union's isolation should be attributed to the revolutionary government's renunciation of its debts, how much to its avowed intent to foster revolution in further European countries, how much to the failure of such revolutions to occur, and how much to deliberate propaganda about a 'capitalist encirclement' which enabled the Stalinist leadership to rally the people behind it – these are questions that must be left to others to debate and decide. The account given here of the formation of the communist power monopoly will not enter into that disputed territory; nor need it. Instead it will support a simple historical judgement about the Soviet Union's isolation which, perhaps

because of its very simplicity, has all too often been passed over in treatments of Soviet political and economic history. It concerns the interdependence between the economic and political systems of Stalinism on the one hand, and the closed frontier on the other.

The state acquired a monopoly in foreign trade early in the revolutionary period. Originating in a defensive action in response to embargoes imposed by powers hostile to the revolution, control was further enhanced by the nationalisation of the merchant marine and by the need, or temptation, to resist Germany's exploitation of the dominance it had gained from the treaty of Brest-Litovsk, signed by the Bolsheviks in March 1918 to end Russia's involvement in the war. Carr concludes that it was due

partly to the comparatively minor role of foreign trade in the Russian economy, partly to the urgent necessities of defence against economic exploitation by the capitalist world, and partly to a series of accidents, that the monopoly of foreign trade was so early, and so firmly, established as a vital part of the Soviet system.[3]

Its value to the leadership when the first five-year plan was launched in 1928 was immense. It constituted a barrier behind which the centrally planned economy could operate. Without that barrier, the system of planning that was instituted in 1928 would have been impossible to maintain. Abolishing the market inside the planned area required that possible sources of uncertainty should be prevented from entering that area. And planning involves, as one of its key features, the maximum elimination of uncertainties from decision-making.

So much is easily stated. But the barrier had much wider implications. Having wagered on its own resources, human and material, the Stalinist leadership set to work to train up its own qualified workforce. Control of the national wages bill was an essential part of the early planning mechanism, and, whilst wage differentials were allowed to act as a stimulus for performance, there was no intention of giving the more highly qualified members of the workforce as great a remuneration as they could then command on the world market. In this case the closed frontier came, by 1939, to act as a barrier to movement out of the country. Spanish supporters of the republican cause who left for the Soviet Union after defeat in the Spanish civil war, some to be trained as engineers but others already having engineering qualifications, found themselves later unable to leave. Nor were their children to enjoy such a privilege. At a later point the indigenous Jewish population, which, because it was more urban, constituted a disproportionate number of professionally qualified people, was to suffer from a similar disability.

This second example of the effect of the closed frontier was partly economic and partly political. A third was purely political. An essential part of the party's power monopoly was its control over the spoken and written word. Through that control it could on the one hand guarantee doctrinal conformity and, on the other, it could choke off the expression of rival sources of ideas. But this, too, depended on the maintenance of a barrier between the Soviet Union and the outside world.

It is easier, of course, to construct a foreign trade barrier and to forbid citizens to emigrate than it is to impose a communications barrier. It may be possible to stop written material at the frontier, but policing the air waves is more difficult. The gradually increasing vulnerability of the communist power monopoly in the Soviet Union was in many ways inevitable, simply because it became increasingly difficult to maintain the ideological barrier. Jamming broadcasts is expensive and ultimately becomes impracticable as the volume of messages increases. In this realm perhaps more than in any other, in the Soviet Union especially but elsewhere too, the power monopoly fell prey to the social developments that it had come into being to promote. It was easy to shut out the world in the early days when possibilities of travel were few, when radio programmes were relayed through loudspeakers rather than through individually-owned receivers, and when few people spoke foreign languages. But in the end economic and technical advances and the very success of its educational programme undermined the party's ability to control communications.

Moreover, isolating the Soviet citizenry in Stalin's day from messages coming from outside the system was far easier than isolating smaller countries at a later time. To prevent citizens of the GDR from watching television transmissions from the FRG was – except for a small corner around Dresden – quite impossible; nor could Yugoslavia develop a thriving tourist industry and maintain an effective censorship at one and the same time. But in the Stalinist Soviet Union the party was able to organise a network of control over the written and spoken word which was an essential element in its monopoly of power.

In sum, not only was the Stalinist system economically autarkic, but it depended upon the closed frontier for the maintenance of the power monopoly that was its chief characteristic. The one fed on the other. Small wonder, then, that an obsession with the frontier grew up, taking the physical form of searchlights and well-staffed regiments of frontier guards. Small wonder also that the propaganda apparatus developed and then made full use of a phobia of the external enemy in its appeals for national solidarity around the party, its leading role and its leaders.

Central command planning
The existence of the sealed frontier was essential for the development of the second component of the communist power monopoly: monopoly in economic life.

The relationship between ownership and control has been a key topic in debate on the socialist project.[4] The Stalinist Soviet Union has represented an important reference point in that debate, both ownership and control being vested to an extreme degree in the state. So strong, however, was the communist political monopoly that the question of ownership was eclipsed and became something of a formality. Once the monopoly had been installed, the question of who owned what in formal terms became largely irrelevant.

The doctrinal position was duly recorded in a set of constitutional and juridical definitions of ownership. These presented a mixture of state, collective and individual forms, and reflected the increasing power of the Soviet state. It will be recalled that the bulk of industry passed into the hands of the state during the revolutionary process. Even under the NEP the state retained its ownership in the industrial sphere, and state ownership in industry was virtually complete by the end of the first five-year plan in 1932.

The trade and distribution networks, which had been to a considerable extent in private hands during the NEP, were brought almost in their entirety into state ownership with the first five-year plan, although in agricultural distribution the resulting pattern was affected by the collective organisation provided for in the collective farm charter of 1935. According to this charter, nationalised land was farmed rent-free, with the members of the collective farm pooling their animals and implements. But until 1958 tractors and other machinery were held in Machine Tractor Stations, and as regards the actual assets of the farm, control by the state rendered collective ownership nugatory, except in the most formal sense. The collective farms coexisted with a smaller number of state farms, which were run effectively as factories on the land.

The largest item in the private sector was the plots of land that collective farm peasants were allotted for their own use. They were also entitled to own a stipulated number of animals. Beyond that a tiny sector of private artisans survived, but not on a scale to signify. The state did not, therefore, enjoy a monopoly of ownership in formal terms. What counted, however, was control, and it was a monopoly of control that the party exercised.

However, once the discussion moves from ownership to control in the economy, questions of a political nature arise concerning the structure of the state, and about who it was, in terms of actual people, that exercised decisive power over this vast pool of public and semi-public resources. A preliminary and brief answer can be given here, which must be left to be filled out further as this chapter moves from the economic to the purely political.

The structure of the Soviet state included an extensive array of centralised ministries, which had charge of running the country. But there was also a parallel if much smaller bureaucracy, comprising the communist party's paid staff, which supervised and to a great extent directed the formal organs of the state, and indeed the collective area of the Soviet economy as well. Much more will be said about the party and its apparatus in what follows, where it will be noted that structurally the organs of the state were separate from those of the party, whilst in functional terms they were so closely intermeshed as to be inseparable.

If it be asked, then, in whom the communist power monopoly was vested, the answer must be the party-state, in a relationship that it will be the task of the remainder of this text to elucidate.

It was in fact in agriculture, where in formal terms the collective farms were neither owned nor run by the state, that the functional link between party and state was at its most evident. Collectivisation had indeed been devised primarily so as to give the party-state control over the grain supply. Through the collective farms the centre could be sure of procuring the grain that the peasantry had been able to withhold until that point if market conditions were not judged propitious. To withhold grain from the market, and thus from the workforce in the cities, could easily be seen as frustrating the socialist goals of the revolution by a class that the Bolsheviks' Marxist ideology deemed suspect. There was thus a grim logic in the elimination and deportation in 1929–30 of the richer peasants – the 'kulaks' – who were the mainstay of the village economy. The policies of de-kulakisation and of collectivisation gave the state virtually complete control of the agricultural economy. If the weather could not be planned, the grain could at least be placed in a single barn, with a lock on the door and an agent of the party-state to hold the key. This was the role performed by the Machine Tractor Stations, whose dismantling in 1958 was a crucial step in the process of de-Stalinisation.

In industry and distribution it was the system of central command planning that revealed the full workings of the communist power monopoly. The launching of the first five-year plan in 1928 brought an end to the NEP and, to a determining extent, to the market relationships that the NEP had permitted. The plan organised the whole economy as a single unit and ran it from Moscow. The invisible levers of the market in industry were replaced by administration by people. At the apex of the system were the state commissions for planning and for supplies; managers became executants of the plan, the enterprise's inputs and its output being determined from above.

The task of running this vast centralised economy was given, as noted, to a formidable structure of ministries. Table 4 illustrates the complexity of the ministerial structure of the Soviet Union as it was in the 1970s. Certain features of it deserve special mention in view of the concerns of this study.

First, amongst these ministerial instances were a number of key bureaucracies that articulated the economic monopoly. The state planning commission (Gosplan) had the task of constructing annual plans for the various ministries and their enterprises, based on a co-ordinated plan for the whole economy. A supply commission (Gossnab) had the hardly less formidable job of allocating the supplies that enterprises needed in order to fulfil their plans and of designating the destination of the product of enterprises. A manager could not lift a telephone and order from a choice of sources the materials he or she needed. Except at retail outlets goods moved around in the economy against dockets signed by the supply agencies. A further central office had the task of setting prices, since these, too, were not left to be determined by the market.

Secondly, the structure left little initiative to the managers of enterprises. From the late 1950s a series of reform proposals in the

Table 4   *USSR Council of Ministers*

PRESIDIUM OF THE USSR COUNCIL OF MINISTERS

CHAIRMAN OF THE USSR COUNCIL OF MINISTERS (1)
FIRST DEPUTY CHAIRMEN (2)
DEPUTY CHAIRMEN (11)

Including: Chairman, USSR State Planning Committee (Gosplan)
USSR Representative, Council for Mutual Economic Assistance
(Comecon)
Chairman, USSR State Committee for Science and Technology
Chairman, USSR State Committee for Material and Technical
Supply
Chairman, USSR State Committee for Construction Affairs
Chairman, Commission of President of USSR Council of
Ministers for Foreign Economic Questions
Chairman, Military-industrial Commission of Presidium of
USSR Council of Ministers

OTHER MEMBERS OF THE COUNCIL OF MINISTERS
(U) = Union Republic Organizations* (A) = All-Union Organizations*
Minister of Agriculture (U)
Minister of Automotive Industry (A)
Minister of the Aviation Industry (A)
Minister of the Chemical Industry (A)
Minister of the Chemical and Petroleum Machine Building (A)
Minister of Civil Aviation (A)
Minister of the Coal Industry (U)
Minister of Communications (U)
Minister of the Communications Equipment Industry (A)
Minister of Construction (U)
Minister of Construction of Heavy Industry Enterprises (U)
Minister of the Construction Materials Industry (U)
Minister of Construction of Petroleum and Gas Industry Enterprises (A)
Minister of Construction, Road, and Municipal Machine Building (A)
Minister of Culture (U)
Minister of Defence (U)
Minister of Defence Industry (A)
Minister of Education (U)

* The All-Union Ministries govern the branch of state administration
entrusted to them throughout the territory of the USSR either directly or
through bodies appointed by them. According to Article 76 of the USSR
Constitution, the Union Republic Ministries, as a rule, direct the branches
of state administration entrusted to them through the relevant Ministries
of the Union Republics; they administer directly only a certain limited
number of enterprises according to a list approved by the President of the
Supreme Soviet of the USSR.

Minister of the Electrical Equipment Industry (A)
Minister of the Electronics Industry (A)
Minister of Ferrous Metallurgy (U)
Minister of Finance (U)
Minister of the Fish Industry (U)
Minister of the Food Industry (U)
Minister of Foreign Affairs (U)
Minister of Foreign Trade (A)
Minister of the Gas Industry (A)
Minister of General Machine Building (A)
Minister of Geology (U)
Minister of Health (U)
Minister of Heavy and Transport Machine Building (A)
Minister of Higher and Secondary Specialised Education (U)
Minister of Industrial Construction (U)
Minister of Installation and Special Construction Work (U)
Minister of Instrument-making, Automation Equipment, and Control
    Systems (A)
Minister of Internal Affairs (U)
Minister of Justice (U)
Minister of Land Reclamation and Water Resources (U)
Minister of Light Industry (U)
Minister of Machine Building (A)
Minister of Machine Building for Cattle Raising and Fodder Production (A)
Minister of Machine Building for Light and Food Industry and Household
    Appliances (A)
Minister of the Machine Tool and Tool Building Industry (A)
Minister of the Maritime Fleet (A)
Minister of the Meat and Dairy Industry (U)
Minister of the Medical Industry (A)
Minister of Medium Machine Building (A)
Minister of Nonferrous Metallurgy (U)
Minister of the Petroleum Industry (A)
Minister of the Petroleum Refining and Petrochemical Industry (U)
Minister of Power and Electrification (U)
Minister of Power Machine Building (A)
Minister of Procurement (U)
Minister of the Pulp and Paper Industry (A)
Minister of the Radio Industry (A)
Minister of Railways (A)
Minister of Rural Construction (U)
Minister of the Shipbuilding Industry (A)
Minister of the Timber and Wood Processing Industry (U)
Minister of Tractor and Agricultural Machine Building (A)
Minister of Trade (U)
Minister of Transport Construction (A)
Chairman, State Committee for Cinematography (Goskino USSR) (U)
Chairman, State Committee for Construction Affairs (Gosstroi USSR) (U)

Chairman, State Committee for Foreign Economic Relations (GKES) (A)
Chairman, State Committee for Forestry (Gosleskhoz USSR) (U)
Chairman, State Committee for Inventions and Discoveries (A)
Chairman, State Committee for Labour and Social Questions (Goskomtrud USSR) (U)
Chairman, State Committee for Material and Technical Supply (Gossnab USSR) (U)
Chairman, State Planning Committee (Gosplan USSR) (U)
Chairman, State Committee for Prices (Goskomtsen USSR) (U)
Chairman, State Committee for Publishing Houses, Printing Plants, and the Book Trade (Goskomizdat USSR) (U)
Chairman, State Committee for Science and Technology (GKNT) (A)
Chairman, State Committee for Standards (Gosstandart USSR) (A)
Chairman, State Committee for Television and Radio Broadcasting (Gosteleradio USSR) (U)
Chairman, State Committee for Vocational and Tecnical Education (U)
Chairman, Committee for People's Control (U)
Chairman, Committee for State Security (KGB) (U)
Chief, Central Statistical Administration (TsSU USSR) (U)
Chairman, *Soyuzsel'khoztekhnika* (Association for the Sale of Agricultural Equipment and the Organization of Machinery Repairs and Utilisation)
Chairman of Board, USSR State Bank (Gosbank USSR)
Chairman, Armenian SSR Council of Ministers*
Chairman, Azerbaijan SSR Council of Ministers
Chairman, Byelorussian SSR Council of Ministers
Chairman, Estonian SSR Council of Ministers
Chairman, Georgian SSR Council of Ministers
Chairman, Kazak SSR Council of Ministers
Chairman, Kirghiz SSR Council Ministers
Chairman, Latvian SSR Council of Ministers
Chairman, Lithuanian SSR Council of Ministers
Chairman, Moldavian SSR Council of Ministers
Chairman, RSFSR Council of Ministers
Chairman, Tajik SSR Council of Ministers
Chairman, Turkmen SSR Council of Ministers
Chairman, Ukrainian SSR Council of Ministers
Chairman, Uzbek SSR Council of Ministers

---

* According to Article 128 of the 1977 USSR Constitution the Council of Ministers of the USSR includes the Chairman of the Councils of Ministers of the Union Republics ex officio.

Soviet Union and Eastern Europe had as their chief focus the responses of managers to the system of central planning, but despite the reformers' best efforts, the problems were never satisfactorily solved.

What mattered for managers was meeting the targets of the plan, since it was on this that their bonuses, or their job, depended. The fact that they did not have to worry about disposing of their product had an obvious effect on quality. Insolvency of the enterprise was not a risk, since losses were funded by the state, and this led to a hoarding of labour and of supplies. What was a risk was non-fulfilment of the plan's targets. These, in the early years, were cast in terms of quantity (so many tyres, tractors, nails) with little regard for the product mix or, again, for the quality of the goods produced. Later reforms increased the range of indicators in an enterprise's plan, but to the end the overriding obsession with quantity remained, coupled with the inefficiencies caused by the lack of penalties in the system for wasteful use of resources.

Thirdly, since all the nation's assets and productive forces were vested in the state, and since their organisation was so centralised, there took place a fusion of economic and political functions at the apex of the system. Factories in the localities, together with schools and hospitals and even the finance departments of local governments were subordinated to the ministerial structure. Moreover, whilst some of this responsibility was devolved down to the level of the constituent republics of the Union, local government budgets were very low, and central control of them extremely tight. Not only did the state monopolise the organisation of production, but it organised it on highly centralised lines.

In recording the extent of the power monopoly it is important, fourthly, to register also its limits. There was a labour market, in the sense that workers could apply for jobs and improve their chances through training. There was a retail market – though local government had a monopoly of control over its organisation. And there was a black market, without which the system could not have worked. The monopoly was not total, nor could it ever have been. But it was none the less extreme; and few have had any reservations in describing the economic system of Stalinism as monopolistic in its essential workings.

Finally, the Council of Ministers – that is, the government – was not accountable to the citizenry in economic or indeed in any other matters. Elections did not involve choice, for reasons that will be explained below. They had no effect on the composition of the government, and only a minimal and entirely indirect effect on the economic policies that it should adopt. But whilst it was not accountable downwards to the people, the entire governmental structure was subordinated to the communist party. This subordination is, in fact, a central link in the chain of the communist power monopoly. It provides the bridge between central command planning in the economy, and the political aspect of the monopoly – the 'party's leading role'. To this we must now turn, in order to examine the precise mechanisms through which the communist party secured its monopoly in economic and political life in the Soviet Union.

The leading role of the party
The ministerial structure that was thus set up to organise a centralised and planned economy soon began to develop characteristics that reflected the difficulties and complexity of its tasks. Never sure that the materials it required for its firms to meet their plans would actually be forthcoming, and having no recourse to a market to ensure supplies, each ministry tended to defend itself by making itself as self-sufficient as possible. This 'departmentalism' was deplored as long as the Soviet system survived as one of its besetting sins, frustrating the planners' aims and causing enormous wastage through the hoarding of materials and spare parts. It also introduced a strong dose of oligarchy into the system as the ministries developed into islands of power. It may be asked, then, how this oligarchy is compatible with a view of the Soviet system as monopolistic. The answer lies in the role of the communist party in the political and economic system, since the party from the start set itself the goal of directing and controlling the entire developmental process, and all the people and institutions involved in it.

This purpose was achieved by the creation of a parallel party bureaucracy to oversee the ministerial bureaucracy and to iron out its many problems. In a sense this only added to the element of oligarchy by bringing into being further institutional interests, but at the same time the party was able, through specific mechanisms which will shortly be examined, to ensure that its committees and officials dominated the governmental structures. This domination was supposed to stop short of actual interference, but in fact it did not, and another besetting sin of the Soviet system, equally deplored throughout its life, was *podmena* – the tendency for party bodies to substitute themselves for governmental bodies, rather than simply providing guidance. In *podmena*, seen as a defect of the system but in fact one of its key characteristics, lies one of the essential clues for understanding the workings of the communist power monopoly, and we return to it below.

The communist party had in fact many ways of asserting its dominance. First, it made party membership effectively a passport to success in an administrative career. It was rare for a factory manager not to be a member of the party, and this reached virtually total saturation at the ministerial level. Indeed, to be appointed a member of the party's Central Committee was a reward and an honour to which anyone with the highest ambitions aspired.

Control was exercised also through overlapping membership of important committees. It was common, for example, for the first secretary of a regional party committee to sit on the executive committee of the regional soviet, and for the latter's chairman to be a member of the regional party hierarchy.

Thirdly, in every soviet throughout the system, and in every trade union organisation, the members of the communist party acted as a caucus, guiding its work in accordance with the established principle of the party's leading role.

But transcending all these as a means of control was a particular political technique which came to be characteristic of communist rule in general, and ensured its monopolistic nature. It was a technique that turned on a central institution – the party's apparatus.

The term 'apparatus' referred strictly to the party's own bureaucracy – those people who were paid by the party to do its work. This means in effect all those who staffed the party's committees at the various administrative levels. The size of the total apparatus of the CPSU was never divulged, though figures in the region of 200,000 were deduced. Structurally the apparatus was composed of the departments of the party's committees at the various levels, headed by powerful secretaries. At the regional level, the first secretary of the party's committee was far and away the most powerful figure in the localities. But in a highly centralised and hierarchical system the central apparatus in Moscow dominated the structure. There, the apparatus of the Central Committee comprised a number of departments. The heads of the more important of these held the rank of Secretary of the Central Committee. These together formed a collective body – the Secretariat.[5] The key political figure in the Soviet political system as a whole was the General Secretary of the Central Committee of the CPSU (entitled First Secretary during Khrushchev's period in office).

Figure 1 presents the overall structure of the CSPU as it was before the Gorbachev period, showing both deliberative and executive bodies at each level. Of these various levels two merit particular attention: the union level, where a massive accumulation of power was retained; and the regional (or *oblast*) level, where the party's apparatus played a crucial role in relaying central decisions to the localities. Figure 2 presents the organisational nexus that lay at the heart of the CPSU's structure and thus at the heart of the Soviet political system. Table 5 shows the departments of the Central Committee as they were before the reorganisation of December 1988. Figure 3 gives fuller details of the party's organisation at the regional level.

Clarity in understanding the role of the apparatus is best achieved by focusing attention on two particular functions that it carried out at each administrative level. It is not too bold a generalisation to say that between them these two functions encapsulated the power monopoly.

The first was that of appointment to positions of political importance, or confirmation of such appointments when other agencies were involved. This was known in Soviet parlance as the 'selection and deployment of leading cadres', but it has been associated with another term which achieved a certain notoriety – the *nomenklatura*.

The latter term was used in both a general sense, and in a more specific application. Specifically, the *nomenklatura* was a list of posts to which the party's committee at a given level was competent to appoint, or to ratify appointment. In a looser sense the term was used to refer collectively to all the beneficiaries of this system of élite recruitment. But here again a distinction must be made between those who were carried on the Central Committee's own *nomenklatura* and the lower *nomenklatura*. Membership of the former brought particular privileges and status. Members of the central *nomenklatura* were connected to each other by a separate telephone system, special shops gave them access to scarce goods and enabled them to avoid queuing. Lower down the administrative hierarchy the privileges were fewer. Here the category extended to responsible posts in local government and local economic management, and to chairpeople of collective farms, where the rewards were less. The most powerful figure at local level – the first secretary of the party's regional committee – was in any case carried on the central *nomenklatura*. At central level the appointments function was

Table 5 CPSU Central Committee departments

Administrative organs	Agriculture
Chemical industry	Construction
Culture	Defence industries
Foreign personnel	General
Heavy industry	Information (from 1976)
International	Light industry and food
Machine construction	Organisational–party work
Planning and finance	Main political administration
Propaganda	Science and education
Socialist countries	Trade and consumer affairs
Transport and communications	

was carried out in Moscow (until a reorganisation in 1988) by the Administrative Organs department of the Central Committee's apparatus.

During the Solidarity episode in Poland in 1980-81, a complete list of the *nomenklatura* of the Central Committee of the Polish United Workers' Party (that is, the communist party) became available (see Appendix 1). This gives a good impression of the scope of a ruling communist party's *nomenklatura*.

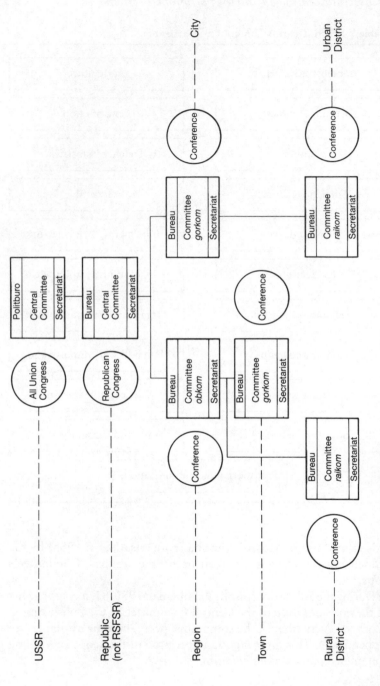

Figure 1 Structure of CPSU, deliberative and executive bodies

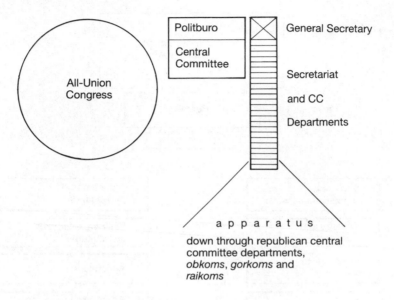

Figure 2 *Central power structure of the CPSU*

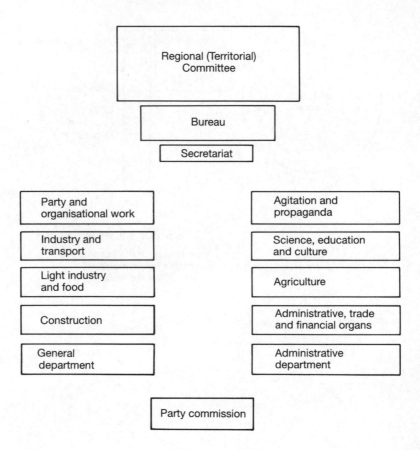

Figure 3 *The CPSU's apparatus at the regional level*
Source: Adapted from *Partiinoe stroitelstvo* (Moscow, 1970), p.152

It is difficult to overestimate the importance for the communist power monopoly of this control over appointments, extending as it did to ministerial and senior administrative posts, editorships at all levels, and the names that were to go on ballot papers as the sole candidate in elections. Indeed the opening up of the electoral system to allow greater freedom of nomination in the election to the new Congress of People's Deputies in 1989 was one of the most important steps in the dismantling of the political power monopoly.

What, then, was the distinction between the apparatus and the *nomenklatura*? The latter was wider than the former. The *nomenklatura* covered many posts that lay outside the party's own structures – positions of responsibility in, for example, the ministries, the collective farms and the trade unions, and often non-party people were appointed to these posts. The apparatus on the other hand was the party's own bureaucracy, the officials who were actually on the party's payroll. Many, if not most, members of the apparatus would themselves be on the *nomenklatura* at a level one step higher than that at which they worked. But whilst this distinction must be made between apparatus and *nomenklatura*, they obviously reinforced each other in functional terms, and formed the organisational hub of the political power monopoly.

The second important function of the apparatus that has underpinned the power monopoly is control of communications, the media, and the written and spoken word in general. It was the Department (from the end of 1988 the Commission) for Propaganda that oversaw this function at central level, and propaganda departments existed also at local level, but this function was rather more diffuse than that of appointments, the party's departments concerned with science, education and culture playing an important part in fulfilling it.

It was through the apparatus that the communist party exercised its 'leading role' in society. If this role is to be presented justifiably as a monopoly, we must clearly go beyond definitions and structures to look at the way in which the apparatus maintained its dominance to the exclusion of other potential sources of power.

First, from the time of the Civil War until the Gorbachev reforms brought the power monopoly into question, there were no free elections in the Soviet Union, either in the party or in the state. The regular and frequent elections that were held functioned as confirmatory referenda in support of the communist party. It fell to the party's apparatus to nominate candidates for election, whilst autonomous organisation for the purpose of contesting an election was ruled out. The role of the propaganda departments of the party was to present the election as evidence of the nation's solidarity with the party in achieving its social goals, and to condemn any proposal to contest an election under the traditional ban on fractional activity. 'It is a secret to no one', wrote a Soviet theorist, 'that our communist party

really accomplishes political leadership of campaigns for election to the soviets, defines their tasks, takes trouble over the election to the organs of popular power of worthy representatives of the working class, the peasantry and the intelligentsia. [The party] sees this as its obligation, and the concrete expression and manifestation of its leading and directing role.[6]

As the example of elections shows, the elements of the power monopoly were mutually supporting. The apparatus held a monopoly in determining the outcome of an election; but it also held a monopoly over the means whereby this situation was presented as right or wrong. The power monopoly was able to cloak its own operations in a way that extruded from the system any public expression of interest or opinion that the monopoly chose not to endorse.

Secondly, whilst the Soviet Union was highly politicised in the sense that the masses were involved in the activity of numerous organisations, virtually all that activity was sponsored by the party. The party created organisations to encadre each strategic sector of Soviet society. The vast majority of school children were enrolled in the Young Pioneer movement, and whilst the Pioneers' activities were only partially political in nature, those of the party's youth league – the Komsomol – were much more so. Almost the entire workforce was enrolled in the trade unions – necessarily, since the chief function of the trade unions was to distribute welfare benefits and to run sanatoria, holiday centres and cultural facilities. The various sections of the creative intelligentsia were likewise encadred by the trade union structure, in the Writers' Union, the Film-makers' Union, the Union of Journalists and so on.

So much organisation may seem to spell pluralism in some form, but in fact it did not, since it was through these 'mass organisations' that the power monopoly worked. In Chalmers Johnson's term, it was a matter of 'pre-emptive organisation'.[7] Through the *nomenklatura* the party's apparatus was able to provide the key personnel in charge of these 'mass organisations', together with the editors of newspapers and the chiefs of the editing houses. Through control of information it was able to present these structures, together with the soviets and the party themselves, as the basic building blocks of socialist democracy, to determine the editorial line and the content of the official printed organs of each mass organisation (each organisation was ascribed an official paper: *Komsomol'skaya Pravda* for the Komsomol, *Trud* ('labour') for the trade unions, *Literaturnaya gazeta* for the Writers' Union and so on), and to prevent any rival views or publications appearing.

The central party apparatus was thus able to create and to control a series of dependent bodies – the Central Council of the Trade Unions, the Central Committee of the Komsomol, the State Committee on Religious Affairs – which in turn controlled a strategic sector of society and maintained the power monopoly in being. A slightly different variation of the mechanism operated within the military. Here a Main Political Administration, whose task was to conduct political work among the armed forces, was at one and the same time a department of the Central Committee apparatus and a section of the Ministry of Defence (see Figure 4).

The existence of these mechanisms meant that there were elections without accountability (or choice, since the *nomenklatura* system has enabled the party to control candidacies in elections), and that there was limitless organisation without political pluralism.

The party's role was, in one sense, quite constitutional. First of all, it was written expressly into the constitution itself – in the Soviet case – at Article 126 of the 1936 constitution, which was reworded as Article 6 of the 1977 constitution. This read – until that article was amended in 1990 in the heat of the power monopoly's crisis – as follows:

The leading and guiding force of Soviet society and the nucleus of its political system, of all state organisations and public organisations, is the Communist Party of the Soviet Union. The CPSU exists for the people and serves the people. The Communist Party, armed with Marxism–Leninism, determines the general perspectives of the development of society and the course of home and foreign policy of the USSR, directs the great constructive work of the Soviet people, and imparts a planned, systematic and theoretically substantiated character to their struggle for the victory of communism.

Secondly, elections did in fact take place, the Council of Ministers was in formal terms elected from the parliament, and the apparatus itself was similarly derived from the party's quinquennial (from

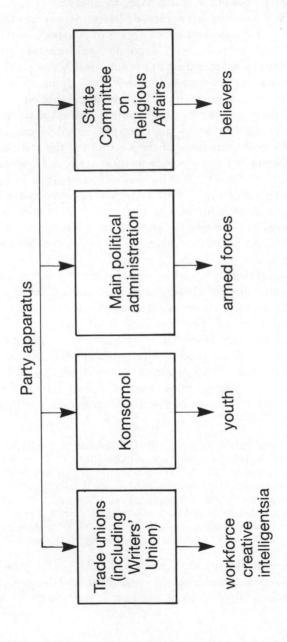

Figure 4 *Party control of strategic sections of society in the USSR*

1961) congresses via the Central Committee. Moreover, the leading role of the party has more than once, at points of crisis in one country or another, been held to represent the norm which a process of 'normalisation' should restore.

It remains to present a conclusion on the relationship between party and state, given the constitutional status of the party's leading role and given the clear overlapping of functions that emerges from the foregoing.

Whether party and state are to be seen as distinct or separate was one of the perennial bones of contention among Sovietologists; nor is it surprising that debate should have focused of this topic, since it lay at the very heart not only of the Soviet system but of communist politics in the broad and, by the same token, of the communist power monopoly itself. All the argument of this book strongly supports the view that party and state, despite all structural arrangements, were analytically inseparable in the Soviet system, and that the predominant characteristic of that system was the monopoly that the party's leadership wielded over the operations of the entire party-state.

First, the principle that 'just as the same item may have multiple functions, so may the same function be diversely fulfilled by alternative items' can be claimed to be axiomatic in the social sciences.[8] Nor should the fact that the party always insisted on the distinction be given too much weight. Authoritative party figures, in their tirades against *podmena*, only too frequently revealed the confusion in their own minds about the supposedly separate functions. 'The CPSU is the ruling party, and everything that happens on Soviet soil is of vital interest to the party as a whole, to each communist. A communist has no right to be a detached bystander', said Khrushchev at the twentieth congress of the CPSU. 'This, of course', he then went on, 'does not mean confusing the functions of party bodies with those of economic agencies or the substitution of party bodies for economic agencies'.[9]

The true situation is well put by Zygmunt Bauman:

We need not be astonished at the far-reaching institutional personal union of these two theoretically separate bodies. Many a body, formally constituting an integral part of, say, the 'party apparatus', owes its existence exclusively to participation in industrial, or transport, or distribution management; but on the other hand, the apparently expert and 'non-political' bodies of professional managers take the most 'political' of all decisions taken in the state. The overlapping of personnel is even more striking: the same group of people on all possible levels of state administration can meet, with only minor adjustments, first in the capacity of a party body, then in the capacity of, say, an industrial board. There is plenty of difference from the legal point of view; from the sociological perspective the difference between the two situations is practically nil.[10]

Central command planning and the leading role of the party have been the most important mechanisms, the one economic and the other political, through which the communist power monopoly has operated. Alone, however, they do not provide an adequate description of the monopoly. For behind these structures has lain a way of thinking about economic, political and social relationships that has not only served to legitimate these structures but has, in a curious way, provided a central part of the identity of a world-wide series of communist parties, most of whom do not exercise governmental power and which therefore have no economy to organise. This way of thinking – to which the term 'democratic centralism' has traditionally attached – will be painted in here with a broad brush. The justification for such treatment is that democratic centralism is so central a concept in the whole field of communist politics that the detail of the matter will appear piecemeal throughout this study – as indeed it has already so appeared more than once.

The 'Leninist principle of democratic centralism'

With very few exceptions, stemming from the strategic rethinking of a number of communist parties in the Eurocommunist period, each and every communist party has claimed to base its organisation on the principle of democratic centralism. Until slightly modified in 1986, this principle was spelled out in the CPSU's statutes as follows:

1 the application of the elective principle to all leading organs of the party, from the highest to the lowest;
2 periodic accountability of party organs to their respective party organisations, and to higher bodies;
3 strict party discipline and the subordination of the minority to the majority;
4 the absolutely binding character of the decisions of the higher bodies upon the lower organs and upon party members.

It is a curious fact that these four clauses describe rather badly the way in which communist parties have conducted their affairs, if election is to involve choice, whilst they describe rather well many of the presuppositions of liberal democracy. True, the second pair of clauses have served to endorse a tradition in which action is subordinated to discussion in pursuit of meaningful social change, and this 'freedom of discussion, unity in action' has indeed been an important part of the way in which communist parties have acted and of their party culture. But on the whole it is in spite of these four clauses, rather than through them, that a full understanding is to be gained of what democratic centralism has meant.

The conceptual scheme of Marxism is, needless to say, particularly congenial to an idea such as democratic centralism which involves a 'dialectical unity' of opposites. But in the discussion on democratic centralism at the most general level, the notion of conflicting pulls within an organisation, be it the party or the state, has been conceptualised in a quite distinctive way. There is a common tendency, discernible in all interpretations of democratic centralism, to see the organisational unit as an organism, the well-being of which outweighs the well-being of the parts. But there is room within this very general conception for differing views on the ideal relationship between centre and periphery, the leaders and the led. In Gramsci's notion of *organicità*, for example, there is an insistence on a constant tension between the 'thrusts from below' and 'orders from above', and it is the 'constant insertion of elements thrown up from the depths of the rank and file' that guarantees this *organicità*. Should the 'birth of oppositional forces' be stifled, the result would be not democratic centralism but bureaucratic centralism.[11]

The Stalinist orthodox version of democratic centralism has shared the tendency to view the organisational unit as an organism subject to good or bad health; but it has seen political tension as a sign not of good health but of bad. It has developed, moreover, in the notion of fractionalism, a negative symbol for such tension.* The ban on fractional activity must be considered part of the definition of orthodox democratic centralism. It is its central requirement, and to

---

* The Russian term *fraktsiya* can be translated as either 'fraction' or 'faction'. I have used the forms 'fraction' and 'fractionalism', following the normal usage of communist parties in English-language texts that refer to the formation of organised groups within the party. There is, in fact, a distinction to be made between fractionalism in this restricted sense and factionalism in a broader sense, which would include less organised alliances and cliques throughout the party and state. The CPSU also used the term *fraktsiya* in a positive sense for the caucus of party members within a soviet or a trade union organisation.

deal with democratic centralism is to deal at the same time with fractionalism.

Fractionalism must be seen as the obverse of orthodox democratic centralism. It has occupied pride of place in the orthodoxy's demonology, and it opposes democratic centralism as chaos is opposed to cosmos. When Lenin first advocated the ban on fractional activity in 1921 he used the analogy with bodily ill-health; and a strong taboo on fractionalism has lived on to become a negative element in the way democratic centralism is conceived and to become also an important element in Stalinism. Stalin's own definition is worth quoting:

The existence of fractions is compatible neither with the party's unity nor with its iron discipline. It scarcely needs proof that the existence of fractions leads to a number of centres; and the existence of a number of centres means the absence of one common centre in the party, the breaking up of unity of will, the weakening and disintegration of discipline, the weakening and disintegration of dictatorship.[12]

Thus, if it is sometimes not very clear what practices orthodox democratic centralism enjoins, it is abundantly clear what practices it condemns: organising to contest the policies of the leadership within the party or of the party within the state is ruled out. But there is more to it than that. Fractional activity has been given the aura of a taboo. It has been seen as abnormal and unhealthy. 'The rejection of democratic centralism', writes Samosudov,

an incorrect interpretation of the norms of party life which stem from it, the destruction of the dialectical interconnection between centralism and democracy in practical activity lead to sickly phenomena in party life, destroy the unity of action and engender crisis situations.[13]

In every party that makes any claim at all to be democratic there is a tension between the competing demands of leadership and of the rank and file, between the formulation of a single policy and the expression of multiple demands. What is at issue is the way in which this tension has been thought of in communist parties, and in particular the way in which the collective will is seen as eclipsing that of individuals. This is well illustrated in Trotsky's celebrated words:

None of us wishes to be or can be right against the party. In the last instance *the party is always right* ... One can be right only with the party and through the party, because History has not created any other way for the realisation on one's rightness.[14]

And Pyatakov in 1928:

A true Bolshevik has drowned his personality in the collective, that is in the 'party', in such a way that he is able to make the effort necessary for renouncing his own convictions and honestly adopting those of the party – this is the criterion by which you can recognise the true Bolshevik. It would be impossible for him to live outside the ranks of the party and he would not hesitate to assert that black is white and that white is black if the party demanded it. In order to be at one with this great party he would lose himself in it and would abandon his own personality to the point where there would no longer be an atom of this own 'I' which did not belong to the party.[15]

There is also in the way democratic centralism is talked and thought about a clear insistence on verticality, discipline and hierarchy, which imparts to the concept a marked military flavour. Illuminating from this point of view is the first occasion when democratic centralism became a contested concept within a communist party. This was during the Civil War period in the Soviet Union when the political practices that had grown up since the revolution were being condemned by an opposition group that called themselves, in fact, the Democratic Centralists. They gave themselves that name precisely because they saw that the practices with which democratic centralism had been associated up to that point were succumbing to the pressures of circumstances. Osinskii claimed that bureaucracy was being 'implanted under the flag of militarisation'. 'We do not need militarisation,' he contended, 'because within our civilian apparatus there is an organic gravitation towards military methods of organisation'.[16]

There are, of course, historical reasons for the fact that communist political organisation had a military flavour. The goals that the ruling parties have espoused, the social discipline that they have enjoined in pursuit of those goals, the evangelising attitude that has been adopted towards the ideology, the circumstances of insurrectionary revolution and civil war in which these parties have become embroiled, and also, certainly in the Soviet case, elements from a national past – all these things have conspired to create a powerful tendency towards military thinking and military patterns of organisation.

This tendency has been manifested in a constant emphasis on unity, discipline and solidarity, and on political practices and attitudes that foster them at the expense of mere discussion, debate and politicking. This attitude of 'theirs not to reason why, theirs but to do and die' is inscribed in the party's fear of degenerating into a 'discussion club' and in the military metaphor of fronts, brigades of socialist labour and so on, which was so characteristic of the Stalinist Soviet Union, and pervaded the discourse of other communist parties.

The ban on fractionalism, the removal of autonomous organisation in the middle regions of the political system, or of horizontal connections within the party, yielded an unstable structure in which the centre was vulnerable to surges of discontent from below, and in which, moreover, the absence of intermediate organisation makes such surges inevitable. In the economic realm the result is, according to Szczepanski, that 'the absence of arbitration structures between employers and employees threatens to convert any work stoppage into a political conflict'.[17] In more strictly political terms, the Yugoslav Eduard Kardelj once claimed that 'We communists must pose the question of how . . . we can overcome the historical practice . . . whereby every political change of government or of policy is always attended by political disturbances reminiscent of a *coup d'état*'.[18]

The problem was put in comparative terms and particularly graphically by Andrei Sinyavski (in 1979):

The Western system is constructed like a hive: the honey cells seem very light and fragile, but they are well built and resilient. Imagine a change of power in Russia. What would happen? People would start to kill each other, the provincials would rush to Moscow, it would be true chaos. For the Soviet system is like a sort of sack full of sand, which stands up only by virtue of being well tied. If you puncture it, everything falls into dust.[19]

The patrimonial system

If a term be sought to catch the essence of the system that the communist power monopoly created in the Soviet Union and that was to prove productive in other contexts, it would be hard to better that which Graeme Gill, in his work on Stalinism, adapts from Weber.[20]

Gill takes as his starting point Weber's definition of patrimonialism as a structure in which political administration is 'treated as a purely personal affair of the ruler, and political power is considered part of his personal property'. The ruler's exercise of power 'is therefore entirely discretionary'. At the centre of this definition of patrimonialism there is an individual ruler – in the

Soviet case Stalin himself. Gill draws attention to the way in which the party became Stalin's patrimony, to his relationship with his lieutenants whose very survival was dependent on the whim of the leader, and to Stalin's organisational power, exercised through his own secretariat, the central apparatus of the party, and the People's Commissariat of the Interior (the NKVD). The writ of this central coercive power, however, ran neither continuously nor firmly, and the so-called 'family groups' that developed in the localities in self-defence against it will be encountered below as evidence of a weakness in the communist power monopoly wherever that monopoly has been exercised.

On this basis it can be shown how both Khrushchev and Gorbachev, the two major post-Stalinist reformers, attacked this patrimonialism, the former, for example, instigating changes in the party's statutes so as to limit the tenure of holders of party officials to two terms in office, which constituted a major challenge to the party's privilege, and the latter not only doing the same but also highlighting abuse of their position by the party's officials through his policy of glasnost.

Gill himself is chiefly concerned to demonstrate how the patrimonial system developed around the individual leader, and then lingered on within the system after Stalin died. At other times, however, he changes the emphasis to talk of 'the primacy of the patrimonial principle in the structuring of party life', and patrimonialism in this broader sense encapsulates rather well the communist power monopoly as it is analysed in these pages. When Stalin died, leaving no explicit heir, the patrimonialism did not wither away; it survived perfectly well without him. And it was not a further individual leader that brought Khrushchev down, but a collective effort on the part of the true patrimonial leader – the party *nomenklatura*. That is, the patrimonialism of the Stalinist system inhered not in an individual leader so much as in the system itself.

Moreover, if the notion of patrimonialism is extended to cover not only the holder of patrimonial power but also the nature of the patrimony itself, it can be seen, in the light of considerations raised in the last chapter, that the Stalinist economic and political system inherited a good deal of its patrimonialism from the revolutionary period.

It will be recalled that it was the period of war communism that began the process whereby economic power was transferred into the hands of the state. It will be recalled also that that process was both seen as desirable in terms of Bolshevik goals, and was furthered by the disruption of the time. The result was the creation of a single pool of economic power, over which the new revolutionary élite exercised a monopoly. This process got under way as the storm clouds of the Civil War were gathering, and was to develop during the war years. Whatever was to happen later under Stalin, the formation of that pool of economic power was a creation of the revolutionary period.

The political monopoly that the new élite exercised was likewise a direct result of the revolutionary process. The determining circumstance here, without any need of ideology – although that, too, was forthcoming – was a simple competition for power, in which the winner took all. There may occur cases where the open competition which revolution involves ends in an enduring compromise between competing forces; if there are such, the Russian revolution was not one of them. By the end of the Civil War the Bolsheviks had freed themselves from their rivals; in power terms they had scooped the pool.

At that point they could say 'all this is ours'. Since that was indeed the case, it would have been surprising if they had not thought and acted accordingly. This they did, converting the pool of economic and political power into a patrimony – a collective good for which they had sole responsibility, to be preserved in the collective interest, but available to the holders of the patrimony as a source of power and privilege. A threat to that power and privilege could then be presented as a threat to the collective interest itself. It must be left to others to make the historical judgement whether this was the result of processes inherent in revolution itself, or whether the Russian revolution was extreme in this regard. Certainly, as far as the creation of a pool of political power is concerned, the French revolution had a similar upshot. As de Toqueville put it in that case:

Napoleon must be neither praised nor blamed for having concentrated in his hands alone all administrative power, for after the sudden disappearance of the nobility and the upper bourgeoisie these powers fell to him unaided.[21]

Notes
1   Alec Nove, *An Economic History of the USSR* (Harmondsworth: Pelican, revised ed. 1982), p. 144.
2   This terminology, adapted from Hirschman, is used here because it will be found to be extremely useful in providing a perspective on the process of change when the Stalinist system began to unravel after that leader's death.

3   E. H. Carr, *A History of Soviet Russia. The Bolshevik Revolution, 1917–1923* (London: Macmillan, 1963), Vol. 2, p. 130.

4   The seminal work on this topic was written by James Burnham, who in 1939 severed a long-standing commitment to the Trotskyist fourth international: *The Managerial Revolution* (New York: John Day, 1941).

5   The central apparatus was reorganised at the end of 1988, and the Secretariat was replaced by six Commissions.

6   A. Lashin in *Kommunist*, 2 (1975), p. 34 (quoted in Ronald J. Hill, 'The CPSU in a Soviet Election Campaign', *Soviet Studies*, Vol. 28, No. 4 (1976), p. 590.

7   J. Chalmers Johnson, *Change in Communist Systems* (Standford, CA: Stanford University Press, 1970), pp. 19–20.

8   Robert K. Merton, *On Theoretical Sociology* (New York: Free Press, 1967), pp. 87–8.

9   *Pravda*, 15 February 1956.

10   Zygmunt Bauman, 'The Second Generation Socialism', in Leonard Schapiro (ed.), *Political Opposition in One-Party States* (London: Macmillan, 1972), p. 235.

11   Quentin Hoare and Geoffrey Nowell-Smith, *Selections from the Prison Notebooks of Antonio Gramsci* (London: Lawrence and Wishart, 1971), pp. 168–9, 188–9.

12   V. I. Stalin, *Foundations of Leninism*, VIII.

13   A. V. Samosudov, 'Demokraticheskii tsentralizm i edinstvo marks-istsko-leninskoi partii', in *Printsip demokraticheskogo tsentralizma v stroitel'stve i deyatel'nosti kommunisticheskoi partii* (Moscow/Berlin: Politizdat/Dietz Verlag, 1973), p. 116.

14   Quoted in Annie Kriegel, *Les grands procès communistes* (Paris: Gallimard, 1972), p. 98.

15   Raphael R. Abramovich, *The Soviet Revolution* (London: George Allen and Unwin, 1962), p. 415.

16   This episode is treated in Roger Pethybridge, *The Social Prelude to Stalinism* (London: Macmillan, 1974), p. 116.

17   J. Szczepanski, *Le Monde*, 7–8 September 1980.

18   See Dennison Rusinow, *The Yugoslav Experiment, 1948–1974* (London: Hurst, 1977), p. 216.

19   Andrei Sinyavski, *Le Monde*, 7 July 1979.

20   Graeme Gill, 'Ideology, Organization and the Patrimonial System', *The Journal of Communist Studies*, Vol. 5, No. 3 (1989), pp. 285–302.

21   Alexis de Tocqueville. *Oeuvres, Papiers et Correspondances*, Vol. 1, *De la démocracie en Amérique* (Paris: Gallimard, 1951), Part 2, p. 305.

Further reading

For a comprehensive text on the Soviet political system
Jerry F. Hough and Merle Fainsod, *How the Soviet Union is Governed* (Cambridge, MA: Harvard University Press, 1979).

For a concise commentary
John N. Hazard, *The Soviet System of Government* (Chicago, IL: University of Chicago Press, 5th ed. 1980).

On specific topics
Abdurakhman Avtorkhanov, *The Communist Party Apparatus* (Chicago, IL: Henry Regnery, 1966).
E. H. Carr, *The Russian Revolution: From Lenin to Stalin* (London: Macmillan, 1979).
Michael Ellman, *Socialist Planning* (Cambridge: Cambridge University Press, 2nd ed. 1989).
Bohdan Harasymiw, *Political Elite Recruitment in the Soviet Union* (Basingstoke: Macmillan, 1984).
Ronald J. Hill and Peter Frank, *The Soviet Communist Party* (London: George Allen and Unwin, 3rd ed. 1987).
Leonard Schapiro, *The Communist Party of the Soviet Union* (London: Methuen, 2nd ed. 1970).
Robert C. Tucker (ed.), *Stalinism: Essays in Historical Interpretation* (New York: W. W. Norton, 1977); and his *The Soviet Political Mind: Studies in Stalinism and Post-Stalin Change* (New York: Praeger, 1963).
Michael Waller, *Democratic Centralism: An Historical Commentary* (Manchester: Manchester University Press, 1981).

3

The transposition of the power monopoly into Eastern Europe

Such were the key characteristics of the communist power monopoly when it had taken on its final shape in the Stalinist Soviet Union. Much of its historical importance, however, and no little part of the interest yielded by its unravelling, has been provided by its capacity to reproduce itself in other parts of the world. In this chapter the manner in which it was transmitted to other European countries will be examined, but it should be borne in mind that it was outside Europe that some of the more spectacular cases of its reproduction took place. For that reason some reference is made to the wider world in this introductory section.

It was said of Islam by Miquel that it has 'travelled only by means of its arms'.[1] For Hugh Seton-Watson, and for many others, the spread of communism, too, has been a matter of imperialist expansion with a strong military component.[2] This both exaggerates and misrepresents the extent to which communism has been propagated by coercion, whether overt or veiled.

True, the effective Soviet occupation of a series of states at the heart of Europe in the aftermath of the Second World War has been one of the central factors in European affairs since that date. But even in Europe, communist parties came autonomously to power in Yugoslavia and Albania, and from 1948 in the former case and 1961 in the latter the Soviet Union was unable to exert any influence on the governments of those countries. In China, in Vietnam and in Cuba, likewise, communism was not implanted by an external power, but emerged from a revolutionary struggle among internal forces. For the victorious communist parties in those countries the Soviet Union represented a model of development congenial to their circumstances.

It is true that in the last two cases, and in a further series of 'states of a socialist orientation' in Africa, Latin America and the Middle East the Soviet Union was able, through extending military and economic aid, to increase its diplomatic weight in the Third World. But in the final analysis, the Soviet dominance of the communist movement which it had done so much to create was more often indirect than direct. Once the revolutionary period had drawn to a close it was only on its western frontier in Europe (with the exception of indirect support in Korea) that it implanted communism by force of arms. To that extent the Eastern European regimes, though relatively numerous, were untypical members of the communist family.

On the other hand, whilst the imperial element in the spread of communism is often exaggerated, arms were frequently involved in the coming to power of communist parties within their own territories, and this had a powerful effect on their political practices and thinking. Whilst the civil war in which the Bolsheviks consolidated their monopoly of power followed the revolution, the Albanian and Yugoslav communists in Europe, like the Chinese and Vietnamese communists in Asia, fought their way to power. The military task bred military structures. Moreover, these other communist parties that have come to power autonomously have done so mostly in agrarian countries whose developmental situation was at times below that even of Russia. There are here two good reasons why the power monopoly in the hands of the ruling communist party should have become a general hallmark of communist politics.

The untypical nature of the East European regimes, however, has been obscured by the fact that once Soviet power had been extended into the region, the Soviet political and economic systems were implanted in the dependent territories, the existing political and social order being set aside in the name of revolution and the 'gains of socialism'. The transformation once achieved, the Eastern European regimes appeared even more 'typically' communist than did, for example, Yugoslavia, simply by virtue of a Soviet influence from which the Yugoslavs had been able to steer clear. But the artificial nature of the situation, and the resentment against the power monopoly that the situation engendered, were to punctuate the post-war history of the region with a series of crises which culminated in the rejection of the power monopoly throughout the region in 1989.

The uniformity of communist rule, therefore, concealed important differences in the situations of the various ruling parties, and of their chances of coping with pressures for change. But the experiences of the ruling parties are only a part, if the determinant one, of the story of the transmission of communism, with its resulting uniformity in organisational norms. The shared circumstances of civil war and relative economic and cultural lag in agrarian societies obviously cannot explain how the non-ruling communist parties of Western Europe, for example, came to be endowed with many aspects of the communist power monopoly as it had developed in the Soviet Union. Nor can they explain how the non-ruling Italian Communist Party came to play an indirect but important part in the process whereby the power monopoly was dismantled in European communism.

The missing explanatory factor is the international organisation that was created in 1919 in the wake of the Russian revolution and membership of which provided a sense of community among communist parties that outlived the organisation itself and still remains one of the few residual factors suggesting that a communist movement still exists at all in Europe. That organisation was the Third (Communist) International, better known as the Comintern. It was through being members of the Comintern that the non-ruling communist parties of the world, including the West European parties, developed a characteristic pattern of political practice that was modelled on that of the Bolsheviks. Moreover, that development followed step by step the evolution of the CPSU itself.

At the very birth of the Comintern, any party wishing to adhere to it was required to accept the 'twenty one conditions for admission of a party into the Third (Communist) International'. This forced splits within many parties by polarising opinion over strategy, and it brought about the final division of the European Left which has been so familiar a part of the furniture of European politics since that day. Since they give so vivid a picture of what Bolshevik 'communism' meant at that turning-point in the history of socialism, they are reproduced in Appendix 2.

Later, with the defeat of the Trotskyist opposition in the Soviet Union in the mid-1920s, the West European communist parties were 'bolshevised', which meant aligning their practices even more closely with those of the Bolsheviks. This involved, for example, the adoption of the 'cell' structure, whereby the parties were required to be organised in basic units in the workplace. We shall see that this highly symbolic feature of the communist power monopoly assumed a high prominence in the final assault on the monopoly in Eastern

Europe in 1989.

With the 'revolution from above' in the Soviet Union in 1928-32 the West European communist parties not only became finally subservient to Moscow, but they absorbed all those features of the power monopoly that were compatible with their non-ruling situation.

The Comintern was dissolved in 1943, at a point in the Second World War when it had become an embarrassment to the Soviet Union. Four years later it was again considerations of Soviet policy, this time in Eastern Europe as the cold war set in, that led in 1947 to the creation of a Communist Information Bureau – the Cominform – but this was restricted to the ruling parties of the day, together with the large French and Italian parties. The Cominform was in turn dissolved in 1956. Its role in the history of communism, and of the communist power monopoly, had been slight in comparison with the massive influence that the earlier Comintern had had in reproducing the CPSU's political forms, within the party and the state, in other parts of the world.

In sum, three factors have played a determinant part in the transmission of communism, and in the creation of the uniformity of organisation that has been so characteristic of communist regimes and communist parties. The first is direct Soviet interference. The second is a revolutionary experience and a post-revolutionary developmental predicament shared by many communist parties which have come to power autonomously. The third is the tradition of politics stemming from membership of the Comintern, in the shaping of which Soviet experience has in turn played a crucial role.

The uniformity characteristic of Stalinist communism was probably at its highest point during the decade between 1947 and 1957, despite the independent stance taken by the Yugoslav party in 1948. The Albanian and Yugoslav parties, both of them members of the Comintern while that organisation existed, had come to power with the defeat of the Axis forces and had set up economic and political structures based on the Soviet experience. This for them, as for many other forces at the time, was the authoritative revolutionary model. Even after Yugoslavia's break with the Cominform in 1948, it was some years before a distinctive Yugoslav organisational model emerged to disturb the uniformity. That break was itself in large part the result of the building up of pressures as the cold war reached its climax of intensity. It was 1947 that saw the culmination of a process, stemming also from those pressures, in which the Soviet Union effectively imposed on Poland, Czechoslovakia, Eastern Germany, Hungary, Bulgaria and Romania a pattern of economic and political organisation that replicated its own. Finally, although it cannot concern us here, another member party of the defunct Comintern came autonomously to power in China at the close of the 1940s and, like the Yugoslavs and Albanians, modelled its initial structures on those of the Soviet Union.

From 1948 onwards, the implications of the independence that autonomous revolution had brought to the Albanians and Yugoslavs began to make themselves felt. Yet, with the hindsight of history, it can be seen that independence, however loudly proclaimed, did not necessarily mean a radical change in policies or in organisational forms. It was not so much a matter of different roads to socialism being followed as substantially the same road being followed in different places. Even Yugoslavia's development remained a variation on the Soviet model until after 1985, although for some forty years Yugoslavia was held to have modified the model in a number of essential ways. In a sense, in fact, Albania and Yugoslavia were the true satellites of Soviet communism, orbiting at a distance the Stalinist tradition which the Soviet Union had done so much to shape; whilst Poland, Czechoslovakia, Hungary, the GDR, Bulgaria and Romania became parts of the single gravitational mass constituted by Soviet power.

The installation of the power monopoly in Eastern Europe

The transposition of Soviet political and economic forms to the countries of Eastern Europe was not immediate, nor did it come about in one single move. What dictated the pace at which it proceeded, and no doubt accounted for some of its brutality, was the sharpening of the tensions of the cold war. Hugh Seton-Watson has provided the now classic description of a three-stage process through which, with Soviet connivance or overt backing, the communist parties acquired a monopoly of political power in the years between the end of the Second World War and the high point of tension in 1947–8. Not all countries passed through all the phases of Seton-Watson's scheme, but it has great value as a model for understanding the way in which the communist parties in Eastern Europe acquired their monopoly of power.[3]

The first stage (occurring in Hungary, Czechoslovakia, Romania and Bulgaria) was the creation of a genuine coalition of left-wing parties, which included communist and socialist parties, but also – except in the Czechoslovak case – agrarian parties. In a second phase the communist party had acquired sufficient power to empty the coalition of any substance, although it retained a formal existence. By this time the communists had normally gained control of certain key ministries, foremost among them the ministries of the interior, justice and defence, and were in a position to dominate political life. Poland and the GDR passed straight into this phase without traversing the first.

Finally the communist party transformed this domination into monopoly by subordinating all political organisation to itself. Existing political parties were not always disbanded. Some were retained and enrolled, together with the trade unions, the party's youth organisation, and other 'mass organisations' in a 'people's', 'national' or 'fatherland' front (the institution was given various names), and it was through this front that the party exercised its control over strategic sections of society. Yugoslavia and Albania proceeded directly to this phase. Given that these two parties came to power through their own resources, and that therefore their circumstances differed in many ways from those of the bloc countries, they might be regarded as falling outside this model, were it not for the fact that the features of the third phase were to become the defining characteristics of the communist style of politics across the region. By 1948 all the ruling communist parties had fallen into the pattern, and the resulting uniformity was to render the final upshot more salient than the steps by which it was arrived at.

Despite the ability of the Soviet Union to order events in the Eastern European countries, it did not incorporate its client states into the Union. At the purely formal level their independence was taken very seriously indeed, and in the concept of 'people's democracies' a doctrinal innovation was found to cater for their independent status within the universe of socialism. But it was from the start an empty independence, and in fact it was the Soviet Union's ability to control them politically that rendered full integration unnecessary.

The question then arises of how that control was exercised. Until Khrushchev modified the original arrangements of the Stalinist period, Soviet domination was maintained through bilateral links between Moscow and its East European satellites, although the Cominform provided, from 1947 to 1956, an international umbrella for these bilateral relations. Another international body existed from 1949 – the Council for Mutual Economic Assistance (the CMEA, better known by its Western label of Comecon), but it was not until the Khrushchev period that the CMEA acquired any real substance. From 1955 it was joined by the Warsaw Treaty Organisation, and from around that date onwards these two multilateral organisations replaced the bilateral links of the earlier period, converting the Eastern European regimes from 'satellites' into 'junior allies'.[4]

But a more general assurance was given to the Soviet Union that its influence was secure by the simple reproduction of the power monopoly in each of the dependent countries. Provided that the 'leading role' of each national communist party was secure in its territory, Soviet influence was safe. Time was to show that the Soviet Union was prepared to see to it, by force of arms if necessary, that the leading role of the party remained intact in each country of the bloc. It was through this congruence between the monopoly held by each country of the bloc parties and by demonstrating its determination to maintain this congruence that the Soviet Union remained master of the game in Eastern Europe; and a call for 'normalisation', as in the aftermath of the Prague Spring, meant the reassertion of the party's role, through the familiar mechanisms.

Thus each of the bloc countries was endowed with mass organisations to encadre strategic sectors of society as in the Soviet Union, with only minor variations – in the GDR, Poland and Czechoslovakia, for example, a number of formally independent political parties were permitted to live on, but they were treated as if they were mass organisations, and were subordinated to the party and its apparatus on an identical footing with the trade unions, the party's youth league, and so on. And the party's apparatus operated exactly as in the Soviet Union – through the two key mechanisms of the *nomenklatura* and control of communications, each of them in the safe hands of the party's apparatus at its various levels. In the Soviet case, however, the CPSU exercised its monopoly of power without the mediation of a 'front', and had disbanded rival political parties before and during the Civil War. The various fronts and the continued existence of a number of political parties in certain of the countries of the region thus distinguished the political systems of Eastern Europe from that of the Soviet Union. But the difference was cosmetic; the party's political monopoly was to all intents and purposes the same in both cases.

In economic life a similar alignment with Soviet norms resulted from the communist assumption of power in the bloc countries. This included the nationalisation of almost all industrial enterprises and the adoption of the system of central command planning on the Soviet model. It also involved a move towards the collectivisation of agriculture, although both the pace and the extent of this varied quite considerably. The determinant factors were state ownership of industry and central planning. These gave the ruling party a control over the economy which, in its substance if not entirely in its detail, replicated the economic monopoly in the Soviet Union.

The fact that the Eastern European countries were not incorporated into the Soviet Union had particular effects in the economic sphere that are worth noting. Whilst the economy of the Ukraine (population approximately 45 million at the time) fell within the monopoly of the overall Soviet plan, that of Czechoslovakia, for example, (with a population approaching 15 million) did not. Instead, a series of autarkic systems was set up, each with its plan, and each therefore enjoying a local monopoly which was to turn out to be resistant to pressures towards integration. Whilst these local autarkies underwent modification with time, they remained an important factor in relations between the Soviet Union and the Eastern European countries.

A frequently cited example of this economic autarky is the Nowa Huta steel works near Cracow in Poland. That country had no substantial existing base in steel production, nor resources of ore, yet for political reasons a giant complex was created which was to serve as a symbol of Poland's commitment to an independent process of industrialisation. Later, under Khrushchev, this early autarky was modified, and the notion of a 'socialist division of labour' was promoted within the Comecon. But there was strong and effective resistance to this, particularly from Romania, which had no wish to have its independent industrialisation curtailed.

The passing of time was to reveal also that the party's economic monopoly in the Eastern European countries was subject to modification, whilst the political monopoly was not. Indeed, the existence and good health of the political monopoly came to be a condition – particularly in Soviet eyes – for slackening that in the economy. Numerous examples can be cited. In 1956 the ruling communist Polish United Workers' Party (PUWP) underwent a crisis severe enough to cause considerable anxiety in the Kremlin. Once assured that the party was capable of sorting out its affairs, the Soviet leadership struck a deal with the Poles which preserved the party's political monopoly, but which allowed for a privatisation of agriculture. This did not seriously affect the system of central planning in Poland, and the party was able to regulate the agricultural economy very closely, but a breach had none the less been made in the economic monopoly.

In 1968 the ruling Hungarian Socialist Workers' Party launched an economic reform which modified the planning mechanisms and made Hungary the standard-bearer in that field among the bloc countries. But it was the fact that the party was in control both of the country and of the reform process that allowed the latter to go ahead. At moments when a party's monopoly has been weak or under threat, not only has economic experimentation been thwarted (as in Czechoslovakia in that same year of 1968), but the Soviet Union, with the support of other apprehensive party leaderships of the region, has taken steps to bolster or reinstate it (as in Hungary in 1956, and Czechoslovakia again in 1968). Yugoslavia, which from 1948 was independent of Soviet control, or indeed influence, presents a rather different case which must be examined separately below.

A case study: Czechoslovakia

The case of Czechoslovakia serves well as an illustration of the way in which the communist power monopoly in both the economy and politics was transmitted to Eastern Europe as a whole.

Highly developed economically, and with a political system that had developed between the wars into a flourishing democracy – surrounded ultimately on all sides by dictatorships of one hue or another – Czechoslovakia was an unpropitious seedbed for the implantation of patterns of economic and political organisation that had been formed in the drive for economic construction in a far less well endowed country. True, Eastern Germany shared Czechoslovakia's economic level, but the status of Germany at the time of the transposition was exceptional in view of the defeat in the war.

Indeed, Czechoslovakia has played a rather special role in the history of communism. In the inter-war years the communist parties of industrial Czechoslovakia and of France were the two largest communist parties of Europe outside the Soviet Union, each of them with a strong worker base. There was therefore no little irony in the fact that it fell to a sovietised Communist Party of Czechoslovakia to grapple with the contradictions between a sovietised economy and the customs and needs of a developed economy – contradictions that were particularly sharply experienced in Czechoslovakia. It was these contradictions and this history that was to give the Prague Spring of 1968 its salience, and to make it one of the major landmarks in the process of de-Stalinisation, and then of the fall of the power monopoly.

The securing of political power

The 'Prague coup' of 1948, through which the Communist Party of Czechoslovakia (CPCz) secured its monopoly of political power, was used from then on by the enemies of communism in Western Europe as a symbol of the danger that communist parties posed, should they win a majority in a democratic election. The CPCz, already strong between the wars and now benefiting from its record in the clandestine struggle against German occupation (and also from having distributed to Czechs and Slovaks the lands confiscated from the expelled Sudeten Germans), had secured, at 38.7 per cent of the poll, the largest vote for any of the parties that competed in an open election in May 1946. The communist leader, Gottwald, was able as prime minister to secure for his party the key government portfolios, of which the ministry of the interior was to prove of particular importance, since it had the organisation of the police in its charge. The minister, Nosek, was to play a crucial role in the take-over of power.

In September 1947 the communists in Slovakia, who had not had the success of their Czech comrades in the 1946 elections, secured, by a feat of political manoeuvring, the resignation of the Slovak government and its reconstitution under the communist Husak, who retained merely five non-communists in his team. This was a prelude to what was to happen at federal level in early 1948, when Gottwald engineered a similar resignation, this time of the non-communist ministers of the national government, through a mixture of intimidation, political sleight of hand, and pressure from massive street demonstrations. The coup of 1948 was therefore not entirely unconstitutional, though it bespoke scant respect for the norms of democratic politics.

But in any case it was not the coup itself, but its aftermath that installed the communist power monopoly in Czechoslovakia. There had existed before the coup a National Front, which was at that time a loose coalition of political parties. It was now refashioned so as to act as the political arm of the single ruling communist party. In the new election of 1948, it was the National Front that proposed candidates for election. Since no other electoral organisation was permitted to exist, the communist party had secured a monopoly of the electoral process. This in turn emasculated the Assembly, which lost its character as a debating chamber. As noted above, it also acquired the function of linking together all the mass organisations under the party's control.

Secondly, Gottwald set to work to reproduce on Czechoslovak soil a party apparatus modelled on that of the CPSU, comprising departments duplicating the functions of the state bureaucracies, but also the characteristic, and determinant, cadre department, which had charge of the *nomenklatura*, and the department for agitation and propaganda, which controlled communications.

Thirdly, the establishment of the political monopoly in Czechoslovakia had its economic counterpart. A process of nationalisation took place through a series of measures. First, in agriculture – and pre-dating the communist seizure of power – almost a quarter of the acreage of the entire territory fell to the state when the Sudeten Germans were expelled and wartime collaborators were dispossessed. A policy of collectivisation in agriculture was adopted by the communist party on assuming power, as a result of which the acreage in socialist ownership of one form or another – and therefore subject to the party's control – rose considerably. By 1960 it stood at 88 per cent.

A substantial part of Czechoslovak industry (between 60 and 70 per cent) had been nationalised before the communist party seized power, but thereafter state ownership was extended to monopoly proportions. First, all enterprises with more than fifty employees were nationalised, but gradually, through various forms of 'intervention', such businesses as remained in private hands in industry, trade and distribution were taken over by the state, leaving only a very small sector of artisans and tradespeople (47,000 units employing 50,000 people in 1956, against 383,000 and 905,000 respectively in

Table 6   Changes in ownership of fixed assets in Czechoslovakia

	Capital equipment in the whole economy (per cent of value)					Agricultural land (per cent of area)						Living houses	
												per cent of flats (1930)	per cent of value (1955)
	1930	1947	1950	1955	1960	1937	1947	1950	1955	1960	1965		
Private property	(78)	(45)	10	4	0	99.5	98.9	77.9	57.4	12.0	10.0	88.4	56.3
Co-operative property	(1)	(1)	1	5	9	–	–	9.1	26.7	67.5	60.2	4.3	} 43.7
State property*	(21)	(54)	89	91	91	0.5	1.1	13.0	15.9	20.5	29.8	7.3	

* State property includes also local government property.

† Machinery, equipment, livestock and buildings excluding dwellings (living houses). Figures for 1937 and 1947 are estimates.

Co-operative property includes private plots of co-operative farmers.

‡ In conurbations with more than 10,000 population only.

1948).[5] The means chosen for organising this nationalised productive capacity was central command planning on the Soviet model. The market was banished from the heart of the economic system, and administration replaced the invisible hand. As in the Soviet Union, it fell to the party's apparatus to sort out the innumerable problems that this created in production and supply.

The emasculation of the trade unions in Czechoslovakia

Finally, the trade unions were deprived of their autonomy and subordinated to the party. This was of especial significance in that Czechoslovakia had a developed industrial base, and the trade unions were strong in both numbers and organisation. The Communist Party was well represented both at leadership and membership level, particularly in certain areas such as 'red Kladno'. Indeed, massive demonstrations organised by the trade unions had helped handsomely towards creating the atmosphere of tension which the CPCz exploited in its bid for power, whilst trade union leaders such as Antonin Zapotocky themselves played a significant role in the coup. To blame the communists for emasculating the trade unions is therefore a complicated charge to lay. None the less, the way in which the trade unions were brought to heel in Czechoslovakia casts an interesting light on certain aspects of the communist power monopoly, and the story is worth telling in some detail.

The trade union movement in pre-war Czechoslovakia presented the fragmented and incremental growth so common to unionism in the industrialised countries. But after the war a reorganisation took place and the Czechoslovak trade unions were consolidated into a single unified movement – the Revolutionary Labour Movement (better known by the Czech acronym ROH).

Already existing at the moment of the ROH's inception was a Central Workers' Council, which had operated clandestinely during the Nazi period within the corporatised trade unions. Communist resistance activists were well represented in this body and indeed the communist Zapotocky became its chairman in June 1945. During the Prague Uprising in the closing days of the war the Central Workers' Council called on all workers to form 'revolutionary works councils which shall exercise control over production and management of the factories', and these works councils became the basic organisational units of the ROH.[6] They were elected by all the workers in a given firm, and although the CPCz was strong in the councils, the control that it exercised in them was far from complete. In fact the works councils and the CPCz followed different tactics at this time, the former often adopting a more radical stance than the latter.

During 1945 the CPCz began the process of dominating the works councils, by using its control of the Central Workers' Council to create a rival set of grass-roots organisations, outside the works councils, which would constitute a parallel hierarchy within the ROH as a whole. Workers were now encouraged to enrol in voluntary 'ROH local groups'. The membership of these would elect 'works committees' and the latter would be articulated upwards to fill the organisational ground between the base of 'ROH local groups' and the national Central Workers' Council. The rivalry, and confusion, that arose from this first step in the process whereby the CPCz gained control of the trade union organisation was eliminated by the second step, which was to put the 'ROH locals' in charge of elections to the works councils.

This was accomplished by a Works Councils Decree, signed in October 1945 by President Benes, which charged the ROH local groups with organising elections for the councils and with compiling a list of candidates. Not only that, but they were given an explicit monopoly in this regard. The list submitted by the ROH local group would offer no choice of candidate, and workers would vote for or against the list *en bloc*. To gain election the list had to receive 80 per cent or over of the votes cast. Should it fail, there would be a second ballot; and if that did not produce the required percentage, the ROH local group would nominate a 'substitute body' in place of the works council. In either case, the ROH local group was in a position to determine the composition of the works councils. It was a system of elections without choice. According to Kovanda's authoritative account of this episode, 'The actual elections were for all practical purposes reduced to a popularity poll for the communist-controlled ROH'.[7] The trade unions had been reduced to an arm of the party, to be run from above after 1948 as mass organisations according to the techniques of control established in the Soviet Union.

The establishment of the communist power monopoly in the economies of the other countries of the Soviet bloc differed in its details from this Czechoslovak case study. The result, however, was in all cases remarkably uniform. All industry was owned by the state and run through a central plan; a largely collectivised agriculture reduced to a minimum planning uncertainties stemming from agricultural interest pressures (even in the Polish case, where it was in private hands from 1956, agriculture was subject to extreme forms of regulation); whilst at the heart of the system the party exercised a monopoly control over all forms of political organisation.

That must be the general historical conclusion. Like all such general conclusions it is open to refinement and qualification by the presentation of detail for which there is no space here. It should be noted, however, that in both Poland and Hungary the crystallising Stalinist system was shaken in 1956 – that is, less than a decade after the advent of communist rule – by major crises to be recorded below. Whilst the chief upshot of these crises was the confirmation of Soviet control in the region, in both cases a new leadership was tacitly to offer its people at least a cushioning of the Stalinist rigour. This was to show itself, as we shall see, far more in the economic than in the political sphere, but it is no accident that when new winds blew with the accession of Gorbachev to the post of general secretary of the CPSU it was in Poland and Hungary that advantage was first taken of the changed atmosphere.

Romania was to display a quite opposite evolution. There, the Stalinist system was to strengthen under Ceausescu to the extent of caricature. Whilst in the Soviet Union itself the death of Stalin had seen incumbency of the power monopoly shift from a personal dictatorship to collective rule by the party's leadership and the apparatus, in Romania Ceausescu was to take up the baton of dictatorship, preventing any coagulation of rival power at the centre of the political system within the bureaucracies of either party or state by a constant shuffling of personnel, except in the case of members of his own family, who provided an inner core of leadership – socialism, as the wits had it, in one family.

Soviet relations with the bloc countries

Two questions in particular arise from this discussion of the transposition of the power monopoly into the countries of the Soviet bloc. The first concerns the extent to which the Soviet Union can be said to have exercised a monopoly of power within its direct sphere of control in Eastern Europe, reproducing the monopoly of the CPSU's leadership within the Soviet Union itself. Might not an extension of the notion of monopoly to this international context rob it of the analytical value that it has when applied to each of the political systems separately? Secondly, how did Soviet control affect the legitimacy of the governments and ruling parties of these client states? Given the subsequent history of Eastern Europe, this question is clearly of the greatest importance.

Certainly many of the monopolistic features that have characterised the Soviet political system were present in its relations with the Soviet bloc as whole. The frontiers of the bloc were, if anything, more firmly marked than those of the Soviet Union itself, with the Berlin Wall standing as a rugged symbol of this. That extended frontier served an economic as well as a political role: trade within the Council of Mutual Economic Assistance (the Comecon) was conducted on an entirely different basis from the trade that each constituent nation carried on with the external world. Whilst the individual communist parties were formally independent, the congruence between the mechanisms through which the leading role of the party was maintained, and the Soviet Union's readiness to use tanks in order to 'normalise' any softening of that role, had the flavour of monopoly.

But many other features suggest that, whilst Soviet control over the bloc states was rigorous, systematic and involved a high degree of coercion, the relationship was not such as to justify extending the notion of monopoly to that level. Moscow's control over the communist party in the Ukraine or Uzbekistan, for example, was organisationally far tighter than its control over the communist parties of Eastern Europe – in fact it was complete. This was well illustrated by the freedom of manoeuvre that Romania enjoyed in international relations between 1964 and the oil crisis of the 1970s. The same country's refusal to allow Warsaw Treaty manoeuvres on its soil illustrates the limits of arrangements within that organisation. And whilst the CMEA constituted an economic unit with its own pricing, barter and clearing mechanisms, its ability to integrate the Eastern European economies was restricted by the high degree of economic autarky of each individual state. Each Eastern European country had its own plan, and it is not too much of a simplification to say that one plan meant one monopoly.

In brief, purposes of clarity are better served by reserving the concept of monopoly for the relations within the economic and political systems of the individual societies concerned, without inviting the confusion that follows from an extension of the concept to the international level.

Time was to show that formal separation from the other states of the bloc that it dominated had both benefits and disadvantages for the Soviet Union itself and the preservation there of the power monopoly. On the one hand, separation provided a buffer against contagion in the event of a threat to the monopoly in one of the units. On the other it was more difficult for the Soviet Union to police and contain popular movements within those external units. It showed itself willing to undertake such policing on a number of prominent occasions. The Brezhnev Doctrine, enunciated in the aftermath of the Warsaw Pact's intervention in Czechoslovakia in 1968, and describing the relationship between the 'brother republics' and the Soviet Union in terms of a 'limited sovereignty', offered a specious rationalisation of this willingness. It was specious in that simple control is not monopoly, and the Brezhnev Doctrine in fact proclaimed more than it could ultimately guarantee.

The second question raised by the transposition of the power monopoly to the bloc countries worth noting in conclusion concerns the legitimacy of the new rulers of those countries.

The fact that communism was imposed on those Eastern European countries that fell within the sphere of direct Soviet influence placed their leaderships in an ambiguous and awkward situation. First, there was no way of testing the acceptability of a given leader to his people, given an electoral system that everyone knew did not involve choice. Secondly, Soviet influence in the region could only be experienced as Soviet domination, articulated through the ruling parties. The leaders of those parties necessarily appeared as stool-pigeons of Soviet power. True, the relationship with the Soviet Union was experienced in different ways: Russian aid in the Turkish wars of the late nineteenth century, and a shared Slav and orthodox cultural background have meant that Bulgarians did not evince the same hostility towards the Soviet Union that the Poles or Hungarians in particular showed.

It is true also that certain Eastern European leaders at various times found ways of acquiring apparent acceptability in the eyes of their people: Gomulka in Poland until the mid-1960s, Kadar in Hungary during the years in which his unspoken 'social compact' lasted, whereby the people put up with communist party rule in return for an undertaking by the party to further the material well-being of the population as far as possible; Gheorghiu Dej and later

Ceausescu in Romania, who were able to gain favour at home through a demonstrably independent foreign policy abroad – again within the bounds of what the post-war settlement allowed. Nevertheless, overall the leaderships of those Eastern European countries that were subordinated to direct Soviet power had a real problem of legitimacy.

The Yugoslav and Albanian leaderships, it should be noted, did not suffer from this disability. Quite on the contrary, the revolutionary struggle there provided an heroic myth which stood the new élite in good stead, at least until, with the passing of time, the idol turned out to have developed feet of clay. Even then, in the ensuing turmoil that will be recounted below, the communists could count on somewhat greater support among the population (or, in the Yugoslav case, the Serb and Montenegrin sections of it) than could the leaderships of countries where communism had been imposed from without.

In sum, Soviet influence led to the transposition of the communist power monopoly from the Soviet Union to those Eastern European countries which fell within that sphere of influence. In each country the monopoly reproduced with considerable uniformity the features of the Soviet monopoly: central command planning, and a 'leading role of the party' resting on the pillars of control of appointments and of communications exercised by the party's apparatus. Whilst in the economic sphere modifications of the monopoly occurred, orthodoxy in the political sphere was maintained. The power monopoly secured the position of the national leaderships in circumstances where their legitimacy was necessarily weak, whilst the security of each party's power was a condition for Soviet security in the region. It was the congruence and interdependence of these discrete monopolies that kept the edifice together, rather than an overt international monopoly of power exercised by a Soviet master over the client states of Eastern Europe.

In one corner of communist Europe – Yugoslavia and Albania – a different story had unfolded. Of these, Yugoslavia offers a special interest, in that for long years it stood as an example of the ability of communism to reform itself.

The development of the power monopoly in Yugoslavia

The communist power monopoly has on the whole had a thoroughly bad press. It had, however, one or two redeeming features to which its defenders have been able to appeal. The case of Yugoslavia offers good examples of such arguments.

First, having come to power in a society marked by wide cultural diversity and differing levels of economic development, Tito's revolutionary government saw it as a major policy objective to reduce the gap between the richer and the poorer areas of the country. Central control of investment gave it the levers necessary to pursue this objective. That is, the monopoly in the economic realm, as in the Soviet case, was functional in terms of realising centrally determined objectives at a certain stage of economic development. We shall shortly see that when Yugoslavia embarked on its reforming course after 1948, one of the major aims of the decentralising reformers was to get rid of central control of invest-ments, and with it an egalitarianism which was seen as hindering the economic development of society as a whole. Defence of equality through central control of investment thereby became one of the strongest arguments of the defenders of the power monopoly.

Secondly, it was possible to argue that in Yugoslavia an open electoral system would threaten the cohesion of the state, since if alternative candidacies to those of the Communist Party (or League of Communists as it became from 1952) were to be allowed, the result would simply be the creation of a series of national parties based on the ethnic and cultural divisions of Yugoslavia.

Time was to reveal that such apprehensions were well founded. But a wider argument was involved that raises central questions about the function of elections and the nature of representation. Control, or manipulation, of the electoral process by the centre can be defended not only on the grounds of protecting the cohesion of the political system, as in this Yugoslav case. It can also be held to be necessary if a full cross-section of society is to be represented. Free and open elections offer no such guarantee. This argument itself, of course, is open to manipulation. Nowhere, for example, has the communist power monopoly been used to ensure that women are represented proportionally to their numbers in society, although such representation as they have enjoyed must be attributed in large part to the power monopoly. But the beneficial aspects of controlled elections have had enough force for them to be used by supporters of the power monopoly in debates over reform in communist parties and communist political systems.

Equality and at least a diminution of ethnic rivalry were thus delivered to post-war Yugoslavia by a communist party victorious in the partisan war fought both against the Chetniks of Mihailovic and against the Axis powers, and exercising a monopoly of power inherited from that military struggle. The story thereafter is one of a slackening of the power monopoly, and a concomitant increase both in the distance between rich and poor areas, and in ethnic rivalry.

Subsequent Yugoslav history largely erased the memory of the early post-war days when opponents of the Communist Party in Yugoslavia were charged with being collaborators and imperialist agents, and were removed from the political scene and in many cases executed after trial by a military court. The circumstances were such, as with the Civil War period in Soviet Russia, to favour rough justice and a sharp centralisation of power. They not unnaturally played a great part in determining the actual form that the power monopoly took in the Yugoslav case, in its political and its economic aspects.

First, the political unit within which the power monopoly was being exercised was sealed off from the external world. The vigorous tourist industry and open borders which were for so long a feature of Yugoslavia, and which were so important a factor in the erosion of the monopoly, were a later development. In the early days Yugoslavia was as good an example as any of the close connection between the closed frontier and the preservation of the party's power monopoly.

Secondly, the party moved directly to ban existing rival political parties and to rule out the formation of new ones. It moved against rival sources of ideological influence in a similarly direct manner, often using wartime collaboration as a pretext, as in the case of the Catholic Archbishop Aloysius Stepinac, who was sentenced to sixteen years in prison.

Thirdly, the influence of the Soviet model in those early days can be seen in the formation of an apparatus which enabled the party to control strategic sectors of society less directly. As in the Soviet Union, trade union organisation was encouraged, but sponsored by the party, and one of the partisan leaders, Vukmanovic Tempo, was placed at the head of the trade union's central council. The apparatus' control was exercised, again as in the Soviet Union, through its departments dealing with nominations and with communications and the media.

Fourthly, the oligarchic character of the communist power monopoly in general is very clearly exemplified in the case of Yugoslavia. The partisan struggle, waged in a relatively small country, had created close bonds within a restricted leadership group drawn from the various Yugoslav nationalities. One by one these founding oligarchs were to fall out with their fellows (the Montenegrin Djilas from 1953; the Serbian Rankovic in 1966), or eventually to die (the Slovene Kardelj in 1979; the Croatian chief Bakaric in 1983; Tito himself in 1980). But in the early years they guaranteed the power monopoly, and in a sense embodied it.

Fifthly, Yugoslav experience, especially in those early days, illustrated equally well a further feature of the monopoly: its dependence on policing. A Department for the People's Defence (OZNa) was set up in 1944, and was later renamed the State Security Administration. Its function, in Tito's words, was to 'strike terror into the bones of those who do not like this kind of Yugoslavia'.[8]

Finally, the Yugoslav communist leadership embraced what had become by the time of their revolution a traditional way of talking and thinking about political relationships, which was described above as a blend of Marxist precept and the Soviet revolutionary experience. Indeed, a translated Soviet textbook was used in university courses on Marxist-Leninist theory, marking not only the lack of a Yugoslav corpus of literature in that area, but equally the authority that Soviet socialism carried at the time.[9] The historic role of the proletariat, together with the vanguard role of the communist party in furthering it, provided the ideational underpinning of the political system; whilst the ban on fractionalism legitimised the moves taken by the party to outlaw dissenters in society, and by the leadership to frustrate opposition within the party itself.

The early policies
The early steps taken in the revolutionary reorganisation of the economy tended equally to monopoly, but contained features that distinguished Yugoslav from Soviet experience.

Two laws on nationalisation were passed, the first in 1946 and the second in 1948, bringing all industry and transport of any significance, together with almost the entire distribution network, into the state's hands. The influence of Soviet experience was shown not simply by the decision to organise this pool of resources through a system of centralised planning, but by the fact that Boris Kidric, who was to be Yugoslavia's planning chief in this early period, made a study of Soviet planning before embarking on his own project. The first five-year plan was duly launched in April 1947.

Administration thereby replaced the market in the whole of industry and distribution; and this was centralised administration. What followed bore a marked resemblance to Soviet experience: the centre was able to determine clear priorities, the targets of the plan favouring heavy industry over consumer production; there was an enthusiasm for large projects; and investment was channelled to the less developed areas – Bosnia-Hercegovina, Montenegro and Macedonia. All these features of early Yugoslav planning reflected the party's monopoly in the industrial realm. Moreover, the foreign capital that had played a prominent role in the pre-war economy was sequestered, and foreign entrepreneurs were expelled. This correspondingly reduced resistance to a monopoly of ownership. The same could not be said, however, for a policy of levelling among the eight constituent republics. That policy was pregnant with future problems; but in those early days, with the discord and the slaughter of the war so recent a memory, the monopoly held up. It was secured, in large part, by the cohesion of the party leadership, its authority and – at that point – the authority also of a Soviet model.

The situation in agriculture was somewhat different. The party's strength when it came to power was drawn to a great extent from the peasantry. An early law restricting land holdings to between 35 and 45 hectares in fact benefited that peasant support, and the party could not bring itself to force the peasantry into collectives. On the other hand, the centre's control over prices and over the marketing of produce meant that the peasants were effectively subjected to the effects of the power monopoly. In Rusinow's words the Yugoslav political-economic system became 'a single, giant, countrywide and monopolistic trust' and he quotes Bilandzic, who described the system as 'an unfissured monolith . . . divided into sectors or subsystems and founded on an all-inclusive State-ownership monopoly over the means of production, over what ends they served, and at whose behest'.[10]

Yugoslavia after its expulsion from the Cominform

It was a major turning-point in the history both of Yugoslavia and of the communist movement when the Yugoslav Communist Party was expelled from the Cominform in 1948. The rupture forced the Yugoslavs to fashion an independent strategy for its future development in a world divided into two camps. The socialist option, and the authority of the party in the country, were guaranteed by the success of the partisan struggle. The power that the party had won in fighting a war was to colour the ensuing reform process. The reforms that the Yugoslavs put in place from 1948, after a very brief transitional period of increased orthodoxy, were intended to constitute an alternative to Soviet bureaucracy, and for almost forty years they were seen in that light. Time was to show, however, that whilst the Yugoslav experiment in market socialism and 'social self-management' was indeed innovative, it retained elements of that initial power monopoly. This was to become increasingly clear after 1985, when the new winds blowing in Eastern Europe were to lead to far more radical solutions than the Yugoslav leadership had ever contemplated. In this study of the communist power monopoly the Yugoslav experience therefore has a rather special place. Since the Yugoslavs' claim to have done away with the power monopoly was such an important part of the history of European communism during the intervening years, it is worth setting out at this point what the Yugoslavs presented as the basis for it.

The claim was framed in terms of a critique of Soviet bureaucracy, the remedy for which was seen to lie in political and economic decentralisation. To achieve this goal, the following steps were taken. First, a system of workers' self-management was put in place, which became *social* self-management later when the system was extended from industry to places of work in other areas, such as hospitals, schools and the like. To be effective, and to give the producer control over the productive processes, economic decision-making had to be devolved down to the enterprise, where a workers' council was to make the strategic decisions. The law establishing such workers' councils dates from 1949 and was one of the earliest practical moves of the reform, although the ordinances regulating workplace decision-making, like all constitutional matters in Yugoslavia, have gone through very many revisions.

Central command planning was clearly incompatible with devolving real decision-making to the enterprise level and it was abandoned. Planning at both the federal and the republican level could henceforth be no more than indicative. Furthermore, as noted above, central control of investment was relaxed.

Since the portion of agriculture that was directly organised by the state was very small, these economic reforms spelled the end of anything that could reasonably be termed a monopoly in the economy. In fact a previously existing situation of monopoly had been replaced by regulation of a highly decentralised system, with a strong element of producer democracy built into it.

Secondly, the Communist Party of Yugoslavia, which had conceived and engineered these reforms, determined to withdraw from its monopoly of power in the political sphere, on the grounds that direct interference in the running of public affairs, particularly in the economy, was incompatible with the spirit of the reforms, but also so as to signal to the citizenry and to the socialist universe that this aspect of Soviet bureaucracy also was being set aside. The party's apparatus was consequently reorganised to accommodate its changed role, and it was considerably cut back in size. To mark the turn the party changed its name from Communist Party of Yugoslavia to League of Communists of Yugoslavia. These decisions were taken at the party's sixth congress in 1952.

The reforms were accompanied at a less practical level by theoretical adjustments to the party's doctrines. The redefinition of the communist party's role has already been noted. Other changes concerned the state and the producer in a socialist society. The basis of ownership, for example, was redefined. State ownership on the Soviet model was claimed to be incompatible with an economic structure where the workers were in control of production, amortisation and distribution of the proceeds of production. 'Social ownership' was therefore defined effectively as no ownership, the critical factor being seen as the use of the means of production by the producers. This was, of course, something of a fudge; it was as open to attack on theoretical grounds by the regime's critics as was social self-management on empirical grounds and of course the leading role of the party itself.

It is of the greatest importance to note that social self-management acquired, or rather was given, a high symbolic status, and was added to the partisan experience as the basis of the legitimacy of the country's rulers. The intervening years have shown that the appeal that the reforms made for the support of the people exaggerated the extent of what the people were actually being given. This will form the substance of later chapters, when it will be seen that debates within Gorbachev's Soviet Union have had much in common with these earlier debates in Yugoslavia, and that when pressure for much more radical reform built up in other countries east of the Oder-

Neisse line, the Yugoslav reforms began to appear in a new light. Yugoslavia itself thereupon became itself affected by the massive and generalised move for change. Yet in all the turbulence that this has caused within Yugoslavia, the fact that the country's development has been autonomous and in that sense organic, has strongly affected the outcome.

Notes

1   André Miquel, *L'islam et sa civilisation* (Paris: Armand Colin, 1977), p. 310.
2   Hugh Seton-Watson, *The Imperialist Revolutionaries: World Communism in the 1960s and 1970s* (London: Methuen, revised ed. 1980).
3   Hugh Seton-Watson, *The Pattern of Communist Revolution: An Historical Analysis* (London: Methuen, 1953), pp. 248–56.
4   Zbigniew Brzezinski, *The Soviet Bloc: Unity and Conflict* (Cambridge, MA: Harvard University Press, 1967).
5   See Jaroslav Krejci, *Social Change and Stratification in Postwar Czechoslovakia* (London: Macmillan, 1972), pp. 12–27.
6   For the details of this account, see K. Kovanda, 'Works Councils in Czechoslovakia, 1945–47', *Soviet Studies*, Vol. 29, No. 2 (1977), pp. 257.
7   *Ibid.*, p. 263.
8   Dennison Rusinow, *The Yugoslav Experiment, 1948–1974* (London: Hurst, 1977), p. 15.
9   A. Ross Johnson, *The Transformation of Communist Ideology: The Yugoslav Case, 1945–1953* (Cambridge, MA: MIT Press, 1972), p. 72.
10   Rusinow, *The Yugoslav Experiment*, p. 22.

Further reading

Phyllis Auty, *Tito* (London: Longman, 1970).
M. Drachkovitch (ed.), *The Revolutionary Internationals, 1864–1943* (Stanford, CA: Stanford University Press, 1966).
François Fejtö, *A History of the People's Democracies* (Harmondsworth: Penguin, revised ed., 1974).
Thomas T. Hammond (ed.), *The Anatomy of Communist Takeovers* (New Haven, CT: Yale University Press, 1975).
Ghita Ionescu, *The Politics of the European Communist States* (London: Macmillan, 1968).
David McLellan, *Marxism After Marx* (London: Macmillan, 1979).
Hugh Seton-Watson, *The East European Revolution*, (Boulder, CO: Westview, revised ed. 1985).

Part II

The power monopoly under pressure

4

Weaknesses in the communist power monopoly

Transmitted in this way beyond the country of its origin, the communist power monopoly was for a half a century a major feature of the European political scene, not only underpinning the power of the CPSU within the Soviet Union and of the Soviet Union within its empire in Eastern Europe, but constituting the framework of power in Yugoslavia and Albania and, by an at times incongruous extension, providing the ground-rules for the political life of a series of non-ruling communist parties in Western Europe. In historical terms it reached its apogee as the cold war itself was at its climax in the late 1940s. With historical hindsight it can be seen to have started decomposing in some countries as soon as Stalin was in his grave, and indeed signs of erosion were discernible even before that. But by the very way in which it worked the communist power monopoly was able to conceal these first intimations of decay. Only after 1985, when a reforming Soviet leadership set in train the policies that were to destroy it, did its true vulnerability and the extent of its decay become apparent. True, many had been predicting its demise; but very few, even of these, actually expected the collapse to happen when it did, and with such speed and thoroughness.

Now that the edifice has finally crumbled, it is possible to analyse in detachment the manner of the collapse. In this chapter the various pressures, internal and external, to which the communist power monopoly came to be subjected will be analysed. The focus will be predominantly on the Soviet Union, the country where the monopoly took shape, and whose development determined the extent to which change could take place in other lands.

A discussion of its weaknesses raises central questions about the nature of the communist power monopoly. Did it carry within itself

the seeds of its own destruction? To what extent had it been eroded
by the time of its fall, even if the signs of that erosion were concealed
from external view? How far was the social and economic development of the countries in which it had been established responsible for
the pressures that led to its fall? Structural weaknesses there certainly
were. But many of these stemmed from the circumstances of the
monopoly's birth, when it was brought into being to address goals of
economic development. Movement towards those goals meant that
society relatively speedily outgrew the early structures, and this
brought on to the agenda the question of the extent to which the
system would be able to adapt to new circumstances. It proved, in
fact, to be singularly inflexible, and that inflexibility itself became a
source of weakness. Social and economic change also affected the
make-up of the group that exercised the power monopoly, dispersing
power more widely in a way that could not but dilute and at the same
time put pressure on the monopoly. Developments such as these raise
empirical questions about the degree of oligarchy that the monopoly
secreted, but also theoretical questions about the relationship
between oligarchy and monopoly in the political sphere.

These questions will be approached by examining first some symptoms of malaise in the communist power monopoly that became
increasingly manifest as the Stalin years receded. The discussion will
then move on to treat two particular structural weaknesses from
which the communist power monopoly suffered, not only in the
Soviet Union, but elsewhere too. The first of these was the impedi-
ments to information flows that the monopoly involved, exacerbated
by the extreme centralisation of the political and economic systems.
The second was the centre's inability to control what was happening
at the periphery of the system, with consequent leakages in the power
monopoly which in some cases all but drained it of its character as a
monopoly, and played a large part in the collapse of communism
overall.

Next, certain factors will be examined that help to explain why the
monopoly fell when it did, and why it fell so abruptly in so many
countries at roughly the same time. The first of these, which applies
in particular to the Soviet Union, concerns the way in which social
and economic development gradually altered the environment in
which the party exercised its monopoly, rendering that monopoly
ever more vulnerable. In a sense, the Soviet Union outgrew the
monopoly structure of its youth, and some of the details of this

growing weakness of the monopoly deserve treatment. But secondly, in the countries of Eastern Europe, and more particularly of East Central Europe, the monopoly was vitiated from its inception by being imposed on those societies by a too powerful Soviet neighbour. In those countries the monopoly was only as strong as the willingness of the Soviet leadership to prop it up there. After Gorbachev's accession to power in 1985 it was vulnerable indeed.

The symptoms of malaise

Many of the familiar and characteristic features of communism, which often themselves appeared to be failings of the system, were in fact mere symptoms of deeper faults. A notable example in the political sphere was the perpetual problems of succession at the head of party and of state. Communist countries tended to change their leaders in one of two ways: either through death, or by forced resignation as a result of crisis. Leaders were not voted out of office by popular election. The problem was one of accountability, and it can be presented either in terms of the absence of mechanisms to ensure accountability or, probably more usefully, as a matter of the existence of mechanisms to prevent it. Apparatus politics, working through the *nomenklatura*, staffed the party and the state, except for the very highest level. The question of who should occupy positions of power at the apex of the system was thus left unregulated. This led at times to intense factional struggles, but it could also lead to long periods of immobility, all concerned preferring to maintain an established balance of forces rather than risk a general movement by proposing or supporting piecemeal changes. Thus it was that the bulk of the inner leadership of the CPSU, and a good deal of the ministerial hierarchy, remained in place for the final decade of the Brezhnev's tenure as General Secretary of the party; meanwhile the problems mounted that finally triggered the reforms which, in turn, revealed the deeper faults in the system that lay below the charade of an octogenarian leadership pressing ever more medals on a visibly decaying Brezhnev.

But it was in the economy that were to be found the most illuminating characteristic features of the system that were themselves only signs of deeper faults. The queue, for example, symbolised for outsiders both the rigours of daily life in communist countries, and the inability of communist governments to feed their people. Rarely was the queue perceived simply as a reflection of the pricing system. Shortages there were, but the queues could have been made to disappear at a stroke by raising prices and putting the goods above the margin for at least some consumers – which is precisely what was done when the communist parties had been divested of their power. On those occasions when, while they were still in power, ruling parties tried to reduce subsidies on items such as meat or bread, riots ensued. The economic and political systems seemed to be inter-meshed, attempted adjustments in the former having immediate and disastrous repercussions in the latter.

The devious responses of enterprise managers to the tasks that they were given to perform provides another example of behaviour within the system that was taken to characterise it, but which was really a symptom of a deeper weakness in the power monopoly. The managers of enterprises in a centrally planned economy were in a difficult position, and were forced into endless attempts to find ways around the problems that the system caused. They were given a plan to fulfil stated in the classic model in terms of quantity, but there was no market for them to turn to if their planned suppliers did not deliver. The result was that black markets and informal networks of various kinds flourished, and enterprises tended to hoard parts, labour and materials, and to produce internally as much as they could of what they might need to fulfil their plan. It has generally been accepted that without this informal lubrication, the planning system would not have worked at all. This behaviour in response to the way in which the system worked was thus at one and the same time frustrating the monopoly's goals, and yet helping it to survive. But whatever its short-term beneficial effects and however it modified the economic monopoly through an element of leakage, it was none the less evidence of a basic flaw in the wider system.

The power monopoly's systemic faults

If this and other fundamental faults are sought, they can be located above all in two features of the monopoly: a severe problem of information flows on the one hand, and on the other the difficulties encountered in securing compliance by the periphery in a heavily centralised system. Both of these problems were inherent in the monopoly from its earliest days, but each of them was to have increasingly serious effects with the passing of time. A further factor in the weakening of the monopoly in the Soviet Union itself, which was almost entirely due to the social and economic development of that society, was the growing dispersal of power at the apex of the system.

The problem of information flows

Shortages, the poor quality of goods, and the lack of initiative and motivation in economic life; in political life the deadening effect of censorship, and the tendency for political change to come about through lurches in policy accompanying either social crises or leadership changes (or, as often, both) can reasonably be attributed in good part to the way in which the functioning of the system was impeded by a quite remarkable restriction of information flows; and this problem was exacerbated by the extreme centralisation of the economic and political structures.

In fact, the two problems were interconnected, since the reason why overcentralisation was dysfunctional to the system was precisely because it shut out signals generated at lower levels. The characteristic way in which communist parties have ruled was not only poor at ensuring the circulation of information, but barriers were deliberately put in its way. These barriers indeed were given constitutional status (through the writing into the constitution of the party's leading role, which has been common practice), and had the force of law (as was the case with the plan which eliminated market signals). It is easily said with the benefit of hindsight, but it is true none the less that the power monopoly paid for this failing with its life.

This drastic blocking of information flows can be illustrated from two major areas: first, from the way in which central command planning worked, and secondly from the political void in which party leaderships framed their policies and enactments. In presenting these illustrations a very simple cybernetic model will be used, involving the notions of inputs of information into the system; outputs in the form of commands, policies and legal enactments; and a feedback loop which transmits information about the effects of outputs back to the core of the system in the form of inputs. The terminology of cybernetics is particularly helpful for understanding the problems that the communist power monopoly encountered precisely because of its focus on information and its circulation. In that terminology, as Klaus von Beyme pointed out in a perceptive article in 1975, economic and political power in communist political systems was structured so as to favour outputs and to block inputs.[1] The information needed to inform policies was therefore generated within the system's core itself. The result, in cybernetic terms, was oversteering.

History has delivered its verdict on central command planning as it was practised in the Soviet Union and in Soviet-type economies. The planning centre did not receive the information it needed in order for it to organise production rationally. Firms produced what they were told to produce by their ministries in accordance with the plan, and not in response to consumer demand or consumer preferences. At the point of sale, consumers bought what there was to buy (or saved their money) whilst what they wanted to buy was often not available. No entrepreneur could step in to fulfil evident needs, because the materials to do so were only available through the bureaucratic mechanisms of the plan. The planners were aware in general terms of what the economy needed to produce, and right up until the system's collapse they were trying to develop mathematical and computing techniques that would enable them to calculate the precise inputs needed to fulfil precise demands. But the matching of supply with true demand necessarily eluded them, since only a clear expression of consumer choice such as is articulated through a market could provide that information. Prices were determined from above; not reflecting scarcity or demand they, too, were deprived of their input function, and became simply a bookkeeping exercise.

Treatments of the way in which both production and pricing were closed off from signals coming from the consumer, and the consequent lack of consumer choice, are standard fare in the copious literature on Soviet economics. Accounts of the *politics* of the Soviet and other communist political systems presented in the same terms of information failures, however, are less frequently encountered. But in fact there is a close connection between the lack of choice in the economy and lack of voice in politics. The system being highly centralised, all major and many minor decisions were made without informed knowledge of the effects of those decisions being fed back to the decision-makers. No channels existed for the articulation of public opinion, no free elections held the decision-maker accountable, whilst the mass organisations, including the party itself, which could have transmitted signals from the grass-roots of society, were prevented from doing so effectively by their being controlled from above. Again, these were devices to channel outputs, and any possibility of their providing inputs was viewed with suspicion. The centre was not only arrogating to itself the right to make decisions, but it was making those decisions in the dark.

This deficiency in the flow of information had other untoward political effects. Most notably – and a common feature of democratic centralism wherever the Leninist principle has been applied – ignorance of the effects that policies were having, coupled with a closeting off of the decision-makers from society, led to extreme inflexibility and a politics of lurches. There was a tendency for changes not to be made until it was too late, and then only to occur when the situation was unblocked either by a major disturbance or by the death of a leader. All change had to come from the top downwards, and even when changes were made in communist parties, they tended to be precipitate (often the result of belatedly recognising previous mistakes) or far too late, or both.[2]

The leadership, closeted off from society in this way, and enjoying complete control of communications and the media, together with the entire education and legal systems, could issue edicts, make ideological innovations, and draft constitutions to suit its own preferences. True, the party-dominated structures of the mass organisations, and the party itself, served to transmit signals upwards to some extent. The population was also encouraged during the Khrushchev and, increasingly, during the Brezhnev periods to write letters to the press and to party instances on topical matters. None the less, the element of sifting and control that these mechanisms involved necessarily restricted the chances of these channels imposing themselves on the making of decisions or on the formulation of policy or doctrine.

As a result the party's ideological statements were made in something of a void. It is not too much to say that they had the air of a fairy-tale about them – a point developed by Alexandre Bourmeystre, who analysed the Soviet official discourse in terms of the *skaz* (the Russian folk-tale), using for this purpose Vladimir Propp's *Morphology of the Folktale* from 1927. Another semiological study 'found that a speech by Chernenko on local soviet and popular needs was structured in such a way as internally to cancel the practical force of the dozens of manifest injunctions which it contained'.[3] Treatments of this kind, taken out of context, admittedly present a caricatural picture of communist – in this case specifically

Soviet – politics. But the system was one that lent itself easily to caricature precisely because of the widely recognised distance between official pronouncements and daily life as it was lived, and also because of the absence of countervailing accounts. And it was the mechanisms of the power monopoly that ruled out those countervailing accounts.

David Easton, who pioneered the application of the systems approach to the study of politics, pointed out that in polities of the Soviet kind the party 'stands as the major gatekeeper over the inflow of demands and their conversion to issues'; members of the system were 'not expected to create new structures to store or to relay their sentiments about outputs to the appropriate authorities'. He was aware, however, that 'in most single-party systems, other channels along which responses can travel tend to come into existence' and he refers expressly to the 'semi-popular administrative organisations' of the USSR. These 'form the eyes and ears of the authorities for continuously taking the supportive pulse of the members in the system'.[4]

It is important to register this qualification. The system did function, if badly, and through the mass organisations and its own structures the party could hope to test the mood of the people and inform itself of the effects of its policies. But, first, these structures showed themselves to be quite inadequate and, secondly, they did not simply, as Easton suggests, take the supportive pulse of the members of the system. A major part of their role was to be active in putting across messages generated from above, thus creating *interference* in whatever messages might be filtering their way upwards. The party not only conscientiously suppressed all autonomous organisations, but it equally conscientiously created its own, controlled, organisations. A lack of autonomous organisation could only spell a lack of information circulating in the system; whilst the energetic sponsoring of dependent organisation could only spell disinformation designed to comfort the ears of higher authority. We encounter here the basic reason why the monopoly survived for so long apparently intact until its final crash. The way in which information was controlled did indeed constitute a major weakness in the system. But at the same time it enabled the party to conceal the full effects of that weakness and to project, without fear of contradiction, an assurance that all was well.

Problems in controlling the periphery

The more centralised a system, clearly the greater difficulty will the centre have in ensuring that its decisions are appropriate to circumstances at the periphery and also that political actors at the periphery can be relied on to carry out the centre's policies. The more the centre tries to retain all the reins of power, the more likely it is that local officials will make common cause against the centre to defend a local interest, or simply their own jobs and portion of power. Such 'localism', which has been lambasted in the official Soviet press continuously over the years, constituted an important source of leakage in the communist power monopoly there and elsewhere. Indeed, the constant emphasis on unity generated by the propaganda apparatus may be explained to a good extent by the centre's need to counter these threats to its monopoly. The more disunity threatened, the louder the assertions that the nation was united.

The communist power monopoly, in whatever country, tried to cope with this problem in two characteristic ways. First, it relied on a cohesive, vertically organised party, backed up by policing under the party's auspices, to provide a framework of political control that would keep these cliques and mafias in check. Secondly, central command planning kept the reins of economic decision-making in the hands of the central holders of the monopoly. These specifics did the trick for as long as the development of the economy did not actually require economic actors in the regions to show initiative, and for as long as the localities had no basis for the development of local autonomy. But, particularly in the Soviet Union and Yugoslavia, and to a lesser extent in Czechoslovakia, the ethnic and cultural factor added a further dimension to the problem of controlling the periphery. By gradually increasing the use made of certain institutional footholds that in time became available to them, national communities which had up to that point had their autonomy severely restricted by the power monopoly, were able to subject it to intense strain.

In the case of the Soviet Union, ever since shortly after the revolution, the numerous minority nationalities remained subjected to the strong centralising power of Moscow. The policy of 'national in form, socialist in content' meant that in economic terms the plan treated the whole Union as a single unit, whilst a degree of cultural autonomy cloaked political subjection throughout the Stalin years and beyond. The autonomy that the constitution gave to the consti-

tuent republics of the Soviet federation meant little beyond the
ability of schools to teach, and local radios to broadcast, in the
national language.

In 1974, however, Teresa Rakowska-Harmstone pointed out that
whilst those national groups that did not enjoy full republican status
were in danger of becoming fully assimilated, the fourteen non-
Russian republics of the Union were faring rather better, to a great
extent because, through a process of indigenisation, they had been
endowed with formal institutions of government – a republican
supreme soviet, a council of ministers. 'The nationally-based units of
the federal politico-administrative system have provided the
minority élites with both the bases and the means for pursuing
national-group interests' against the centre. It did not add up to
much but it did at least suggest that the power monopoly of an earlier
year was being weakened in this realm.[5]

Gorbachev's arrival in power added a further dimension to this
apparent ability of republican leaderships to withstand pressures
from Moscow. As the drive against the corruption of the Brezhnev
years gathered momentum, it became clear that Rashidov, the First
Secretary of the Uzbekistan Party and a non-voting member of the
Politburo, had been at the centre of a vast network of embezzlement
involving a good part of the republican administration. The case was
illuminating from many points of view. It illustrated first the
'localism' alluded to above – the formation of cliques and mafias that
formed to frustrate the intentions of the central power-holders. That
is, this case was not simply one of national self-assertion, since cases
of local corruption of this kind were being revealed throughout the
Soviet Union. It showed also how the structures not only of the
federation, but of the party itself, could be used to limit the powers of
the centre. It illustrated further the oligarchic nature of the power
monopoly. As a member of the Politburo Rashidov was in the inner
circles of the holders of the monopoly, and yet he could use that
position to run his satrapy as a microcosm of the central monopoly.
His role was that of a prefect, embodying the monopoly in the
periphery.

Finally, the fact that Rashidov could have been running so extensive a local mafia for so long illustrated the effects of the party's
control over the means of information, which was so fundamental a
component of the communist power monopoly. The central holders
of the monopoly must have known at least something about the

corruption in Uzbekistan, but it would have threatened the monopoly to reveal it – and they were safe in the knowledge that they could stop anyone else using it. Gorbachev could take the bold step of revealing all for the simple reason that he wanted to undermine the monopoly itself.

In Yugoslavia, the period during which the party succeeded in dominating the centrifugal local power of the national republics lasted for only some twenty years, the eighth congress of the League of Communists in 1964 marking the watershed. The decision to decentralise the economy after the break with the Cominform in 1948 had been a political one, but, the decision once taken, political and economic decentralisation proceeded more or less in tandem, with the constituent republics providing the major impulse in both cases. This process will be examined in greater detail in a later chapter, where an answer will be given to the question of how real was the party's withdrawal from the centre of political life in Yugoslavia in the years from 1952 to 1989, and to what extent its earlier monopoly of power was modified. It will be seen that, whilst the economy was decentralised to such an extent as to make it impossible to talk at all of an economic monopoly in federal or even republican hands, the League maintained the monopoly in existence in the realm of political organisation – including a modified monopoly in other areas, such as communications and the media.

But even whilst the League was able, in fact until 1990, to prevent the formation of autonomous political parties or trade unions, the federal nature of the constitution gave the federating republics a good deal of autonomy. It was they, more than the enterprises and far more than the workers' councils (on to which power had been theoretically devolved), that were the chief beneficiaries of the policy of decentralisation. The monopoly had to that extent been divided, without any pluralism resulting. The republican party organisations exercised an effective, if tolerant, monopoly within their fiefdoms, and if freedom of association was ruled out by central ordinance, or by centrally endorsed practice, the republican leaderships benefited as much from that as did the federal unit – in fact more, since the federal unit was thereby reduced to a battleground on which the republics fought to defend their interests. Decentralisation in that country meant the devolution of economic decision-making at the micro level to the enterprise and, in constitutional terms, to its workforce. This diluted the economic monopoly to such an extent that little is gained by using the term in that context. On the other hand political power gravitated no lower than to the republics. Given the monopoly that the League continued to exercise in the realm of political organisation, this meant that power had been redistributed among the holders of the political monopoly. Moreover, as events in 1971–72 were to show, the centre still had, at that date, the power to dismiss republican leaderships.

In neither the Soviet nor the Yugoslav case, then, was power in the hands of a republican leadership incompatible with the maintenance of the power monopoly overall, but it necessarily qualified it, and could threaten it quite categorically when other factors entered to weaken the monopoly. In any complex economic system there is a tension between the need for devolution and the danger of local initiative creating problems for central policy-making. Equally, in any multinational state ethnic tensions will render the role of a centralised organ of government difficult. Yugoslavia and the Soviet Union have had to deal with both of these problems to a greater extent than have most other states. They differed in the strategies through which they attempted to resolve these problems. But in each case – both the Soviet attempt to make a thorough-going centralisation stick, and the Yugoslavs' more flexible approach through wide republican autonomy and a controlled experiment in industrial democracy – centre–periphery relations pressed increasingly hard on the communist power monopoly, and in the end played an important part in its downfall.

The functional dispersal of power

The communist power monopoly fell largely through its own internal failings. But those failings were amplified in the Soviet Union, and in certain East European countries, by a developmental factor that began to operate with the passing of time. A political and economic system geared to tasks of political mobilisation was ill fitted to provide mechanisms of mediation appropriate to the efficient functioning of a large-scale technology-based society. Moreover, the differentiation of functions that economic development involved was bound ultimately to affect the power monopoly by reorganising the composition of the group that held the monopoly. In the case of the Soviet Union, economic and social development brought increasing complexity to the industrial and administrative bureaucracies, and with it a dilution of power at the apex of the political system.

When Jerry Hough claimed in the late 1960s and early 1970s that the Soviet Union had developed a form of 'institutional pluralism' he found himself attacked by many who objected that to term the Soviet political system pluralist in any sense obliterated the crucial differences between it and the Western liberal democracies to which the term was conventionally applied. But Hough was right in drawing attention to the 'whirlpools' that could be discerned in the policy-making process in the Soviet Union, where there 'seemed to be occurring a devolution of *de facto* power from the leader or leaders collectively . . . to a type of differentiated "leadership echelon" that cut across the line between state and interest group'.[6] He was also one of the first to point out how the party's apparatus would make common cause with equivalents in the ministerial apparatus to press for a particular policy outcome:

The categories of 'party' and 'state' have little relevance for understanding the way in which Soviet appropriations are made, at least once the basic investment level for the country has been decided. The conflicts arise between one group of industrial and party officials who support one project and another group of industrial and party officials who support another project.[7]

Hough later refined his position, moving to an analysis in terms of corporatism; but in any case he was not alone in claiming that, even if pluralism was not the word for what was happening, the power monopoly was by no means as streamlined as the common assumptions made out.

The views of Hough have been privileged here, but others were making similar claims at approximately the same time. A notable further example was the important work edited by Gordon Skilling and Franklyn Griffiths in 1971, entitled *Interest Groups in Soviet Politics*, which recorded important changes in the way policy options were being pressed.[8] The emerging group pressures that the editors and authors of that work claimed to discern did not have a fully autonomous status – 'tendencies of articulation' Franklyn Griffiths termed them – and the suggestion that they might constitute a form of pluralism was, as in the case of Hough's view, widely attacked. 'Whatever else may be going on in communist systems', remarked Joseph LaPalombara, 'it seems fair to say that pluralism is not included. Pluralism as doctrine, normative orientation, or basis for making political allocations is simply and clearly not acceptable to the élites of such systems'.[9] But the evidence of change was there for all to see, and could not easily be gainsaid. What jarred was the fact that the power monopoly was also still there for all to see.

This paradox can be resolved by taking an historical view of Soviet development. The constraints imposed on the written and spoken word through the power monopoly meant – and continued to mean at the time that Hough and Skilling were writing – that no real public opinion existed in the Soviet Union, nor indeed in the other communist party-states. With brief interludes such as the Prague Spring, and with due qualification for Yugoslavia, on which more below, this remained the case until the coming of Gorbachev. It was restricted, quite specifically, by the party's control of communication.

On the other hand, one of the major achievements of the Khrushchev 'thaw' in the 1950s was that, whilst public opinion continued to be ruled out, *specialist* opinion was allowed to develop, pushing ever further on the boundaries of what was possible. It was from 1957, for example, that sociology and cybernetics were no longer labelled 'bourgeois pseudo-sciences'. What the public press lacked the specialist press was being granted, and the boundaries of what could be discussed openly in official and specialist circles expanded remarkably fast.[10]

This evolution extended to a certain extent to the non-specialist press. Robert Miller in the 1970s made a detailed study of the extent to which various national newspapers carried readers' letters on a particular proposed item of legislation – the collective farm charter of 1969. In the discussion attitudes diverged on the question of collective farm trade unions and collective farm autonomy in general:

Izvestiya, the main government newspaper, carried not a single comment on the unions – a clear expression of disapproval – whilst *Pravda* . . . and *Sel'skaya zhizn'* [Village Life] were largely favourable to the idea. Regionally, *Sovetskaya Moldavia* was consistently favourable, while *Sovetskaya Estoniya*, perhaps reflecting Estonian Party First Secretary Kebin's opposition to creating a separate collective farm administrative hierarchy, published no comments on the issue.[11]

Newspaper editorships were still at that point subject to the party's *nomenklatura*, and the independence of *Izvestiya*, to say nothing of the very official *Pravda*, was then heavily circumscribed. Moreover Miller's own comment reflects the power that a republican first secretary held in matters of the press. But examples such as this reveal the beginnings of a process of change which was becoming much more established in the ever extending labyrinth of the bureaucracy's corridors.

By the 1980s, when public opinion was still fettered, the role played by specialist opinion was coming close to dissidence, and at times crossed that boundary which the power monopoly, simply by the way in which it operated, rendered particularly sharp. This time the clearest evidence comes from Eastern Europe, where we find in 1986 Wlodzimierz Bojarski, head of the energy section of the Institute of Technical Problems of the Polish Academy of Sciences, publicly expressing his reservations about nuclear power. In Hungary Janos Vargha, an eminent biologist, was prominent in the activities of the Danube Circle which protested against the construction of the Gabcikovo-Nagymaros dam on the Danube, whilst in the GDR scientists in Koenigswalde contested the official view in the early 1980s that in the GDR economic growth should have priority over the protection of the environment.[12]

A prominent case occurred in the Soviet Union in 1983. A complex of institutions of the Soviet Academy of Sciences in Novosibirsk in Siberia had become, by that date, a base for innovative work, including in the social sciences. It was there that Tatyana Zaslavskaya published what is known to history as the 'Novosibirsk report', forcefully arguing that economic structures framed for the 1930s had outgrown their usefulness, and urging reform.[13]

At other times the emergence of an assertive expert opinion took a rather different form in the Soviet Union. In fact it fell into the Russian cultural mould, with very real debates being conducted indirectly and in an Aesopian manner which itself testified to the lingering grasp of the monopoly. For example, Gilbert Rozman has shown how the reform debate in the Soviet Union was reflected in the rival analyses of Chinese development by the various Soviet scholarly institutions and individual specialists concerned with China. Supporters of orthodox and reformist positions among Soviet specialists used comment on China as a surrogate for comment on the Soviet Union itself, covering such issues as moral as against material incentives, the enhancement of state power as against the rule of law, and, of course, central planning as against decentralisation in the economy.[14]

Similarly, events in Poland in 1980–81 were accompanied by wide-ranging controversies within the Soviet academic and official establishment, whilst, in a celebrated article in *Kommunist* at the beginning of 1989, the Soviet theorist Naumov admitted that in the recent disputes that had divided the Italian Communist Party and the CPSU, the Italians had been in the right. Once again, a reference to an external dispute was being used as ammunition in the internal Soviet debate.[15] The work of Archie Brown provided, even before the arrival of glasnost, many further examples of these debates among specialists in the various institutes of the Academy of Sciences and in the departments and research institutes of the party's central committee.[16]

Thus, in the Soviet case, even before the arrival on the scene of glasnost, whilst the party's Politburo made the ultimate decisions, it was within a framework of specialist debate and institutional pressures that was bound ultimately to threaten the power monopoly. When glasnost did eventually come, many of the protagonists in the earlier debates were now to be found arguing these and other causes on the floor of a Congress of People's Deputies. A corner had been turned in Soviet politics, although the question of what this contributes to the demise of the power monopoly can only be answered when evidence of other kinds is adduced below.

One, perhaps minor, development illustrates well how social development was pressing on the traditional functioning of the communist power monopoly. The party's control of communications had an active as well as a passive role. It not only prevented unwanted ideas and policy suggestions from emerging, but it ran extensive programmes of political education. The party made no bones about its intent to shape the ideas of society. The 'agitation and propaganda' department of the apparatus was charged with just this task, the distinction between these two activities being that agitation was supposed to mean (following a distinction made by Plekhanov) presenting many ideas to a few people, whilst propaganda involved a more detailed and better informed treatment of many ideas to a few people.

As the cultural level of Soviet society rose – steadily and quite spectacularly, for which the party has to be given due credit – people waiting in queues or in cinema vestibules were no longer content to be harangued by an agitator whose grasp of current affairs was often less secure than their own. It was in the 1960s that a new figure entered the scene – the *politinformator* – whose role was to provide political information in a more sophisticated guise. At the same time the work of the All-Union Society 'Knowledge' (*Znanie*) was upgraded, to become a part of the adult education system.

The contrast is stark between the views of the 'qualified pluralist' theorists, such as Hough or Skilling, and those of commentators who, during this same period, were emphasising the still existing traditional mechanisms. 'The most salient feature of communist systems', wrote T. H. Rigby in 1972,

is the attempt to run the whole society as a single *organisation* in which almost no socially significant activities are left to autonomously interacting individuals and groups, but instead are managed by centralised, hierarchical agencies, themselves subject to close coordination, principally by the apparatus of the party.[17]

Can such contrasting views be reconciled? The answer is that they can, since they focus on different aspects of a changing system which contained within itself strong contradictions arising from the process of social and economic development. But if they are to be reconciled, obviously a little further discussion is required.

First, it was only at the apex of the political system that real change was taking place. In another place Rigby discussed the power structure characteristic of communism in terms of the distribution of powers, and of the connection between effective participation and the appropriation of '"free power" floating in the interstices of the formal structure'.[18] Organisational societies abhor 'free power' because it is potentially

disruptive of their more or less rigid structure, and they seek a maximum identification of power with powers, whilst at the same time tending to an overwhelming concentration of 'free power' at the apex of the power structure.

It remained the case that the monopoly's mechanisms reduced 'free power' to a minimum, and also that it attempted to concentrate it at the apex of the system. What was happening – and here Rigby's observations require qualification – was that 'free power' was becoming a more widely distributed commodity. But only at the top of the structure.

Secondly, the power monopoly disposed of mechanisms – the strength of which admittedly weakened over time – to weld this potentially dispersed power into an interdependent system. Those mechanisms, which will by now be familiar to the reader, were formidable. They were in part practical – the *nomenklatura*, the overlapping membership of party and state positions, control of the

means whereby discrepant independent voices might make themselves heard; and in part ideological, in the sense of the word so
peculiar to communist systems. As Rudolf Tokes put it:

'effective mutual guarantees' based on shared beliefs concerning the regime's
long-term goals are an indispensable condition for the transformation of
specialist-élite-party *interaction* into mutually binding political *interdependence* of all participants involved in decision-making processes.[14]

The central committee of any ruling communist party has been
perhaps the most prominent locus for the promotion of this
integration of the country's élite. Interestingly, despite this powerful
integrative role, the dispersal of power that Hough and others noted
at the higher levels of both state and party in the Soviet Union began
also to affect the standing and the composition of the central committee. It was a major turning-point in the history of Soviet communism when in 1957 Nikita Khrushchev, in danger of being dismissed
from his post at the head of the CPSU by a majority in the Politburo,
convened the central committee, put his case to it, and was confirmed
in office. One of his subsequent reforms was to have the record of
central committee meetings published.

There is no doubt that the central committee came to play an
important role during and after the Khrushchev period – as the
reformer found to his cost when he repeated his manoeuvre of 1957
in 1964. This time the central committee confirmed the Politburo's
decision that he should step down.

As for the Soviet Union, so for Eastern Europe. A number of the
authors of Stephen Fischer-Galati's edited work on the communist
parties of Eastern Europe, published in 1979, concluded that the
central committee was gaining in influence within the system, Miklos
Molnar noting that in Hungary the central committee had become 'a
battleground for fights over different views', and Manfred Grote
reaching a similar conclusion in the case of the GDR.[20] In the latter
case Peter Ludz had already published an influential study of the
GDR's 'changing élite', in which he observed that the central committee had come to include a wide range of administrative and
technological expertise and that its role was consequently changing.
On this basis Ludz concluded that a trend to 'consultative
authoritarianism' was under way in the GDR.[21]

However, any conclusion as to whether such developments constitute a dilution of the power monopoly, this time within the party's

higher echelons, must take into account the basic role that the party's central committee played within the overall monopoly, since that role thrusts into the shade any increase in its visibility or in its ability to debate freely. It was the central committee that embodied the integration of society's élites. Apart from the secretaries who headed up the central apparatus, it typically contained the more important chiefs of the regional party apparatus together with a number of senior ministerial heads, and a sprinkling of newspaper editors, ambassadors and military leaders. In integrating those members who drew their salary from jobs outside the party's apparatus into the central nexus of power it was a powerful buttress of the power monopoly.

The power monopoly in Eastern Europe: an unsuccessful graft

The pressure put on the power monopoly by factors stemming from social and economic development has been discussed here with particular reference to the Soviet Union. There are good reasons for this given the dominance of the Soviet Union over its client states, which meant that no radical change could come to Eastern Europe until the Soviet Union itself changed. By that very token, however, the power monopoly suffered from one particular and overriding weakness in Eastern Europe. There the party's monopoly of power, whilst it was as complete as it was in the Soviet Union itself, did not rest on an organic base. It was imposed, and was seen as such. It was an imposition in two senses. First, it was brought in from without and maintained in being ultimately by Soviet power or the threat of its use. But secondly, it was imposed in the sense of being more an overlay than a true graft. The leading role of the party, as described above in terms of the monopoly of power in the hands of the party's apparatus, could be secured by outright political leverage. But the ideological underpinning of the monopoly – the image, that is, of an organic unity of party and people – stood very little chance in countries where the party was perceived as a Soviet stool-pigeon.

The rejection of the Soviet graft was more categorical in Poland, Hungary and Czechoslovakia than in Bulgaria or Romania. But in no case, with the important exceptions of Yugoslavia and Albania, did orthodox democratic centralism become accepted as a part of the structure of legitimacy, as it had in the Soviet Union itself, which was the cradle of that way of thinking. Elsewhere, as soon as the body was able to reject the graft it did so, and with this rejection what had been a reasonably uniform pattern of politics from the Oder-Neisse to the Bering Straits broke up. This consideration is of the first importance. Whatever the weight to be attributed to economic factors in the pressures for change in Eastern Europe, change when it came was made possible by a single all-important political fact – the withdrawal of Soviet support from the regimes of the region.

Thus the party's power monopoly in the Soviet Union itself, at the moment when Gorbachev became General Secretary of the Central Committee of the CPSU was already being undermined from within. The party leadership maintained its prerogative of final decision-making; it was able also to preserve its control over the base of society through the mass organisations; by controlling communications it was able, above all, to prevent signs of change from becoming manifest and from being built on. But within the carapace of the monopoly, important changes were taking place. Meanwhile, in the Eastern European countries the monopoly rested on the shakiest of foundations, and was doomed to extinction the moment that Soviet support was removed from the Eastern European regimes. But because of the characteristic way in which the monopoly worked, these facts remained concealed to the very end by the cocoon that orthodox democratic centralism has been so good at weaving around itself.

Notes

1 Klaus von Beyme, 'A Comparative View of Democratic Centralism', *Government and Opposition*, Vol. 10, No. 3 (1975), pp. 259–77.
2 These are the words that Malcolm McEwen uses in describing party life in the non-ruling Communist Party of Great Britain. They are equally applicable to the ruling parties and, of course, it was from the CPSU that the CPGB acquired its organisational norms: 'The Day the Party had to Stop' *Socialist Register* (1976), p. 37.
3 Michael Urban, 'Local Soviets and Popular Needs: Where the Official Ideology Meets Everyday Life', in Stephen White and Alex Pravda, *Ideology and Soviet Politics* (Basingstoke, Macmillan, 1988), p. 151.
4 David Easton, *A Systems Analysis of Political Life* (New York: John Wiley, 1965), p. 419.
5 Teresa Rakowska-Harmstone, 'The Dialectics of Nationalism in the USSR', *Problems of Communism*, Vol. 23, No. 3 (1974), p. 10.
6 Jerry F. Hough, *The Soviet Union and Social Science Theory* (Cambridge, MA: Harvard University Press, 1977); for a nuanced presentation see his 'Pluralism, Corporatism and the Soviet Union', in Susan Gross Solomon (ed.), *Pluralism in the Soviet Union: Essays in Honour of H. Gordon Skilling* (Basingstoke; Macmillan, 1983).

7   Jerry F. Hough, *The Soviet Prefects: The Local Party Organs in Industrial Decision-making* (Cambridge, MA: Harvard University Press, 1969), p. 265.
8   H. Gordon Skilling and Franklyn Griffiths (eds), *Interest Groups in Soviet Politics* (Princeton, NJ: Princeton University Press, 1971).
9   Joseph LaPalombara, 'Monoliths or Plural Systems: Through Conceptual Lenses Darkly', *Studies in Comparative Communism*, Vol. 8, No. 3 (1975), p. 325.
10   Skilling and Griffiths, *Interest Groups in Soviet Politics*; also H. Gordon Skilling, 'Interest Groups and Soviet Politics', *World Politics*, Vol. 18, No. 3 (1966).
11   Robert F. Miller, 'The Future of the Soviet Kolkhoz', *Problems of Communism*, Vol. 25, No. 2 (1976), p. 45.
12   Michael Waller, 'The Ecology Issue in Eastern Europe', *The Journal of Communist Studies*, Vol. 5, No. 3 (1989), pp. 308–10.
13   Tatyana Zaslavskaya, 'The Novosibisrk Report' (introduced by Philip Hanson), *Survey*, Vol. 21, No. 1 (1984), pp. 83–108.
14   Gilbert Rozman, *A Mirror for Socialism: Soviet Criticisms of China* (Princeton, NJ: Princeton University Press, 1985).
15   Vladimir Naumov, 'IKP pered s"ezdom', *Kommunist* (Moscow), No. 1 (1989), pp 101–12.
16   Archie Brown, 'Pluralism, Power and the Soviet System: A Comparative Perspective', in Susan Gross Solomon, *Pluralism in the Soviet Union*, pp. 61–107.
17   T. H. Rigby, 'Totalitarianism and Change in Communist Systems', *Comparative Politics* (April 1972), p. 451.
18   T. H. Rigby, *Communist Party Membership in the USSR, 1917–1967* (Princeton, NJ: Princeton University Press, 1968), p. 30.
19   Rudolf Tokes and Henry Morton, *Soviet Society and Politics in the 1970s* (New York: Free Press, 1974), p. 41.
20   Stephen Fischer-Galati, *The Communist Parties of Eastern Europe* (New York: Columbia University Press, 1979), pp. 217 and 184.
21   Peter C. Ludz, *Parteielite im Wandel* (Cologne: Westdeutscher, 1968), p. 125.

Further reading

Hélène Carrère d'Encausse, *L'empire éclatée* (Paris: Flammarion, 1978).
Moshe Lewin, *The Gorbachev Phenomenon: A Historical Interpretation* (London: Radius, 1988).
Richard Lowenthal, 'Development vs Utopia in Communist Policy', in Chalmers Johnson, *Change in Communist Systems* (Stanford, CA: Stanford University Press, 1970).
Peter C. Ludz, *The Changing Party Elite in East Germany (Cambridge, MA: MIT Press, 1972).*
Gilbert Rozman, *A Mirror for Socialism: Soviet Criticisms of China* (Princeton, NJ: Princeton University Press, 1985).
Tatyana Zaslavskaya, *The Second Socialist Revolution* (London: I. B. Tauris, 1990).

5

Getting rid of Stalinism: state and society in Eastern Europe

Stalin died on 5 March 1953. By that time the Soviet Union had emerged from the test of the Second World War as a superpower. It had also acquired a series of client states in the rest of Europe which it had endowed with its own political and economic structures. A world-wide ring of communist parties acknowledged the doctrinal authority of the party of Lenin.

By 1953, however, there had already been movements away from Stalinist orthodoxy in two parties, one ruling and the other non-ruling. In Yugoslavia Tito and his communists had resisted the consolidation of the Soviet Union's sphere of influence, and had struck out on a path of development which was to lead them some way from the monopoly of orthodox communism; whilst in Italy the Italian Communist Party under Togliatti had taken the first steps that were to lead, twenty years later, to the movement known to history as Eurocommunism, which was to play an important, if indirect, role in the communist power monopoly's demise.

Yet the final fall of the communist power monopoly in the country of its origin was still three and a half decades in the future. In this and the following chapters the long and gradual sequence of events that was to culminate in the abrupt collapse of the communist power monopoly will be recorded. To reiterate a theme that has run through this study, the very way in which the power monopoly worked ruled out adaptation until the pressure of circumstances brought about its implosion.

In this chapter the various pressures to which the communist power monopoly was subjected in Eastern Europe in the years from the onset of the cold war to the epic year of 1989 will be put into a single perspective. This period was marked by a series of crises. They arose more from political than economic causes, but this account will start by recording a debate about economic reform the high points of which sometimes coincided with the political crises, but which otherwise followed its own rhythm. The political crises will then be treated. Thirdly and fourthly, a most important shift in Soviet policy towards the Western European left was to form part of the backdrop to an equally important shift in the evolution of dissent from 1975 in Eastern Europe, and these both merit attention.

It should be noted that from early on in the story of attempts to reform the Stalinist system it was clear that the political power monopoly in the traditional form of the party's leading role was impeding economic reform, but it was none too easy to show exactly how it was doing it. And yet that relationship was crucial since, for a full understanding of the collapse of communism, it is necessary to know how much to attribute to economic and how much to political factors.

The reform debate

In the record of the various attempts to reform the system of central command planning as it had operated in the Stalinist years, experimentation in the Soviet Union and in the countries of Eastern Europe had proceeded at differing rhythms, but broadly in parallel. For that reason a single record will be presented here.

Designed as a tool for rapid industrialisation in circumstances of austerity, the system of central command planning in the Soviet Union was bound to show its inadequacies as the need for basic and infrastructural goods gave way to the demands of an increasingly complex industrial society. This shift in the pattern of development from extensive to intensive growth was occurring by the time of Khrushchev's stewardship as First Secretary (as the party's leading post was then called) of the CPSU. But until Khrushchev had succeeded in changing the political climate in the Soviet Union, it was still impossible for well-thought-out proposals for economic reform to be forthcoming.

It is not surprising therefore that the story of the critique of the economic power monopoly should have started outside the Soviet Union, in 1948 in Yugoslavia. After the break with the Cominform, the Yugoslavs were not only free to develop their own economic and political forms, but their detachment from the Soviet bloc that was forming required them to do so. In the Yugoslav economic reforms associated with social self-management economic decision-making was devolved to enterprise level, and in order for self-managed forms to be able to do business with each other central planning had to be abandoned, and prices had to be allowed to form through the operation of a market. These structural changes in Yugoslavia, which will be treated more fully below, were to serve as a reference point elsewhere as debate on economic reform developed.

It will be recalled that in the unreformed Stalinist economic system an enterprise's plan was formulated in terms of physical output, and a manager's rewards and penalties were related to the quantity, rather than the quality, of what the enterprise produced. The market having effectively been abolished, there were few consumer signals, either within industry or at the point of sale, to regulate production. Such signals as there were, in the form of queues and unwanted goods on the shelves, had no effect on what was produced, and were in fact an abiding feature of the system. That role was certainly not performed by prices, which were centrally determined, and served only to facilitate the bookkeeping involved in moving goods within the economy by administrative means.

This meant endless bottlenecks, and production little related to demand. Since managers were sure of being able to dispose of what was produced, they had little cause to worry about quality. Moreover, the constraints on managers were 'soft', in the sense that the mechanisms of planning imposed no penalties for hoarding labour or stocks, whilst any losses incurred were absorbed by the state budget. This means that enterprises which performed badly did not for that reason go bankrupt. In sum, the existing mechanisms operated in such a way as to keep motivations, productivity and the quality of goods necessarily low, and wastage of labour and stocks equally necessarily high.

In the countries of the Soviet bloc, the movement for economic reform is conventionally dated from an article published in 1962 in the USSR by the Kharkov economist Evsei Liberman, entitled 'Plan, Profits and Bonuses', although reform ideas, including earlier and more radical proposals by Liberman himself, had been circulating since at least 1959. Liberman's primary target was the tendency of managers to keep the enterprise's plan low so that it could be easily fulfilled. By thus concealing the capacity of their enterprise they could increase their bonuses, which were based on production in excess of the plan. A second aim was to make enterprises more responsive to the requirements of their customers, and to make it more difficult for managers to turn out low-quality goods simply to fulfil the quantitative requirements of the plan.

Liberman proposed that managers be rewarded only for planned production, but he also aimed to give managers greater flexibility in fixing their plan through negotiations with customers. The aim was thus two-fold: to make the economy more responsive to customer needs, and to ensure a greater return from an enterprise's capital. Indeed it was profits, defined as a percentage of an enterprise's capital, that were to be the key measure of success. Liberman's article was hailed as a real attempt to come to grips with the key problems of running the system of central command planning as it had thus far operated, and it proved to be the beginning of a debate that was to lead to various experiments at loosening the economic monopoly in the Soviet Union and Eastern Europe.

The ideas that were being put forward by Liberman and others were included in reform measures adopted first in the GDR's 'new economic system' in 1963, and then in the reform of 1965 in the Soviet Union, associated with the name of Aleksei Kosygin, who was prime minister at the time. In both these reforms, profit was used as one of a number of indices by which performance would be assessed, and managers were given more freedom of action in choosing the instruments for achieving their plan. The GDR was to take its reform further, with an adjustment of the pricing system which did not, however, change the basic function of prices. Both reforms were to run into the sand, but the GDR went on to pioneer a method of rationalising the existing system by creating associations of enterprises (VVBs), with the creation of combines constituting a further step in the same direction. Both the Soviet Union and Poland followed suit by setting up associations of this kind between ministerial level and that of the enterprise itself.

The reforms in both the GDR and the Soviet Union failed partly because gross output remained the key indicator of success, profit merely being added to the list of indicators, and partly because the inertia of an economy set up on central command principles constantly pulled those whose job it was to operate in it to conform with requirements originating higher up in the system rather than with demands arising from below. But they failed in good measure also because the party's grip on the political power structures exercised a pull back towards the orthodoxy of central planning. In other words, modification of the power monopoly in the economy was being impeded by the power monopoly in the political sphere.

The implications of this consideration were immense. It was one thing for the ruling party to use its monopoly of power to put in hand reform of the economy; it was quite another to acknowledge that economic reform could be achieved only at the cost of giving up that monopoly. Whatever any individual academic economists thought, it was in the interest of any party that wished to carry out economic reform to maintain that economic and political reform were separable, and that the economic monopoly could be given up without at the same time ceding the political monopoly. There was one exception to this – the Czechoslovak reformers of the Prague Spring, who made quite explicit their belief that there was an intimate connection between economic and political reform. Subsequent history was to show that in each case where a ruling party did not accept that there was this connection – either covertly, as in Yugoslavia, or expressly, as in Hungary in 1968 – the result was a contradiction that was bound to be resolved one way or the other in the end. In both of these particular cases, as we shall see, it was resolved by the collapse of the political power monopoly.

The link between economic and political reform was made particularly clear in the contrasting fates of the Czechoslovak reforms from 1963 and those launched in Hungary in 1968. In each country a wide-ranging economic reform was proposed. In the Hungarian case, the leadership made it plain that economic reform would not interfere with the leading role of the party. Indeed, the stability that the policies pursued by Kadar in the years since the 1956 uprising had produced was seen as an important guarantee for the success of the reform. In the Czechoslovak case it was the snowballing of political demands, and the effective abandoning by the party of its political monopoly, that led to the intervention by the Warsaw Treaty forces to protect the leading role of the party and the 'gains of socialism'. It was to defend apparatus politics and the political power monopoly that the Warsaw Treaty states went to war.

The intervention put a stop to the process of economic reform, which makes it difficult to assess the economic achievements of the Prague Spring. But changes proposed from 1963 on, and to an extent implemented by 1968, show that the Czechoslovak reforms were following very much the same priorities as the Hungarian reforms

Table 7 *Income distribution in Czechoslovakia, 1930–65*

(Individual incomes from all sources – approximate global data)

Income recipients quintiles	Per cent of the sum of income		
	1930	1946	1965
Lowest fifth	2.5	3.8	6.3
Second fifth	8.5	11.0	14.0
Third fifth	16.0	18.0	19.7
Fourth fifth	26.0	24.1	25.6
Highest fifth	47.0	43.1	34.4

launched in 1968 were to follow. Prices were to perform the role that they play in a market economy by reflecting scarcity, but only on a limited range of products – chiefly consumer goods – would prices be completely freed. On a second range they would be allowed to fluctuate, whilst over a substantial range of products – particularly capital goods – they would remain fixed. Enterprise managers were to be given far greater freedom to decide on the product mix, on wages, on the number of workers to be employed. They were to be enabled to enter into trading relations with other enterprises, and also with foreign firms. Enterprises were to be allowed to fail, and go out of business if they could not cover their costs with sales. The narrow wage differentials of the existing system were a specific target of the reformers (see Table 7), and the unemployment that would follow from the reforms was accepted as a necessary consequence of them.

The intervention of the Warsaw Treaty forces in August 1968 meant that the Czechoslovak reform was never implemented in its entirety, although some elements were salvaged, to place Czechoslovakia in the category of moderately reformed economies. The Hungarian 'New Economic Mechanism', on the other hand, which was launched in the same year of 1968, took root, and Hungary was to become, like Yugoslavia, a reference point for those pressing for reform elsewhere, but this time within the confines of a retained system of central planning.

This time the reform was put to the test of experience. It embodied very much the same mechanisms as the Czechs had proposed. The same three-tier system of prices was introduced, although the category of prices that were to be freed from central control was much wider in the Hungarian case. On the other hand, whilst the

Hungarian reformers intended, as had the Czechs, to allow insolvent firms to go out of business, the degree of control that the centre retained brought it almost inevitably to prevent such cases occurring and, should they none the less occur, to allow the shock of failure to fall on the public exchequer. Unemployment could thus be kept within bounds, but the continued subsidising of firms and of prices meant that the reforms did not in full achieve the 'hard' constraints that the Hungarian economist Janos Kornai claimed were essential to any true reform of the traditional system.

No other country in the region was to imitate the bold steps that the Hungarians, let alone the Yugoslavs, had taken in economic reform. On the other hand, a number of attempts were made during these years to render the system of central planning more efficient. Particularly in the Soviet Union sophisticated mathematical techniques were developed, and greater use was made of computer technology. Also, as noted, the 1970s saw the development in Poland, the GDR and the USSR of a system whereby enterprises were grouped in 'associations' in order to draw benefits from the resulting integration. In the Soviet Union itself, apart from the application of these various techniques to make the existing system work better at the central and intermediate levels of the economy, a number of experiments were conducted in individual firms and groups of firms – often through the initiative of a particular management – which set out to solve some of the basic problems of central planning, such as the inefficient use of labour.

In any assessment of these various attempts to reform the system of central command planning there are two cardinal considerations that must be borne in mind. The first is that, whilst the possibilities for reform were greater, and the proposals more cogently pressed, outside the Soviet Union than within, nothing fundamental could change until change occurred in the Soviet Union itself. Thus the Hungarian experiment remained precisely that – an experiment – for nigh on twenty years.

Secondly, such attempts as were made in the Soviet Union itself either to reform the system of central command planning or to make it work more efficiently, were being designed and applied in an evolving society. Whilst the death of Stalin and the radical change in the political climate that the Khrushchev thaw ushered in made it possible for Liberman's proposals to be formulated and discussed, we have seen that they were called forth by a fundamental change in the developing Soviet economy, a change from extensive to intensive growth. The most graphic illustration of this is the use of forced labour – effectively slave labour – during the Stalinist period. The gulag could do the simple jobs in the infrastructure that were needed in the early years of accumulation – lumbering, digging canals, simple construction works. Neither quality nor productivity were the essential considerations. By the mid-1960s they were (though the gulag was effectively dismantled already from 1956); and the requirements of intensive growth were to put a growing pressure on the economic structures. No longer was it possible to squander labour in this way.

If these various proposals for economic reform are considered, then, it can be seen how they relate to the wider story of the development of the Soviet Union and of Eastern Europe. They came on to the agenda when the developing Soviet economy required a shift from extensive to intensive growth, and the difficulties of making that adjustment were to prove to be literally insuperable. Far from being overcome, they in the end overcame the system, and forced its eventual abandonment.

If reasons are sought for this failure of adaptation and adjustment, they can be readily located in cultural and political factors. On the one hand, during the quarter of a century of Stalin's rule citizens' attitudes had been fashioned in a mould appropriate to the rugged tasks of development at a forced pace, and where the stick predominated over the carrot as a means of ensuring performance. There was little in the cultural soil of Stalinism or indeed of the Russian past to favour the growth of new habits and attitudes that would take the economy and society into a new phase. Meanwhile, the entrenchment of the party's officials in positions of power which they were naturally loth to surrender blocked the organic assertion of the class of managerially skilled people which the party, whatever its failings, had succeeded in bringing into being.

Lessons could have been learned by the Soviet Union from the more advanced economies of some of the East European states. To an extent it did learn. But ultimately the political factor was to act as a brake here too. Just as the CPSU's bureaucracy was jealous of its prerogatives at home, so it was not prepared to let economic change go ahead in Eastern Europe if that spelled political risks, which could be seen in terms either of instability in the region, or as a threat to the local party's power. In the series of crises that provides the landmarks in the history of post-war Eastern Europe, political factors in fact predominated. But the mix of the economic and political was complex, and that series of crises, so important a part of the back-drop to the events of 1989 in the region, calls for separate treatment.

Crises of the power monopoly in Eastern Europe

It will be recalled that in 1948 the Yugoslav communists, having fought their way to power without significant Soviet military assistance, were able to resist the attempts of the Soviet Union to bind its client states in the east of Europe more closely to itself. The expulsion of the Yugoslavs from the Cominform was, in fact, the first in a series of crises in the region, each of which defined in a particular way the geographical extent of Soviet power and its political implications. In the case of the Yugoslav crisis the upshot was clear. Soviet power was rebuffed and the Yugoslavs were free to develop their own form of communist rule along the lines indicated in an earlier chapter.

In 1953 – the year of Stalin's death – strikes and worker disturbances broke out in the GDR (in Berlin in particular), in Czechoslovakia (where Pilsen was the epicentre of discontent), and in Plovdiv in Bulgaria. These disturbances, however, did not put the new regimes to any severe test. They were the result of high-handed government action which, in the first case, caused severe food shortages, and in the second brought about a sharp devaluation of earnings. The Czechoslovak case, however, does serve to illustrate a frequently encountered effect of the power monopoly. The monopoly placed the setting of prices and the determining of policy in the hands of the centre. Since – again through the monopoly – the centre was not only isolated from social voices, but believed that it could rely on force to counter popular discontent, it frequently misjudged the possible impact of a rise in prices. This was no invisible hand of a market, but the all too visible hand of a party leadership. Policy decisions that had the effect of sharply raising prices, often at crassly chosen moments, were responsible not only for the Czechoslovak disturbances of 1953, but for much more substantial crises in Poland in 1970 and 1976, and in Novocherkassk in the Soviet Union in 1962.

1956: the testing of the parameters of soviet power
Far more serious in their implications than the disturbances of 1953

in Czechoslovakia, the GDR, and Bulgaria, were the crises of 1956 in Poland and in Hungary. These were a direct result of the death of Stalin and of the adoption of a 'new course' adopted in the Soviet Union under Stalin's immediate successor, Georgi Malenkov. In terms of policy, the new course was directed towards redressing the imbalance in the Soviet economy between heavy and light industry in favour of the latter, but in Eastern Europe it was interpreted as an attempt to make a political break with the Stalinist past. It created an atmosphere of expectation and of instability, and in Hungary and Poland this atmosphere was to provide the background to major disturbances, amounting in the Hungarian case to an attempted revolution. Although they occurred in the same year, these two crises illustrate very different aspects of the communist power monopoly.

What came to be the crucial issue in the Hungarian case was the post-war settlement itself and, within it, the parameters of Soviet power in the region. The withdrawal of occupying Soviet troops from neighbouring Austria and the subsequent provision made for Austria's neutrality in 1955 had an important impact on the Hungarians and was to lead to an acute raising of the political temperature in the country in the following year. National feeling, stimulated by a reinvigorated intelligentsia, focused on the figure of Imre Nagy and on his proposals for reform. Having been ousted as prime minister in the spring of 1955 by his Stalinist rivals in the communist Hungarian Socialist Workers' Party, Nagy was reinstated in that post as tension turned into mass demonstrations at the end of October 1956. With the Hungarians on the verge of withdrawing from the Warsaw Treaty Organisation, Soviet forces intervened on 4 November, placing Janos Kadar in power at the head of the party.

Any doubts about the boundaries of Soviet influence in Eastern Europe which the Yugoslavs' independent stance in 1948 might have generated were thereby laid to rest, and it was within those clearly demarcated parameters, and from that very unpromising starting point, that Kadar embarked on his quest to find an accommodation with his people based on the realities of the position.

But behind this drama, other developments had been taking place in Hungary that affected the power monopoly. It was in 1953 that, on Soviet prompting, Nagy had first become premier and was thus in a position to counter the Stalinist Rakosi, who retained his base at the head of the party. Nagy thereupon proposed economic changes which moved away from the economic autarky characteristic of the Stalinist period, when the economic monopoly was at its most extreme. Interestingly, as Fejto tells us, it was Mikoyan, a highly-placed member of the Soviet leadership, who pointed out that the 'disproportionate development of iron-smelting indicates a somewhat rash attitude. Hungary has neither iron mines nor coke'.[1]

The Soviet leadership apparently also approved Nagy's intention, within 'the Leninist principle of democratic centralism', to reduce police powers, democratise political life, and institute religious freedom. What this would have meant in practice cannot be known. Nagy was removed from office in the wake of Malenkov's own fall in March 1955, and by the time he was reinstated in 1956 a strong movement for national self-assertion had welled up. When Hungary's participation in the Warsaw Pact was brought into question the Soviet leadership acted, securing the leading role of the party with their own nominee at the party's head.

In Poland the crisis was triggered by worker protests in Poznan in June. These were put down with some severity, with 54 killed, but the crisis had invaded the party's leadership where the death of the Stalinist Bierut earlier in the year had led to factional tension. A key figure in this struggle was Wladislav Gomulka, who had been imprisoned during the purges that affected the entire region in 1948, but who now came to embody the atmosphere of the 'new course'. Alarmed at the increasing tension in the party, which was leading to further manifestations of popular unrest, and apprehensive at what a reinstatement of Gomulka might portend, a delegation from the CPSU's Politburo arrived in Warsaw. Having sized up the position, it accepted the wisdom of a compromise that included installing Gomulka as party leader. With the party's control of society thus confirmed, the worst had been avoided; and, despite having re-entered the arena as the leader of the forces opposed to Stalinism, Gomulka was, for the next fourteen years, to prove as adept a defender of the communist power monopoly as were his Soviet sponsors.

As regards that power monopoly, two developments in Poland in and after 1956 merit attention. First, the collectivisation of agriculture was abandoned. This opened an obvious breach in the economic monopoly, although this was not necessarily how it seemed to Polish farmers who found that, whilst they could indeed sell their goods on a free market, they were dependent on a planned industry for machinery and supplies. Secondly, Gomulka's appointment as party leader raised hopes that a degree of democracy would be introduced into political life. In particular the establishment of workers' councils in the workplace appeared to mark an achievement on the part of the protest movement of 1956. The gradual clawing back of this concession, until the workers' councils had been reduced to the role of the mass organisations characteristic of the power monopoly, was to lodge in the popular mind and to make workers ever more suspicious of party gestures in their direction at future times of tension.

In Hungary, then, a blanket restoration of monopolistic power followed the uprising of that year, and the 'social compact' between party and people that was gradually to emerge, with the latter tacitly agreeing to accept the party's rule if the party for its part made life as agreeable as possible for the people in a difficult situation that neither could do anything about, developed within the confines of the power monopoly. In Poland, an apparent air of democratisation gradually dissipated as the monopoly closed in again, with a privatised agriculture remaining the only clear gain from the events of 1956.

The crises of 1956 thus marked out clearly the parameters of the Soviet sphere of influence in Europe, and in both Poland and Hungary the political power monopoly was, if anything, confirmed by the events of that year. On the other hand, the privatisation of Polish agriculture revealed that divergences in economic organisation could be tolerated. Later events in the region were to confirm this differentiation between the economic and political fields. That is, the economic monopoly was open to experimentation and change, whilst threats to the political monopoly would be resisted with all available means.

Twelve years later, these conclusions were to be given further confirmation, on the one hand in the Hungarian economic reform, and on the other in the major political crisis of the Prague Spring. The failure of the Prague Spring came to have a particular symbolic value in the long, wide-ranging and until 1985 apparently fruitless struggle to dismantle the communist power monopoly.

The Prague Spring
It was not until January 1968 that Antonin Novotny, the old Stalinist party boss, was edged out of power in Czechoslovakia. His political longevity had, in fact, contributed handsomely to the pent-up

pressures for change that were to lead to the historic events of that year. From 1963, an impatience with the country's dismal economic performance had led to vigorous proposals for economic reform. The fateful development was that these proposals came to be linked to demands for *political* change. Novotny's departure was one victory for those demands, but they were to go much further, and were, at least in the short term, to achieve much more.

The major landmark in the process of political change was the publication by the reformist party leadership under Alexander Dubcek of a sixty-four page Action Programme in April 1968, but even before the Action Programme was published a number of things had changed that challenged the power monopoly quite categorically. This was clearest in the case of the party's control of information. In early March political censorship was suspended, marking a victory for the intelligentsia, which was the spearhead of the pressures for change. In a now unfettered press the battle could be waged for a new press law which would finally consecrate the censorship's abolition. This demand for a law that would 'rule out the possibility of advance censorship' was duly included in the Action Programme.

The Action Programme did not recommend that the party's leading role be abandoned as such. But it stated that the party could not 'impose its authority by force but must constantly earn it by deeds', and it called expressly for an end to the 'monopolistic concentration of power in the hands of the party'.[2] The political control exercised by the party's apparatus was attacked indirectly by an insistence on free elections, and on the right of public associations to autonomy. Taken together with the call for an end to the censorship and for free circulation of ideas, these recommendations amounted to a dismantling of the political monopoly. They would have made vast inroads into the party's *nomenklatura* function. The *nomenklatura* was indeed abandoned as part of the reform process, although the party's presidium did continue to supervise or to make key appointments in a less formal way.

With changes such as these either already made, or sanctioned by the Action Programme, whatever political regime might emerge from the reforms could not credibly be termed monopolistic. There is no doubt whatsoever that the Prague Spring did propose an end to the power monopoly in the political, just as in the economic, sphere.

The theoretical debates on the shape of the future political system that accompanied these proposals are a further major feature of political interest contained in the events of the Prague Spring. They were interesting in themselves, within the context of Czechoslovakia alone at that time. But they acquire a much wider interest when they are seen against other debates that were to take place in the Soviet Union when the power monopoly was brought into question there.

First of all, a distinction was made – in fact, if not expressly – between the free circulation of information (what later was to be recommended in the Soviet Union as 'glasnost') on the one hand, and multi-party pluralism on the other. There was no problem with the first; the censorship had to go, or at least to be deprived of its political power. The question of the party's privileged role, however, was much more complex, and was bedevilled by the fact that the collectivist thinking of democratic centralism retained a purchase that extended beyond the hardline faction that was opposed to change of any kind.

At the heart of the debate about pluralism and the party was the double interpretation to which the latter term is susceptible. There is a distinction to be made between parties that see their role in terms of a social force whose aim is to promote some transcendental value and, on the other hand, parties that see themselves as the organised expression of one section or interest in society engaged in competition with others for political power and influence. The logic of the first view is necessarily exclusive, quite simply because the party's main concern, for which it is in business as a party, transcends any other, and this gives it privileged status in the political arena. The Stalinist tradition, from the formation of which in this respect Lenin cannot be exonerated, has been categorical not only in seeing 'the' party as transcending other political formations, but also in justifying the party's use of whatever power is at its disposal to subordinate to itself, to outlaw or to eliminate rival political formations of any kind.

In the debates of the Czechoslovak reform movement, the constraints imposed by Soviet tutelage over the bloc countries, but also the fact that the views of orthodox communists within the CPCz had to be taken into account, meant that many of the attempts to move in the direction of pluralism strove to retain elements of both concepts of the political party. Thus Michal Lakatos, much of whose writing at this time was directed towards recommending an open arena for the expression of group interests, put forward the notion of a 'one party pluralism', in which the communist party would retain its

function as watchdog of the 'gains of socialism' but without being
the embodiment of state power, whilst competing interests would be
able to take the form of political parties in a relationship with the
communist party that Lakatos did not fully spell out. Indeed one wag
commented that such recommendations would lead to naming 'new
parties Communist Party A, Communist Party B, and so on alpha-
betically until all interests and opinions were catered for'.[3]

Views such as that of Lakatos were to crop up time and again as
reform of the political system came more clearly on to the agenda in
both the Soviet Union and in Eastern Europe. They clearly represented a commonly-held view of how a communist party might move
from monopoly to a position of authority which allowed it to retain a
watching brief on social development. It is the point of view on
which the Yugoslav party based its positions in the aftermath of the
1948 split, and it has much in common with the thinking of
reformers whom we shall encounter below, such as Imre Pozsgay in
Hungary, or indeed Mikhail Gorbachev himself.

On 21 August 1968 the Warsaw Treaty forces invaded
Czechoslovakia. The Dubcek leadership was removed, and a process
of 'normalisation' was put in hand. The 'norm' in question was the
power monopoly as it has been described in these pages: a
reimposition of the censorship, the restitution of the party's leading
role, and a cadre policy giving preference to 'trusted comrades'. And
whilst Czechoslovakia was able to retain at least some elements of its
economic reforms, in the political sphere apparatus politics ruled
supreme, with heavy police backing. The ideas of the Prague Spring
went into limbo.

They were not lost, but lived on as an important reference point in
debates among communists, where such debates could take place
and had any purchase in the world of action. And, as noted, they
were to be brought out of limbo by proposals for economic and
political change emanating from no other source than the Soviet
Union itself.

It was only two years after the suppression of the Czechoslovak
reform movement that a further crisis erupted, this time in Poland.
During his twenty-four years as party leader, Wladislaw Gomulka
had presided over a process of deep social change. The agrarian
Poland that he inherited had, by 1970, become urbanised and the
industrialisation that had been embarked upon in the post-war years
was now well advanced. Social change brought social strains: in

particular the shift of people from agricultural to industrial employ-
ments spelled problems of integration for the expanding working
class. In the circumstances it is not at all surprising that it was the
urban workers who provided the spearhead of protest movements in
1970, 1976 and in the sensational climax of the Solidarity period in
1980–81.

Solidarity
Riots in Gdansk and the towns on the Baltic seaboard in 1970,
caused by insensitive government handling of a price rise, were put
down with considerable severity. The events created no movement
that would have modified the power monopoly, which was able to
reassert its sway by a savage resort to force by the Gomulka leadership, as a result of which a considerable number of workers lost their
lives. The party leadership changed hands, passing to Edward Gierek
who was hailed at the time as an enlightened technocrat. Discontent
smouldered, however; and in 1976 further worker disturbances
occurred in Radom and at the Ursus works near Warsaw. This time a
development did take place that was to have a significant impact on
the ability of citizens to fight back against the power monopoly. In
the wake of the disturbances a Committee for Workers' Defence
(KOR) came into being, its leading light at the time being Jacek
Kuron, co-author with Karol Modzelewski in 1967 of an 'open letter
to the party' inspired by New Left and to some extent Trotskyist
ideas. The KOR was later renamed the Committee for Social Self-
Defence (KOSS), but history was to continue to know the organisation by its original title.

Ten years after the worker disturbances and the subsequent
oppression that had brought to an end the Gomulka period in 1970,
strikes broke out again in Gdansk, Szczecin and Jastrzebie. The
Lenin shipyard in Gdansk was to become the focal point of the
drama that was to unfold, and Lech Walesa its focal personality. On
16 August, an Inter-Factory Strike Committee was formed, which
wrote down a number of demands as a basis for discussions with an
alarmed party leadership. On 31 August Walesa announced that the
strike was over. The party's negotiator, Jagielski, had finally agreed
to the twenty-one points put to him by what had by then become the
Independent Self-Governing Trade Union, better known by the title
of its bulletin – Solidarnosc.

The KOR was quick to react to the crisis, first its local members joining the strikers, and later its national leaders arriving in Gdansk with other 'advisers' drawn to a great extent from academic and dissident political life. The links between the strikers and these advisers were not easy to fashion or maintain, many of the more prominent worker leaders resenting this interference in the guise of advice. None the less, if Solidarity gave the communist system in Poland a jolt from which it never really recovered, and was to dominate the politics of the immediate post-communist period – providing in the figure of Lech Walesa Poland's first post-communist president – the role played by the KOR as think-tank, strategist of dissent, and co-ordinator of contestatory activity at both the national and international level was of the greatest significance.

It was in good part owing to its 'advisers' that the Solidarity movement in the crisis of 1980 expressly made no claim to be attacking the mainsprings of the party's power. The lessons of 1968 had been learned, and great pains were taken to reassure the party that its leading role was not being threatened. What was under way was a 'self-limiting revolution'. With hindsight this claim can be seen to be somewhat disingenuous. The very existence of an autonomous Solidarity was a flagrant challenge to the party's control over strategic sections of society which was a traditional part of its leading role, and the intense political struggle involved in having the autonomous trade union registered revealed that fact. Perhaps above all, the fact that at one point Solidarity could claim to have 10 million members on a population of some 36 million, completely destroyed the myth of the indissoluble link between party and people. This was a voice that the party's control of the means of communication could not drown out.

But during the Solidarity period from August 1980 to 13 December 1981 the party itself proved not to be immune to attacks on its monopoly of power from within its own ranks. Pressures for change mounted as the extraordinary party congress, called for 13 June 1981, approached. When delegates were being elected to that congress it was no longer possible for a party secretary to produce a name from his briefcase and have it endorsed by a branch or local conference. With the ending of these 'portfolio candidacies' went also the ability to control cross-representation, and the number of workers elected as delegates to the congress correspondingly dropped. When Kania was elected first secretary of the party at that congress it was probably the first time that the leader of a ruling communist party had ever been freely elected.

By that time, too, the party's membership had in places revolted against the verticality in the way in which the party conducted its internal affairs, which made it impossible for members in one local organisation to discuss common problems with members of another, or to press together for policy choices. In the town of Torun there arose a 'horizontal' movement to establish links of this kind, and the idea was to spread to other areas.

When the call to order came on 13 December 1981 with the imposition of martial law the clock could to some extent be put back, but no credibility could be restored to the party's legitimacy. Poland was not to know the savage police repression of Czechoslovakia or the GDR, and in the 1980s a quite wide range of associations with partially political aims maintained a foothold in Poland, whilst the Catholic church was able to benefit from a Polish pope to increase its political profile. But the attacks on the communist power monopoly, both from reformers within the party and from dissenters without, were rebuffed in December 1981, and it was to be the better part of a decade before they were to resume – and with a vengeance.

By then circumstances across the region had been totally transformed with the arrival in power in the Soviet Union of Mikhail Gorbachev. Even before that turning-point, however, the Soviet relationship not only with the East European states, but also with the constituent elements of the West European left, had changed dramatically.

From coercion to diplomacy – the first signs

These crises served to secure and to confirm Soviet influence in Eastern Europe. They also, however, did little to improve the Soviet Union's image in the West. Yet, ironically, the Soviet Union's interest in escaping from its isolation was increasing throughout these years, and the question of its image was consequently becoming more important. From this point of view the intervention in Czechoslovakia in 1968 was a Pyrrhic victory. The signing of the Helsinki Accords in 1975 represented a step away from isolation, but the use made of the Accords by dissidents in Eastern Europe, and Soviet pressure on Poland during the Solidarity period appeared to cancel out that advance. None the less, from the early 1970s it was clear that in order to escape from its economic isolation, the Soviet

Union was seeking a new image, and clearly this could not be achieved without new policies and new relationships. The hostile face turned to the West was consequently replaced by a multi-faceted diplomacy; whilst in Eastern Europe the Soviet Union accordingly moved to modify its previous strategy of demarcation and coercion: demarcation, that is, of a sphere that it could control, and coercion within that area.

The shift in policy is simply stated, but it had immense implications, many if not most of which were bound to affect the political and economic structure of the country – that is, the power monopoly itself. We shall not be concerned here with the Soviet Union's diplomacy at inter-state level, although that, of course, was an essential part of the background to the fall of the power monopoly. What will be treated here is diplomatic activity at a lower level, a mini-diplomacy which was to open up in a quite remarkable fashion the options open to dissenting groups in Eastern Europe and indeed to the regimes of that region, and was to bring about a highly complex interaction between the CPSU and the parliamentary and extra-parliamentary left of Western Europe.

An early straw in the wind was the increasing attention paid by the CSPU to social-democratic parties in Western Europe, often, and increasingly, at the expense of the communist parties which had been for so long the privileged channels of Soviet influence in Western Europe. This development accompanied a more general increase in the importance of inter-state relations as opposed to inter-party relations, and by the 1970s it was clear that the two were inter-connected. The quest for an improved standing among the nations of Europe was clearly being seen to pass through a better relationship with the non-communist political forces of the left.

At the CPSU's twenty-seventh congress in 1986, held within a year of Gorbachev's assumption of office as general secretary, representatives of a number of West European socialist parties found themselves, to their surprise as much as to everyone else's, seated as guests in the Palace of Congresses in the Kremlin. It was not long before Gorbachev's economic advisers were making visits to social-democratic Sweden, and references to Sweden and Austria – both of them conveniently neutral territories – began to stud the Soviet press in articles presenting those two countries as models worthy of emulation.

By that time Western European communist parties had begun to experience a steep decline in their fortunes, and it was a landmark of no little importance when an article appeared in *Izvestiya* of 3 May 1988, from the pen of Aleksandr Bovin, berating the French Communist Party for its dismal performance in the presidential elections of that year and charging it with having no programme and no appeal to 'broad sections of the population, including the working class'. 'The negative processes and phenomena that have for so long characterised our country', he added, 'are making themselves felt in the weakening of the authority and influence of the [French] communists.'

Indeed, by that time another development of importance in the change of image that the Soviet Union was setting out to effect had manifested itself. From before Gorbachev's arrival in power, the Soviet party began to talk less and less about a communist movement. As Dev Murarka put it, 'the new leaders have quietly perceived that the erosion in the prestige and power of the communist movement is worldwide, and especially [eroded] in Europe'.[4] The place of communism in the party's rhetoric was taken by peace. Although peace was no newcomer to the CPSU's stock of honorific terms, there was novelty in its being promoted at the expense of communism. But this shift of rhetoric was important for another reason.

During the heyday of the power monopoly, the communist parties of Western Europe had sponsored peace councils whose policies had devotedly followed those of Moscow and had consistently presented the Soviet Union as the unwilling protagonist in the arms race. Created in the period immediately following the war, at a time when the stock of the Soviet Union and of the West European communist parties stood high on account of the role that they had played in the war, on the front and in the resistance respectively, the peace councils were part of a world-wide organisation dominated by the CPSU. The pro-Soviet attitude of these peace councils did not prevent autonomous peace movements from acting at times together with them. But in certain cases, the existence of a strong communist-dominated peace movement stunted the formation of autonomous peace organisations. This was the case in France, where the communist party's strong links with the Mouvement pour la paix discouraged the formation of other, independent peace groups. In such cases the iron curtain ran, so to speak, not only between the communist and social democratic parties, but between the sponsored peace councils and autonomous peace movements. The latter, critical of Western establishments and their defence policies, were equally critical of the Soviet Union's record on human rights.

It was therefore an interesting moment when a group formed in Moscow originally to foster trust between the Soviet Union and the United States established links with Western autonomous peace movements in the late 1970s. The KGB under Yuri Andropov, which had by that time, with considerable assiduity and perseverance, cleared all other dissenting organisations from the scene, might have been expected to show the same assiduity in this case. But it did not. As Peter Reddaway pointed out at the time, 'this exceptional situation can be explained by the Group's caution in not criticising directly any Soviet policies, and, more importantly, by the Politburo's reluctance to alienate the Western "peace movements"'.[5]

There was therefore nothing new in the Soviet Union's pursuing a vigorous peace offensive during these years: it had all the machinery in place to do it. What was new was the way in which that machinery was being used, and the targeting of its activities. In turning away from communist parties whose appeal was waning in many Western European countries, the Soviet Union was at the same time setting out to woo peace movements other than those that were sponsored by the communists. This aspect of the Soviet Union's new diplomacy was to have a profound, if somewhat indirect, effect upon the evolution during the 1980s of the relations between Eastern Europe, the West European peace movement and the CPSU itself.

That the peace movement should find itself playing so prominent a role was due in good part to the prominence of the peace issue as the crisis over intermediate-range missiles in Europe developed at the end of the 1970s and in the early 1980s. It was during the development of that crisis that there occurred a sequence of events which, taken together, spelled out the nature of the epoch that was being ushered in, and opened the door through which Gorbachev was to walk.

The shift in the Soviet Union's stance towards the Western European non-communist left and the Western peace movement was accompanied by a loosening of its coercive relationship with Eastern Europe. But for a number of reasons the latter was difficult to discern at the time. First, reporting in the West concentrated on what was after all a rather surprising change in the Soviet Union's attitude towards the Western world. More importantly, the Soviet Union's aim was to transmit a public message to the West, whilst at the same time seeking to avoid the dangers inherent in making too public any shift in policy towards the Eastern European regimes.

It might none the less be asked why the Eastern regimes themselves did not seek to derive a benefit from making public such a shift in Soviet diplomacy.

That they did not do so can be explained by one simple factor. Just as the Soviet Union had relied on its satraps in Eastern Europe for the maintenance of its control over the region, so the regimes had depended, and continued to depend, on Soviet support for their existence. We shall see that the Polish leader Jaruzelski and the reform wing of the party in Hungary were eventually to build on the change in Soviet strategy in an attempt to salvage at least a portion of the power that had been guaranteed them under Soviet tutelage. Jaruzelski, in fact, must have started preparing for that day from soon after, if not actually during, the Solidarity crisis of 1981. But the direction of his manoeuvring did not become apparent until the second half of the 1980s. Before then, the signs of a loosening of the relationship between the Soviet Union and Eastern Europe were slender, but, given the past of that relationship, they were none the less remarkable.

In the spring of 1984 the secretary of the Hungarian party with responsibility for international affairs, Matyas Szuros, wrote an article that raised the possibility of a conflict arising between the national interests of small nations and socialist internationalism. In his view smaller nations could expect to play a role that was independent of the superpowers. The timing of this questioning of the Brezhnev doctrine is important, occurring as it did in the aftermath of the INF missile crisis, with all the emotions that the crisis had given rise to in the centre of Europe. The same factor no doubt explains a second example of Eastern European independence, this time in the case of the GDR. In the same year of 1984, Erich Honecker's declared intention to visit the FRG met with a broadside from the Soviet *Pravda*. *Neues Deutschland*, the GDR's official party newspaper, thereupon printed a sharp reply. In the event, Honecker was forced to cancel the visit, but the exchange had revealed, as in the Hungarian case, a readiness on the part of the Eastern European regimes at least to express an independent position.

A previous episode in the GDR, however, had involved more than mere words. In the 1970s the Honecker regime set about cultivating its German cultural roots, going so far as to lay claim to Martin

Luther as a part of the GDR's heritage. This policy was capped in 1978 by a concordat with the Evangelical churches, which was to offer those churches the chance to play a remarkable role in the early 1980s as the focal point of an upsurge of pacifist and environmentalist activity. The details of this activity will be discussed below. But it could not have occurred had the regime not itself been able to take advantage of a small degree of latitude that had opened up in its relations with the Soviet Union.

It is possible to see in this example how the various reactions to the Soviet Union's new diplomacy were interconnected. To improve its image in the West in general, but also to open up credibly to the non-communist forces of the West European left, the Soviet Union was withholding from coercive action in Eastern Europe. Knowing this, the East European regimes were aware both that it offered them a degree of latitude, but also that a new threat would face them when dissenting movements realised that the Soviet Union would no longer support the regimes in their oppression. The situation was extremely complex. Small wonder that unexpected repercussions continually occurred, and that changes consequent upon this novel situation took place at different rhythms in different places.

The evolution of dissent in Eastern Europe from 1975

There was one area where the indirect implications of this new Soviet stance were particularly marked. It was noted above that the manner of presenting political relationships associated with democratic centralism emphasised the well-being of the organism – be it the party or the state – over the interests of the individual, and the power monopoly gave the party the means to determine, promulgate and enforce its own view of what guaranteed the organism's well-being. The dissenter was thus cast into the role of either a madman in arguing against his or her own true well-being, or a traitor in questioning the established interest of society. Dissent in such circumstances was not simple to contemplate, whilst it was repressed with vigour.

Moreover, until about 1975, a dissenter's struggle was normally a matter of a losing battle contained within the state in which he or she resided. Links between dissenting movements in one country of the region with those in another were scarce, as indeed were movements

of any scale themselves, apart from the churches of various denomi-
nations, which survived as organisations in all the countries of the
region, though subject to party control. In this period before 1975
the West's disapproval of all that went on in the communist East of
Europe could be assumed, but it brought no succour to a harassed
dissenter beyond a diffuse sympathy.

But after the signing of the Helsinki Accords in 1975 there was a
significant shift in the nature of dissent in Eastern Europe. Whilst it is
part of the argument of this book that the communist power monopoly expired through its own weaknesses and through the economic
and political results of those weaknesses, it was none the less helped
on its way by its enemies in the countries where it was being
exercised.

By signing the Helsinki Accords the governments of the Soviet
Union and Eastern Europe had committed themselves to the protection of human rights. This did nothing to affect directly their
treatment of dissent, but it did offer the dissenters, if other factors
were to enter into the equation, a grip on a stick with which they
could beat their oppressors. Just such another factor was the Soviet
Union's acceptance of the need to open itself to the world economy,
which in turn meant making its image acceptable in Europe. With the
birth of Charter 77 in 1977 in Czechoslovakia a new phase in the
history of East European dissent opened up, based upon this
strategy. Charter 77 had its counterpart in the Soviet Union itself in
the Helsinki Monitoring Group.

Further events were soon to occur that would add momentum to
this development. The first was the rise, and then the failure, of the
Solidarity movement; the second was the emergence of a strong
peace movement throughout Europe stemming from the Soviet
Union's installation of a new generation of intermediate range
nuclear weapons, and NATO's 'dual-track' decision of 1979 to
counter this by installing an opposing set of nuclear weapons, whilst
continuing to negotiate for the removal of both series; and the third
was Chernobyl. Behind these lay a fourth factor: the emergence of a
generational cleavage in Eastern Europe. These factors were to
favour the development of an 'anti-politics' (as articulated by Adam
Michnik in Poland and Gyorgy Konrad in Hungary) or a 'counter-
culture' (Agnes Heller in Hungary, Christa Wolf in the GDR)
opposed to the regimentation imposed by the party; they led also to
an important shift in the strategy of the major dissenting movements

and in the ordering of the priorities of the causes for which they were mobilising support; and, finally, they enabled dissenting movements to establish international links, not only within the region, but across Europe.

The idea that dissent should promote a cultural universe separate from that which the party so insistently attempted to shape gained handsomely from the failure of Solidarity. Faced by the mobilisation of a large part of the population, including a working class in whose name it claimed to speak, and with little internal support apart from the organs of coercion, the Polish party had shown itself able none the less to protect – and to use – its monopoly of power. If it were to falter, behind it stood the Soviet power monopoly. It had been made abundantly clear that no social forces could win in an open confrontation with the party-state. This conclusion provided grist for the mill of those who advocated the promotion of a counter-culture. If the party and machinery of indoctrination could not be directly opposed, a different culture and a separate politics could be generated alongside it.

Such thinking was given a strong momentum by the generational factor. Already in the 1970s youth was distancing itself from the party's values in a new and very visible way. The prime vehicle in this case was music. In Czechoslovakia, the early prominence in the 1970s of the rock group *Plastic People of the Universe* and of singers such as Marta Kubisova (who was later to be a spokeswoman of Charter 77) was echoed in the wide-ranging activities a decade later of the Jazz Section of the Prague musicians' union. As dissent built up during the 1980s, John Lennon became a cult hero, his long solemn face adorning many a wall in Budapest and Prague. But music was not the only medium. In Poland a group styling themselves the Orange Alternative staged happenings that evoked the absurd, whilst on 15 August 1989 a Czechoslovak 'Society for Merrier Times Today' staged an 'unsuccessful action by merry policemen', in which young people wearing water-melon helmets attacked a political demonstration with truncheons made of salami, gherkins and inflatable elephants. Such events, recalling similar antics of the Strasbourg *situationnistes* of twenty years earlier, served to reinforce an impression that 1968 had arrived in Eastern Europe.

Moreover, the generational factor was to continue to have an impact when the process of party formation first got under way, one of the earliest and most successful parties to form in Hungary – the

Alliance of Young Democrats (FIDESZ; 9 per cent of the poll in the 1990 election), restricting membership to those under thirty-five years of age.

Meanwhile the generational factor was being harnessed in the GDR at a different level and in a different way. Here, as noted, the Evangelical churches had in 1978 arrived at a concordat with the ruling Socialist Unity Party which offered them a small window of autonomy, which they used to voice their fears of growing militarism in the GDR. As the INF missile crisis mounted, the Evangelical churches found themselves sponsoring a movement in support of peace, and of the protection of the environment. Young people were prominent in this movement which, with its symbol of 'swords into ploughshares', offered an alternative to the party's dreary appeals.

But the rise of a Europe-wide peace movement at that time had more far-reaching effects. When the Western peace movement's leaders strove to co-operate with the dissenting groups, which they took to be their obvious Eastern counterparts, they were at first faced with a problem of communication, which led to a debate of no little historical significance. Certain spokesmen of Charter 77 in particular voiced strong misgivings over putting peace at the forefront of their campaigning. The pseudonymous Vaclav Racek in vitriolic terms, but Vaclav Havel, too, if less stridently, claimed that the party had so distorted the symbol of peace through its propaganda as to void it of any mobilising appeal in Eastern Europe; meanwhile the crucial battle was to secure the civil rights that their Western partners could, in their view so short-sightedly, take for granted.[6]

It was not long, however, before the dissenting movements found that this collaboration with a Western peace movement offered new strategic possibilities. Just as Helsinki had given them a weapon to use against their own governments, so a generalised peace movement, to which their governments could not but subscribe, gave them the chance both to demonstrate the lack of sincerity of those governments, and also to forge links of solidarity with sections of a European left which the Soviet Union, and by implication their own rulers, were anxious to woo. Later, Chernobyl was to add a further string to this strategy, and by the turning-point of 1989 the major dissenting movements of Eastern Europe were mobilising support around the three universalising symbols of peace, the environment and human rights. Once it was accepted that the symbol of 'peace' was worth contesting with the party, Eastern European dissenting movements could present their own ideas of an alternative society based upon a concern for the quality of life and for life itself. And they could do this arm in arm with kindred spirits from beyond the iron curtain, which gave their movement a European dimension.

This international involvement was a further feature of the evolution of dissent in Eastern Europe from the mid-1970s, and it was an internationalism at two levels. First, the dissenting movements established links among themselves. Some celebrated snapshots record a summer meeting between prominent members of Charter 77 and Solidarity on the mountainous border between Poland and Czechoslovakia in 1978, and links were to develop more widely in the region, a Hungarian appeal of 23 October 1986 'on the anniversary of the Hungarian revolution 30 years ago' carrying a substantial list of signatories from Hungary, Poland, Czechoslovakia and the GDR. But more important, even, was the wider internationalisation. The peace movement had created an international army of dissent, and for a few years the leading dissidents of Eastern Europe found themselves the focus of attention and of support in Western Europe, in the heady days before they were catapulted into office as ministers for defence, foreign affairs and the environment, or indeed as state presidents, in the new polities that were to replace communist rule.

But this account of the formation of political parties and of more general aggregating movements does not give a full indication of the immense upsurge in political activity of one sort or another in the region in the era of perestroika. There was change, for instance, within organisations that in the past were an integral part of the power monopoly. Thus in some cases the 'mass organisations' acquired a new autonomy and a new vigour. This was particularly striking in the case of the party-sponsored youth movements, but it affected also the 'peace councils', erstwhile faithful ambassadors for Soviet defence policies. It was the Czechoslovak Socialist Youth League that in 1988 orchestrated a celebrated protest action against the building of a dam in the Berounka Valley at Krivoklat; whilst Miklos Barabas of the Hungarian peace council even applied for membership of END's Convention Liaison Committee – although admittedly that episode ended in the regeneration of past suspicions on the part of the Western peace movement.

In sum, by the time Gorbachev came to power in the Soviet Union the monopoly of power in the hands of the communist parties in Eastern Europe had shown itself to be invincible in the short term through the coercive apparatus that it could command, but fatally vulnerable through its own weaknesses in the long term. Above all, it depended for its maintenance on Soviet backing, and it could not for long survive when that was withdrawn. But until the arrival in power of Gorbachev the ruling parties affirmed, in a series of major crises in the region, their ability to crush internal opposition. They contrived to modify the economic monopoly through various reform mechanisms, none of which dismantled completely the system of central planning, although a wide range of experimentation was developed which in some cases, most notably the Hungarian, at least diluted the monopoly. The monopoly of political power remained intact, but it had to adjust to a shift in Soviet diplomacy that foreshadowed an opening to the world economy and co-operation and a withdrawal from confrontation with Western Europe. The regimes were able to use these new circumstances to develop some very small opportunities for autonomous action, but they had to cope with a similar exploitation of the evolving circumstances on the part of dissenting movements.

With hindsight it can be seen that from 1985 the Eastern European regimes had to plan for a future in which Soviet support could no longer be relied on. Some of them were to move slowly towards attempting to modify their monopoly of political power so as to meet that uncomfortable future. Others, however, continued to act within the logic of the power monopoly itself, but aware now of the increasing permeability of the screen that protected the monopoly in the ideological realm, and of the growing tendency for a younger generation to listen to its own sounds and not to those of the party.

The voices that were raised against the communist power monopoly in Eastern Europe, in economic or political life, within the communist parties or outside them, could have little real impact as long as the monopoly held in the Soviet Union itself. They were not, however, the only voices that were being raised against the monopoly. In Yugoslavia and in Western Europe, in very different ways stemming from obviously differing contexts, the power monopoly had long been under attack by the time Gorbachev acceded to power in the Soviet Union. It will be recalled that in Yugoslavia the League of Communists had, after 1948, instituted economic reforms which effectively dismantled the economic monopoly, whilst retaining a firm political control which suggested that in that realm some elements at least of the monopoly remained. In Western Europe, the distance that the Italian Communist Party had long taken from the CPSU's political practices was to build up, in the 1970s, into a generalised movement among many of the West European communist parties under the sobriquet of Eurocommunism. Each of these contributions to the story of the decline of the communist power monopoly merits separate treatment.

Notes
1   Francois Fejto, *A History of the People's Republics* (Harmondsworth: Penguin, 1969), p. 38.
2   H. Gordon Skilling, *Czechoslovakia's Interrupted Revolution* (Princeton: Princeton University Press, 1976), p. 219.
3   See Morton Schwartz, 'Towards One-Party Pluralism', *Problems of Communism*, Vol. 16, No. 1 (1967), pp. 21–7; Jiri Franek in *Rude Pravo*, 26 Feb. 1966.
4   Dev Murarka, *Gorbachev: The Limits of Power* (London: Hutchinson, 1988), p. 33.
5   Peter Reddaway, 'Dissent in the Soviet Union', *Problems of Communism*, Vol. XXXII, No. 6 (1983), p. 13.
6   Vaclav Racek, 'Letter from Prague', in Jan Kavan and Zdena Tomin, *Voices from Prague* (London: END/Palach Press, 1983), pp. 13–16.

Further reading

Rudolf Bahro, *The Alternative in Eastern Europe* (London: Verso, 1981).
Karen Dawisha, *Eastern Europe, Gorbachev and Reform* (Cambridge: Cambridge University Press, 2nd ed. 1988).
Michael Ellman, *Socialist Planning* (Cambridge: Cambridge University Press, 2nd ed. 1989).
Galia Golan, *Reform Rule in Czechoslovakia, 1968–1969* (Cambridge: Cambridge University Press, 1973).
Elemer Hankiss, *East European Alternatives: Are There Any?* (Oxford: Oxford University Press, 1990).
Vaclav Havel *et al.*, *The Power of the Powerless* (London: Hutchinson, 1985).
Alec Nove, *The Economics of Feasible Socialism* (London: Allen and Unwin, 1982).
Teresa Rakowska-Harmstone, *Communism in Eastern Europe* (Manchester: Manchester University Press, 2nd ed. 1984).
Jadwiga Staniszkis, *Poland's Self-Limiting Revolution* (Princeton, NJ: Princeton University Press, 1985).
Vladimir Tismaneanu, *In Search of Civil Society: Independent Peace Movements in the Soviet Bloc* (London: Routledge, 1990).
Roger Woods, *Opposition in the GDR under Honecker* (Basingstoke: Macmillan, 1986).

6

Hide and seek in Yugoslavia

Yugoslavia occupies a quite special place in the history of the communist power monopoly in Europe. Having fought their way autonomously to power, and having retained their independence in the polarisation of Europe that accompanied the high point of the cold war, the Yugoslav communists could claim a legitimacy that was denied to the ruling parties of the bloc countries. Independence, however, did not mean the abandoning of Marxism-Leninism and the subscription, shared by all Marxist-Leninist regimes, to the view that history had endowed the communist party with a duty to lead or guide (the distinction was to become important in the rhetoric) the process of social development.

Later, once it had deliberately distanced itself from Soviet economic and political practices at the close of the 1940s and had developed its own distinctive form of Marxist-Leninist socialism, Yugoslavia was to be taken as a point of reference in any discussion about ways and means of reforming the Soviet system. The assumption was that monopoly had been abandoned in favour of a unique and adventurous form of decentralisation, and Yugoslav social self-management became an important case-study in the discussion on industrial democracy. This assumption has not been universally shared. Inside Yugoslavia itself the development of social self-management was accompanied by a critique on the part of the radical left, for whom the journal *Praxis* served as a rallying point. The view of internal critics was that there was a fundamental incompatibility between social self-management and the leading role of the party, even in its diluted Yugoslav form, and that, in the words of a celebrated dissident, 'the possibilities of social change towards democratising Yugoslav society will largely depend on whether the

legitimacy of the monopoly usurped by one segment of society . . .
will be brought into question'.[1] But despite these external and
internal criticisms, the conventional wisdom held that Yugoslavia's
experience had been special in being an example of Marxism-
Leninism without the monopoly of power displayed by the Soviet
system and reproduced in the bloc countries.

   The ferment in Eastern Europe in 1989, together with the process
of change in the Soviet Union, at the time distracted attention away
from Yugoslavia. Yet in fact one of the more remarkable features of
the movement in 1989 to disestablish the communist power monopoly was that it affected some of Yugoslavia's republics hardly less
than it struck the bloc countries. The reason why some of the
republics were affected more than others is a matter to which we
must return below. But the point of interest was that the country that
had represented for so long the model of Marxism-Leninism without
a central monopoly of power was now being subjected to calls for the
abandoning precisely of that monopoly. Moreover, the response to
these calls in the republics of Slovenia and Croatia was very similar
to responses in the Eastern European countries.

   This suggests that the Yugoslav League of Communists, whilst it
had indeed modified the power monopoly, had not entirely abandoned it. The League had promoted a high degree of economic and
administrative decentralisation, and had diluted its political monopoly sufficiently to support its *bona fides* as an agent of purposive
change; but it had none the less remained master of the political
game and, moreover, had succeeded in reserving the high ground of
the political system for itself. In claiming in 1952 to be abandoning
its administrative role it was setting out, as it were, to play hide and
seek. The role that it was to perform was far less visible than in the
past, but, in politics if not in the economy, it retained a monopolistic
character. Until further details are presented this may seem to be a
play on words. But the situation can be described in other terms. For
long years the fact that workers in the workplace were empowered to
run their own affairs distracted attention from certain other facts –
for example that the League was not prepared to put its own power
at the centre of things to the test of a free and open election. That was
what was demanded in certain of the republics in 1989 and after, and
the impact of that simple demand is ample demonstration that the
League had departed far less from its earlier position of monopoly
than many had thought to be the case.

The Yugoslav reforms moved through a series of phases and were punctuated by a number of crises. Changes instituted after 1948 led to tension between proponents of pursuing the momentum of the reforms on the one hand, and those who were alarmed precisely at this prospect on the other. These tensions came to a head in the early 1960s and resulted in a victory for the reformers at the eighth congress of the League of Communists of Yugoslavia (LCY) in 1964. Within a decade a crisis of both economic and political origin brought political retrenchment, but left the economic reform intact. The account that follows will focus first on the early reforms after 1948, before examining the turning-point of the mid-1960s and then the 'Croatian spring' of 1971–72.

The move towards the market

In an earlier chapter it was seen that when the Yugoslav Communist party came to power in the closing stages of the Second World War it modelled its economic and political practices on those of the Soviet Union. A staunch member of the Cominform, it even provided the geographical base for that organisation in Belgrade. This close relationship with the Soviet Union and its party foundered as the tensions of the cold war mounted, and as Stalin sought to increase Soviet dominance over what was becoming a series of satellite states. Faced with this threat to their independence the Yugoslav communists forced the issue, and found themselves consequently excluded from the Cominform in 1948. In order to maintain a stance independent of both blocs, they set out to innovate within the socialist frame of reference to which they were committed and which provided the basis of their legitimacy.

From plan to market

The decision to innovate was not taken immediately. The Yugoslav party's first reaction to expulsion from the Cominform was, on the contrary, to attempt to show that its independent stance did not spell any departure from the norms of Marxism-Leninism established by the Soviet Union. The second nationalisation law of 1948 completed the work of the 1946 enactment, bringing hotels, retail outlets and cafés into the state's hands. In agriculture, a reticence earlier shown towards collectivisation was forgotten, the party going so far as to call for the 'liquidation of the capitalist elements and hence the kulaks as a class'.[2] Yugoslavia's application to join the CMEA in 1949 represented a further earnest of this temporary reinforcement of orthodoxy. These early moves must be seen as a response to Soviet criticisms, which the Yugoslavs clearly took seriously at that point, determined though they were to remain masters in their own house. But by 1950 the party had veered away from this aggressive socialist stance, and the turn away from monopoly, at least in the economy, had been made.

Milovan Djilas tells us that it was he who first suggested that the workers should be involved in decision-making down at the point of production as he was sitting with Boris Kidric and Eduard Kardelj in a car in front of Djilas' house.[3] Whatever the individual roles involved, Yugoslavia's renowned experiment in industrial democracy was certainly conceived at leadership level in response to circumstances. At that point in their history, those leaders had not developed political structures through which such innovating policies could emerge from below, whilst they did still carry the authority necessary to carry the reforming measures through.

A first series of reforms had as its aim the economic decentralisation that this new policy required. These measures included the Basic Law on the Management of State Economic Enterprises and Higher Economic Associations by the Work Collectives of 1950, which introduced workers' control; the Law on the Planned Management of the National Economy of 1951, which, despite its name, spelled the end of central command planning in Yugoslavia; and a reform decree of December 1953, which introduced the concept of profit-sharing between the work collective, the commune, and higher public authorities, thus bringing in political adjustments through a reorganisation of the communes to take account of the increased role that they would be playing in a decentralised economy.

Central command planning was replaced by 'social' (that is, indicative) planning. Control over investment, which was one of the key mechanisms through which monopoly was exercised in the economic realm, was at this stage not relinquished by the centre, although investment funds were made available to firms in the form of credits, repayable with interest, and no longer in the form of direct grants. This retention of the investment function was to be a bone of contention as momentum developed behind the reform. In agriculture, collectivisation – which elsewhere had served to extend the power of the state into the countryside – was abandoned, a measure enabling collectives to dissolve being passed on 30 March 1953.

This early establishment of 'workers' self-management' and the move towards 'market socialism' followed from the decision to reduce severely the role of the state in production, and to escape what were seen as the bureaucratic distortions of socialism as exhibited in the Soviet Union. In the early years, during post-war reconstruction, the measures could not be given full effect. But they did lay down clear guidelines for a decentralised future. Workers' councils did form the basic building blocks of an experiment in industrial democracy, with workers' self-management being extended in 1963 beyond the industrial field to embrace other occupations in 'social self-management'. Moreover, the implication that for social self-management to work, relations between enterprises had to be governed by a market and not by human administration was accepted, and the resulting market socialism did spell an end to central planning.

Politics in command

The changes mounted in the political realm appeared to be equally far-reaching. The professed aim of the entire reform was to make a start on a dismantling of the state. Bureaucracy in politics was to be attacked therefore at the same time and with the same vigour as the central monopoly in the economy. Since it will be shown below that the centre in Yugoslavia retained far more power in the political realm that in the economic, it is important to examine carefully the measures that were taken.

The crucial element in the political system whose role would have to change if claims that the system had been reformed were to be taken seriously was, of course, the ruling party itself. Here the cardinal event was the sixth congress of the Communist Party of Yugoslavia in 1952. It was at that congress that the party expressed its intention to abdicate from an administrative role in society, and to limit its activities to political guidance. This indeed seemed to be required by the changes in economic organisation that had been made and which the congress endorsed. A new set of statutes embodying this reformed image contained no reference to a 'leading role' for the party. To mark the occasion the name of the party was changed to 'League of Communists of Yugoslavia' – a move that reflected rather well the curious mixture of Marxist-Leninist fundamentalism and pragmatism that the Yugoslav reforms constituted.

The sequel to the congress did in many ways bear out the intention to remodel the party's role. The central and regional apparatuses of the party – now the League – were cut back significantly, to an extent that really did restrict its ability to intervene in regular administrative tasks. The reforms of 1952 were in certain areas carried further in later years, in particular a requirement that state and party should be structurally separated. By the 1960s a firm convention had been established that no one should hold office in both state and party structures.

But in certain other respects that separation of party and state was less than complete, and the League retained a presence – if not of an outright administrative kind – at all levels of society and, most importantly, in the workplace. In 1952 party organisations were withdrawn from the various departments of the state bureaucracy. But by 1964 many cases of their return were being recorded. Moreover, whilst it was made possible for the party to organise on the territorial principle, workplace organisation in the factories was retained, and in the history of the communist power monopoly, the workplace 'cells' have played a crucial role in relaying central policies and decisions to the grass-roots of society. The statements of some of the leaders at the sixth congress in 1952 made it clear that the new ideas were neither universally shared, nor their implications fully appreciated. The very orthodox Aleksandar Rankovic deplored the idea entertained by some party members that democracy implied, amongst its other attributes, 'a right to discuss the correctness of the party line'.[4]

But the innovation that, with the hindsight of history, can be seen to have secreted most clearly the League's continuing central role and its unwillingness to relinquish its control over the political process was the way in which it set out to reform its role in society in organisational terms through a Socialist Alliance of Working People of Yugoslavia. It was intended that the SAWPY would differ from the mass organisations characteristic of the party's political monopoly as it had been exercised in the bloc countries. There, these were grouped under an umbrella organisation which bore the title variously of the 'patriotic', 'national' or 'fatherland' front, and it was this front, rather than the party itself, that proposed candidates for elections (see Chapter 3 above). In Yugoslavia, in the early years before 1952, the People's Front had played this role.

At the sixth congress the League's chief ideologue, Eduard Kardelj, announced that henceforth, instead of the Front taking its orders from an interventionist party, 'concrete political and ... social questions should be settled directly in the organisations of the Socialist Alliance'. But the SAWPY never lived up to these expectations, if indeed they were ever seriously entertained. By pre-empting the party political field through, for example, control of elections, it prevented rivals to the League's monopoly of political power at the centre from emerging. It was run on looser lines than its counterparts in other communist countries, and it did provide opportunities for discussion, and thus aided communication between the centre and strategic sections of the population. But ultimately, as perhaps with more of the Yugoslav reforms than history has been willing to admit, it merely diluted the power monopoly, and thus gave it a longer lease of life.

As for the structures of the federal state, economic reform was accompanied by a significant decentralisation. The reorganisation of the communes to cater for this decentralisation has already been mentioned. At central level not only was the Federal Planning Commission abolished (in April 1951), but so too were most of the remaining federal economic ministries which had until that point organised the centralised economy. This did indeed break up the central monopoly of economic and administrative power, and the beneficiaries of this change included the enterprises, their work collectives, and the communes. But before much time had elapsed it became clear that the major beneficiary was government at the republican level. It is not too much to say that the history of Yugoslavia since 1950 was dominated by the rivalry among the six republics and between the republics and the federation. The League struggled to stay on top of these very strong tensions, and on more than one occasion it was clear that it was only the monopoly of power that the League had retained, however diluted, that enabled it to prevent those tensions from destroying the state, at least until the general collapse of communism in Eastern Europe.

If the reforms of this period are checked against the features of the communist power monopoly suggested above, the record can be seen to be mixed.

First, that prime condition for the maintenance of the monopoly – the closed frontier – had begun to dissolve. Circumstances played a role here; expulsion from the Cominform meant, for a country as small as Yugoslavia, an opening to the world in one sense or another. That stick was matched by the carrot of the benefits that might accrue from opening up one of Europe's finest coastlines to tourism, even though the tourist industry as we were to know it today was in its infancy at that time. Restrictions on foreign trade were to an extent reduced. To the economic effects of an open frontier were added the political: traffic across the border spelled an end to the party's monopoly over information. The opening of the frontier and its consequences set the tone for Yugoslavia's development over the next thirty-five years. Economy and society were open to influences from outside, which a centralised party would contrive to control, just as it strove to stay on top of massive internal tensions stemming from both economic and political sources, by retaining one crucial element of the earlier monopoly – its prerogatives at the very heart of the political system.

Secondly, monopoly in the economy had begun to give way to a strongly regulated market. Central command planning had gone, although at this stage the centre still retained a determinant influence through the 'social plan', and through control over investment and prices. Both that influence and the momentum behind the forces that the reform had set in motion were to become visible in a crisis that was to develop in the early 1960s.

Thirdly at the level of the party's relationship with society the record was mixed. The party had given up its role at the heart of the administration, and had taken steps to separate itself structurally from the state, as noted changing its name in the process, and converting the People's Front into a Socialist Alliance. But these new arrangements did not accommodate any possibility of a challenge to the League's power to set the political agenda and to control the developing process of reform. Yugoslavia continued to be ruled by the same leadership that brought the regime to birth, and none of the mechanisms that had been put in place in the reforms offered any purchase to a rival leadership that aspired to challenge it.

For commentators at that time, Yugoslavia represented a departure from the Soviet norm within the family of Marxist-Leninist regimes, one white sheep in a black flock. Moreover, the departure was real. But what was concealed at the time – perhaps even from many of the Yugoslav actors in the drama – was that the party had chosen to surrender a large part of its monopoly of power whilst retaining one element of it – a refusal to countenance autonomous organisation such as might contest its political power.

The authoritarian context in which the reforms were introduced is well illustrated from the realm of policing. The rigours of the post-war period, when the revolution was still being consolidated, had generated a formidable political police in the hands of Aleksandar Rankovic, a Serb, and a consistent defender of orthodoxy in the debates within Yugoslavia. The OZNa (*Odeljenje za zashchitu naroda*), later renamed the UDBa (*Uprava drzhavne bezbednosti*) was set up, as noted, to consolidate the party's power – a role that it performed with some vigour. After the nervousness of the split with the Cominform, when Rankovic's police had understandably been particularly active, the UDBa confessed to having been over-enthusiastic during that crisis. But its continuing concern for rooting out 'Cominformists', and the fact that it continued to be headed by one of the inner circle of partisan leaders, gave the party assurance when embarking on its reform policies. We shall shortly see that the UDBa, and Rankovic's role within it, were to become a bone of contention when the reform entered a later stage.

Finally, as might be inferred from the above, the attachment to the orthodox norms of democratic centralism, with the abhorrence of fractional activity and an insistence on the organic unity of party and of society, was retained. It was indeed strengthened as a defence against the dangers of 'anarchy' (the term was frequently invoked by the more traditionalist of the leadership) that the reform policies contained.

No doubt, given the substantial qualifications to its power that the regime had introduced by this time, monopoly is too strong a word to use for the resulting economic and political arrangements. It is, moreover, more important to register the actual changes that took place than to fix a word upon them. Yet much later events in 1989 do force a new perspective to be taken of Yugoslavia's development, and the fact of the matter is that, when communist parties fell or were driven from power in that year elsewhere in Europe, it could be seen that the claims that the Yugoslav League of Communists had been making to have departed from communist orthodoxy in the 1950s had been only partly justified. It is with that in mind that the conclusion can be advanced that, in remaining clearly master of the political game, the League had retained its power monopoly, but with a high degree of tolerance.

That tolerance was put to the test on two particular occasions,

before later events in the region as a whole brought the whole
Yugoslav edifice down. The first was a crisis brought about by the
very success of the economic reforms; the second arose from the
besetting problem of Yugoslav politics – the assertion of republican
interests against the federal principle.

The economic reform crisis of the 1960s

Throughout the period between the launching of the first reforms in
the aftermath of 1948 and the final collapse of the Yugoslav federation at the end of 1991 a continuous struggle was waged between
those pressing to deepen the reform process and those concerned to
restrain its centrifugal influences. That this was inevitable is
illustrated by the view frequently stated by those at the centre of
affairs that the reforms had yielded an ambivalent system half way
between central planning and a free market. The position was
rendered more complex by the fact that the republican units of the
federation exercised a powerful pull towards decentralisation even
within the League.

Whatever their public commitment to social self-management,
there were many within the League's leadership for whom an attack
on centralised power amounted simply to an attempt to relocate
power in the republican capitals. The Serbs, however, as the most
numerous component of the federation, had an interest in maintaining a centralised state. It was no accident that the most prominent spokesman of the 'firm hand' in the 1960s was the Serbian
Rankovic. It was possible at that time to remove such a leader on the
grounds that he was promoting goals of Serbian domination. We
shall see that a day was to come when the League was not powerful
enough at federal level either to restrain republican demands for
autonomy from Belgrade or to prevent a Serbian leader from rousing
Serbs outside Serbia to take up arms to defend a Serbian patrimony.

But this is to run ahead. In the early 1960s, when pressures for
further reforms came to a head, the options were debated within a
League that still contained the leaders of the revolutionary years. At
that point the aim was still seen as being to make sense of a process of
decentralisation which was clearly incomplete, and therefore
untenable. In the years immediately preceding the League's eighth
congress in 1964, and at the congress itself, a number of measures
were taken which deepened the reform process and thereby modified

further the League's earlier monopoly of power.

First, foreign trade restrictions were loosened in 1961, and quantitative restrictions on imports were reduced, apparently under pressure from the US and the other Western nations with whom Yugoslavia had been trading since the turn in 1948, and with a view to integration in the General Agreement on Tariffs and Trade (achieved in August 1966). This left the Yugoslav government with some control over the flow of goods across the border, but it was seen as an important part of the reform that Yugoslavia should be integrated in the world market. Should the movement of world prices be imported into the Yugoslav economy and result in inflation, this was seen as a cost to be set against the benefits of competition. Thus the autarky that had in the very early days protected the centre's monopoly in the economy was further undermined.

Two steps taken in the internal economy revealed how slowly the reform process had been moving. Only now, in 1961, were enterprises given the right to dispose of the proceeds of production, in the sense of choosing the balance between investment, savings and distribution to the workforce. Meanwhile a move was made to reduce the central control of pricing, which at that point was still significant. In July 1964 abrupt price rises were brought in on a wide range of products with a view to ending subsidies and promoting equilibrium prices. This was taken further in 1965, when a further adjustment sought to take world prices as the yardstick. Important, too, in view of the debates of the period, was a decision to dismantle the centre's control over the balance of investment between the republics. This in the past had enabled the poorer republics to secure privileged funding. Now goals of equality were required to give way to goals of economic efficiency: a dinar invested in Slovenia would yield more than a dinar invested in Macedonia, where technical skills and supporting industries were scarce and the infrastructure less developed. A Fund for Underdeveloped Areas was set up in compensation, but the centre's control over the disposal of the country's overall income was reduced by one more notch.

Just who had inherited the power thus released took some time to emerge. Attention focused in the immediate aftermath of the 1965 reforms on the banks, which in turn had been liberated from central control, and found themselves wielding considerable economic power as self-managed institutions. But ultimately the chief beneficiaries of the reform were the republics. In constitutional terms decentralisation meant placing economic power in the hands of the organs of social self-management; but in real terms the republican authorities retained a good part of the power wrested from the central federal government. In circumstances where political controls were strong decentralised economic power was translated into political power in the hands of the republican Leagues.

In the debates of the early and mid-1960s it was accepted by most participants that deepening the economic reform implied instituting political reforms too. Certain it was that those who resisted change frequently found themselves the target of intense pressures. The strong movement in the early 1960s to take the reform process further necessarily polarised opinion at the head of the League. But it was not until after the League's crucial eighth congress in 1964, when the economic reforms were proposed, that the conflict between reformers and hardliners took the centre of the stage. When it did, in a political crisis in 1966, it centred on Rankovic, one of the leaders of the revolutionary years, and in many ways Tito's right-hand man.

Rankovic was at that point the League's organisational secretary and thus in a position to influence appointments to senior posts in party and government. He was also the effective chief of the Serb-dominated State Security Service, and it was his activities in this role (which apparently included tapping Tito's own phone) that gave his enemies the opportunity they needed to drive him from his positions of power, and thereby to mark the political defeat of the defenders of the power monopoly. In view of later developments it is to be noted that in Yugoslavia at that time the defeat of Rankovic was generally seen in national terms as a victory for the Croats.

The political monopoly underwent less erosion than did the economic monopoly in the reforms of the 1960s, as subsequent events were to reveal. None the less the changes that were made in the political realm were wide-ranging, particularly at the central federal level.

Perhaps most significant were those that concerned the League's apparatus. It will be recalled that in the Soviet Union and in Eastern Europe the apparatus, at the heart of which lay a secretariat grouping the most powerful heads of the departments of the Central Committee, was the cornerstone of the power monopoly in the political realm. On coming to power the Yugoslav communists had reproduced this model of political control. The adjustment of the party's role to match the policy turn after 1948 had seen a reduction in the size of the apparatus. On the eve of the political crisis of 1966 the League's central apparatus was already far less substantial than that of any of the ruling parties of the Soviet bloc. Four commissions dealt with organisational matters and a further four covered ideology and political education. These will be recognised as the functions central to communist rule in however modified a form.

There were also five commissions covering social, economic and political affairs, and five dealing with social science, culture and relations between the Yugoslav nationalities. But the staff of these commissions seems to have been small. One source records a total figure of forty-seven senior 'political workers' at this time, which is hardly compatible with a major interventionist role.[5]

With the political crisis of 1966 the secretariat as a collective institution was abolished, and whilst this left the commissions in existence, it clearly represented an intention to reduce the central apparatus' weight within the political system yet further. The *nomenklatura*, as an instrument in the party's hands, none the less continued to function, but in a decentralised fashion and not as an institutionalised central agency.

Elections within the League were opened up to allow for multiple candidacies, without the list system itself being abandoned (it was defended on the grounds that it allowed for prior discussions and consultations), and in elections to most of the republican League congresses of 1968 there was a choice of candidates.

The question of organisation at local level was given a good deal of attention, and a year after Rankovic's fall the practice whereby party members formed numerous small cells within the workplace was abandoned in favour of single consolidated party organisations in each enterprise. This was matched by the creation of single organisations at the territorial commune level.

Finally, a running debate took place on how the principle of democratic centralism should be interpreted in the new circumstances. It is to be noted, first, that the debate was seen as important. That is, the League still adhered to the communist tradition, and this had implications both for the way in which the League perceived its role in society and for the organisational practices that it believed should support that role. The debate turned to a considerable extent on whether a continued ban on fractional activity within the League was not incompatible with the reforms in society at large. Cokrevski quoted Gramsci to support the view that conspiratorial ideas were not appropriate for the changed conditions.[6] But many of those who argued for greater freedom of expression within the League were concerned merely to defend the right to hold and propagate minority views; this involved no great departure from orthodoxy, since the main phobia of fractionalism has concerned the organisation of rival centres within the party, and not merely the expression of views. There was no suggestion that the reform wind that was blowing should lead to a multi-party system, and even those who advocated a new look at the ban on fractionalism were aware that any such suggestion would weaken their position. No doubt all were alive to the nationalist dangers that would result from allowing competitive party politics to invade the Yugoslav system.

As with the debate, so with the reality. However wide-ranging the reforms, there was one area that they did not touch. The party retained its control of society through the traditional mechanisms. The Socialist Alliance, subordinated to the League, organised the strategic sections of Yugoslav society in mass organisations (such as the trade unions) which in their form closely followed the traditional communist pattern. The League was able to maintain this role even with a much reduced apparatus.

The evident decentralisation that the reforms embodied concealed this continuing element of the power monopoly. First, the fact that there had been a real and demonstrable decentralisation of economic decision-making suggested of itself that politics, too, had seen a parallel development. Secondly, the League's rhetoric of withdrawing from an interventionist role and of a dismantling of the state carried a certain persuasiveness in view of the League's independent stance within the universe of Marxist-Leninist socialism. And thirdly, the shedding of a substantial number of jobs and functions at the central federal level could reasonably be indicated as evidence of an abandoning of the power monopoly; but in fact it masked what was in reality largely a distribution of the monopoly into the hands of the republican leaderships. This was to be made alarmingly clear in a major crisis that rocked the Yugoslav state in 1971.

The Croatian crisis

In many ways Yugoslavia has acted out in miniature the tensions and struggles that have punctuated the relationship between the Soviet Union and the Eastern European regimes. The dubbing of the crisis that erupted in 1971 as the 'Croatian Spring' is more than a mere journalistic parallel with the Prague Spring. In both cases a communist party leadership, in a community which felt that it was being held back by being enrolled against its will in a larger and overall less developed unit, was making an attempt to gain greater freedom of manoeuvre within that unit. The differences were that the Croatians' grievance was at that point more specific – they wished to retain a greater portion of the substantial amount of foreign currency earned from tourism and from remittances from Croatian guest workers in the FRG – and that there were very strong supports for outright Croatian independence, both from internal cultural organisations such as the Croatian Motherland (*Matica Hrvatska*) and from an extensive Croatian emigration.

The forthcoming crisis gestated over a long period within the Croatian League leadership itself, a division developing between those – such as Miko Tripalo and Savka Dabcevic-Kucar, the publicly most prominent members of the leadership – who believed that the League's claim to leadership should involve using the rise of national feeling as a support for regenerative policies, and those, on the other hand, for whom the emergence of autonomous organisation, either national or of any other kind, spelled a threat to the forms of democratic centralism, and thus to the power monopoly. The growing organisational strength of the *Matica*, whose journal *Hrvatski tjednik* was now joined by other independent newspapers, represented just such a threat.

Mounting tensions faced the Croatian League's leadership with a dilemma: either to lose its credibility in the republic by turning on the *Matica* and the strong movement that the latter was now leading, or to go with the tide of Croatian national feeling and to hope to guide it. It chose the latter course. A students' strike in Zagreb in November 1971 forced the issue, and the federal centre intervened. It did so in the form of Tito himself, who proceeded to demonstrate that the centre still had the capability – which many at that point doubted – to rein in recalcitrant republics. The Croatian League leadership was dismissed; and to balance the books Tito secured the removal of the Serbian and Slovenian leaderships into the bargain.

In the aftermath of this crisis, voices for 'normalisation' became more audible within the League. In the words of Stane Dolanc, the League had 'never ceased to be the basic revolutionary force of our society'.[7] The year before he had said that 'it must be made clear that communists are in power in this country . . . Communists are those who form the government, the Parliament or wherever power is generated, and they hold it firmly in their hands'. The party should 'return to its former practice of democratic centralism, and must use the power that it holds in the administration, the judiciary . . . in education . . . and in the security services', even at the risk of being 'accused of reverting to past practices'.[8] In the period between the crisis and the tenth congress of the League in 1974, Tito himself called for a reassertion of the traditional mechanisms through which the League had exerted its influence in the past – stricter censorship, and closer attention to appointments to politically important posts. These mechanisms, however, had clearly by now lost a good deal of their earlier force.

The 'Croatian Spring' gave rise to a further round of reforms which, whilst on the surface introducing greater democracy into the political system, in fact, if anything, restricted it. The structure of social self-management was refined, with 'basic organisations of associated labour' forming the foundation blocks and with a highly complex system of delegation linking them to the representative bodies at the communal, republican and federal levels. The principle of delegation, as with much else in the Yugoslavia reforms, was intended to embody Leninist notions of direct democracy. But it also left the League, through the Socialist Alliance, playing a dominant role in selecting the delegates. It was a gesture in the direction of democracy, but in terms of pluralism it was a mere distraction.

In Yugoslavia, then, reform had effectively brought to an end the League's power monopoly in the economy. In political life, however, the mechanisms through which the monopoly of power had been exercised in the past remained in place, even if they were used with a high degree of tolerance. That tolerance benefited above all the republican leaderships, and with Tito's death in 1980, Yugoslavia entered a period of uncertainty and increased tension. In such circumstances the radical changes introduced in the Soviet Union by the Gorbachev leadership could not but have repercussions in Yugoslavia. The League was then in a position somewhat similar to that of the Eastern European regimes despite all the moves towards decentralisation that it had made. Its power was being undermined by the abandoning of orthodoxy by the party which until that point had been the guardian of that orthodoxy; and there were forces on hand that stood ready to take full advantage of the changed circumstances.

The point has come to examine those steps through which the CPSU yielded its monopoly of power. Before that, however, it is important to introduce a final and perhaps rather surprising factor in the collapse of the communist power monopoly – the communist parties of Western Europe.

Notes

1 Zagorka Golubovic, *Yugoslav Society and 'Socialism': The Present-Day Crisis of the Yugoslav System and the Possibilities of Evolution* (Munich: Research Project on Crises in Soviet-Type Systems, 1986), p. 44.
2 *The Soviet-Yugoslav Dispute* (London: Royal Institute of International Affairs, 1948), p. 66.
3 This is the account given by Milovan Djilas in *The Unperfect Society* (New York: Harcourt, Brace, 1969), pp. 220–3.
4 *Kommunist* (Belgrade), Nos 5 and 6 (1952), p. 123, cited in A. Ross Johnson, *The Transformation of Communist Ideology: The Yugoslav Case, 1945–1953* (Manchester, Manchester University Press, 1972), p. 209.
5 April Carter, *Democratic Reform in Yugoslavia: The Changing Role of the Party* (London: Pinter, 1982), pp. 123–4.
6 *Ibid.*, p. 75.
7 *Konferencija IV Saveza Komunista Jugoslavie*, 10–11 May 1973.
8 *Borba*, 22 Sept. 1972.

Further reading

Dusko Doder, *The Yugoslavs* (New York: Random House, 1978).
Branko Horvat, *An Essay on Yugoslav Society* (White Plains, NY: International Arts and Sciences Press, 1969).
Mihailo Markovic, *From Affluence to Praxis: Philosophy and Social Criticism* (Ann Arbor, MI: University of Michigan Press, 1974).
Dennison Rusinow, *The Yugoslav Experiment, 1945–1974* (London: Hurst, 1977).
Gershon Sher, *Praxis: Marxist Criticism and Dissent in Socialist Yugoslavia* (Bloomington, IN: Indiana University Press, 1977).
Duncan Wilson, *Tito's Yugoslavia* (Cambridge University Press, 1980).

7

Reflections of the monopoly in West European communism

The final fall of Stalinism in Eastern Europe and the Soviet Union at the end of the 1980s was abrupt. In the space of a few years communism imploded in the territories that had formed its heart. After that point it was impossible to talk of a communist movement except in an historical sense, and even that came to be questioned. The cataclysmic events in what had been the Soviet bloc, and then in the Soviet Union, followed by the long agony of the break-up of Yugoslavia, naturally absorbed the world's attention, and it is developments in those countries that are the chief concern of this book. But for a true understanding of the passing of Stalinism a broader lens is required than that provided by the Soviet Union with Eastern and Southeastern Europe.

Space does not admit a treatment of the way in which, for example, economic reform in China has brought with it pressures for political reform that are germane to this study of the power monopoly. The events in Tiananmen Square in June 1989 presented a challenge to the power monopoly in that country, which the holders of the monopoly were able to rebuff. In rebuffing it so energetically and effectively they showed that the communist party's power still held good, but in fact the economic monopoly in China, which had always been prone to leakage, was dealt a severe blow with the economic reforms from 1978; whilst a number of factors, among them the historical ability of the provinces to resist central pressures and the separate identity that the armed forces have been able to retain ever since the years of revolutionary struggle, have meant that the monopoly has throughout been both divided and subject to leakage.

Despite the added perspective that a treatment of them would bring to this account of the fall of the communist power monopoly, the ruling communist parties beyond the confines of Europe must be left aside. On the other hand, the experiences of the non-ruling parties of Western Europe form an integral part of that account. True, their contribution to the collapse of the Stalinist system was indirect, but their evolution was none the less closely intertwined with that of their sister parties in the Soviet Union and Eastern Europe, and they were an important sounding board for Soviet policies in a part of the continent which was vital to Soviet interests. In fact, a quite distinct link can be established in the process of de-Stalinisation between developments in the Western European communist parties, movements to reform communism in Eastern Europe, and the final process of undoing the Stalinist system in the Soviet Union itself. However, since it is a monopoly of power in the hands of ruling communist parties that is the major theme of this book, and since this monopoly involved power at the level of the state, some words of justification are required if the discussion is to be widened to admit political parties that are often so far removed from power as to be marginal within their political systems.

It will be recalled that it was with the authority given them within the socialist movement of the day by success in bringing about revolution that the Bolsheviks called for the creation of an international movement that would be modelled on the Bolshevik pattern, would oppose reformism, and would be based on 'centralised, almost military discipline'. That organisation was the Comintern, whose birth was recorded above, and the qualities that were being elicited from its members were to become an integral part of the communist identity. They were shortly to be confirmed in the process of 'bolshevisation' which was bound on the Comintern member parties, or more strictly sections, with the defeat of the Trotskyist opposition in the mid-1920s. The organisational norms that were being insisted upon were naturally more appropriate to the context of a state than of a political party. They were in fact at that time being moulded by the particular experiences of the Soviet state. As that state entered the Stalinist period proper, the West European communist parties continued to absorb the organisational practices that were evolving in the Soviet Union. The result was that they incongruously acquired organisational forms appropriate to a drive for economic construction in a developing nation, with an authoritarian leadership closeted from the membership through a centrally controlled apparatus. So it was that, whilst the West

European communist party leaderships were obviously not in a position to exercise over their memberships the power that a state exercises over its citizens, they not only behaved at times as if they could, but did so in the very particular manner of the Stalinist Soviet state. When, for example, André Marty and Charles Tillon were denounced in a period of power rivalry in the very orthodox French Communist Party in the early 1950s, the way in which the affair was conducted had all the style of the purge trials that were taking place at approximately the same time in Czechoslovakia.[1] Similarly, the same party contrived to bind an effective censorship on its members by forbidding them to write anywhere other than in the party's press, on pain of exclusion from the party.

But there is one particular reason of the greatest importance for mentioning the way in which the Western European communist parties became Stalinised. It was in these parties that the process of de-Stalinisation first began.

Togliatti and the *svolta di Salerno*

The very earliest discernible roots of de-Stalinisation lie in the period immediately following the Second World War – that is, before the dictator's death – and in the reconstitution in Italy of a communist party that had been outlawed by Mussolini's fascism, and had therefore not passed through a formative organisational phase, as had its French sister party, during the Stalinist period. Moreover, the leader under whom the party was reconstituted, Palmiro Ercoli, had spent a great part of the inter-war years involved in Comintern affairs, from February 1926 as delegate of the Italian Communist Party (PCI) to the Comintern's Executive Committee. This had led to his adopting the name by which history will know him – Togliatti. Joan Barth Urban has shown, however, that Togliatti maintained a degree of detachment from the Comintern and the Soviet party leadership, despite his dependence on them.[2] This detachment from his erstwhile hosts, and his familiarity with their ways and thinking, was one of the chief factors that led to the innovative policies that the PCI was to adopt after Togliatti's return to Italy in 1944, and after his statement in March of that year that the PCI would co-operate with the Badoglio government – a statement that has gone down in history as the 'Salerno turn' (*svolta di Salerno*).

Another major factor in the PCI's innovating stance was the

political legacy of Antonio Gramsci, whose views on 'hegemony' – articulated before his death in one of Mussolini's prisons – conflicted with the exclusiveness and siege mentality that had by the 1940s come to be associated with Stalinist communism, and were to become more entrenched in the more orthodox parties as Western Europe turned towards Atlanticism in the cold war.

Those policies, of opening up to the intermediate sections of society so as to build up a bloc of support on the left of the Italian politics and integrating the party into the mainstream of Italian political life as a credible and acceptable 'party of government' presented certain imperatives that conflicted with the Stalinist norms that the Comintern parties had developed, and were bound, by the logic of things, to render the PCI critical of certain features of the power monopoly in the Soviet Union. In particular, to have the party's *bona fides* accepted, it was essential to make it clear that, should it come to power, it would not use that power to impose a coup of the kind that the Czechoslovak communists had staged in 1948. Further, whilst the PCI's views on the virtues or otherwise of a planned economy could only be those of an interested bystander, the judgements that it made would necessarily be conditioned by the kind of image it wished to cultivate within Italian society, and would affect its chances in the electoral field. These accommodations to the political practices and political culture of Western Europe will be recognised as part and parcel of a more general movement that was later to develop in Western Europe under the title of Euro-communism.

There was therefore a consistency between this early innovative stance of the PCI, its approval of the Czechoslovak reformers of the Prague Spring, and its condemnation of the Warsaw Treaty intervention in August 1968. The link in particular between the PCI's positions and those of the Prague Spring, which at first could have no effect on the policies either of the Kremlin or of the CPCz, was later to have a very important impact on the evolution of the crisis of European communism. In fact the process of de-Stalinisation can be seen in its clearest outline by focusing attention on three moments in the history of European communism since the war. The positions of Togliatti and the PCI, the reform ideas of the Prague Spring, and the policies of the Gorbachev leadership, are the nodal points across which flashed the spark of de-Stalinisation.

But that simple view of the process must be qualified with one complication: the time sequence was not in that order. As long as Stalinism held up in the Soviet Union, no innovation by a leadership of a Western European party, however large and influential, nor any reforming ideas of a bloc party, could make any real impression on a power monopoly which, we have seen, had strongly built-in mechanisms for its own defence. This can be illustrated by considering the position at the close of 1981, when Jaruzelski had just proclaimed a state of war in Poland. All the earlier promise of Solidarity had therewith evaporated, and its leaders had been consigned to prison or to house arrest. With this there perished, in Poland but also far beyond, the last vestige of credibility of the myth of an 'unbreakable bond between party and people'. The PCI at that point issued the strongest condemnation of the Soviet Union it had ever made. But no words of the PCI could remove the threat of execution that hung over Solidarity, lift the anathema imposed on the ideas of the Prague Spring or warm the lives of the subjects of a Czechoslovak police state.

The revival of ideas associated with the Prague Spring that followed the adoption of Gorbachev's policies had indeed all the marvel of a fairy-tale kiss to awaken a sleeping beauty. At a stroke all the orthodox Stalinist communist leaderships of Western Europe were thrown on to the defensive, and all the regimes of the bloc found themselves without a guarantee of support to their east. The process of de-Stalinisation which from one point of view had been a lengthy struggle waged now here, now there, now with some small gain, now with a greater loss, suddenly was happening across the continent, and all at once.

Looking back in time to 1968, it is possible to see that the Prague Spring punctuated a long and slow process of de-Stalinisation that was taking place in the communist parties of Western Europe. The Prague Spring was perceived at first as evidence that communism could in fact be reformed. If Marxist-Leninist socialism could be given a human face in Czechoslovakia, why could not change filter further east, to affect the heartland of communism? Normalisation from 1969 in Czechoslovakia dashed those hopes. The entire series of events drove deeper the wedge between those non-ruling communist parties that saw their salvation as lying in distancing themselves from Soviet positions, and those that clung to orthodoxy and the Soviet connection. That division within Western European communism has centred on the notion of Eurocommunism, which was prefigured in the recommendations that Togliatti made to the Italian Communist Party in the post-war years. The story must now be developed further.

Before that, however, it is important to draw out from these introductory remarks two reasons for including a treatment of the West European communist parties in an analysis of the decline of the communist power monopoly. First, those parties maintained a distinctiveness within their political systems which derived in good part from organisational practices borrowed from Soviet experience. They present a strong reflection of the political power monopoly as it was exercised in communist regimes. Thus, whilst not themselves exercising a monopoly of power, the West European communist parties serve as an interesting additional illustration of some aspects of the way in which the monopoly worked. As we shall see, a celebrated and wide-ranging criticism of the French Communist Party's norms launched by Louis Althusser in 1978 pointed a finger of accusation at a number of features of the communist power monopoly as it is portrayed in these pages. No account of the monopoly, in fact, would be complete without a treatment of these non-ruling communist parties which lived in its shadow and shared a good number of its characteristics.

This first reason for including the non-ruling communist parties in this account is analytical. A second simply concerns the story itself. The collapse of the communist power monopoly in Europe was, precisely, a European event. That it involved the Eastern European countries no less than the Soviet Union itself needs no argument. But the role of the West European communist parties, if less central to the story, is none the less also an important part of it. The communist power monopoly had important supports in the world external to it. It mattered to the Soviet Union that a series of parties in Western Europe were prepared to defend it and to endorse its policies and economic practices, just as defence of the Soviet Union and what it stood for was an important part of the identity of those parties. The story of the relationship between the CPSU and its sister parties in the west of the continent is very much a part of the story of the evolution of the Soviet Union itself, and thus also of the communist power monopoly. Once again, no account of the communist power monopoly would be complete without this component.

In sum, the relevance of Western European communism to the decline of the communist power monopoly in Europe is a matter of illustration, and only marginally one of causation. The West European communist parties could not cause the monopoly to crumble. But their whole history was so bound up with that of the Soviet Union that they were bound, first, to reflect the CPSU's norms and, secondly, to become involved in the events that led to the power monopoly's fall.

The birth of Eurocommunism

In March 1977 a meeting took place in Madrid between the leaders of the Spanish, the Italian and the French communist parties – respectively, Santiago Carrillo, Enrico Berlinguer and Georges Marchais. At that particular moment those three parties, which, with the Finnish, were the most substantial communist parties in Western Europe, were prepared to put forward a common view of the strategy appropriate for communism in the West European context. In the following year Carrillo published a book entitled *Eurocommunism and the State*, in which the main lines of that strategy were set down and defended. In it he hailed

a new tendency, which has arisen mainly in the advanced capitalist countries, which remains faithful to the principles of Marxism, which takes to itself, in a critical way, the gains made by the revolutionary movement so far, which strives to incorporate in the successes of theory the analysis and elaboration of structural, economic, social and cultural change, and which demands democratic roads and independence in order to work out its own strategy.[3]

The Madrid meeting has often been hailed as the high point of the Eurocommunist phenomenon – as indeed it was, in a certain restricted sense. It was the closest the Western European communist parties got to establishing an organisation, even in the limited form of regular conferences and contacts, to unite those parties that wished to distance themselves from the Soviet Union. Later in that year, however, the French party sharply reversed its position, returning to its long-standing and well-entrenched orthodoxy, whilst the Spanish party, weakened by an exceptionally severe electoral reverse in 1982, was to split into three. There was to be no organisational sequel to the Madrid meeting, whilst from the abundant literature that blossomed in the aftermath of 1977 it was difficult to winnow out a consistent and coherent view of what Eurocommunism was.

And yet, in hindsight, Eurocommunism can be seen to have been a clearly defined development in the history of the European left. To obtain a clear view of its contours, and thus of its relevance to the crisis of the communist power monopoly, the whole period from the twentieth congress of the CPSU in 1956 has to be taken into consideration, when Nikita Khrushchev, in his report to that congress as the CPSU's leader, not only expressly endorsed the parliamentary road to socialism, but also took the first steps in renouncing the Stalinist past.

But first, what did Eurocommunism comprise? It was an attempt, on the part of the leaderships of a number of non-ruling communist parties (including some outside Europe, such as the Japanese) to end their parties' isolation from the political life of their countries and, since to a great extent it was the Soviet connection that lay at the root of that isolation, to detach themselves from Soviet doctrines and Soviet political practices.

The attempt to end their isolation took various forms. First, they set out to widen their electoral appeal in two ways. They became less exclusive in the social categories from which they sought support. Whilst they had in many cases always had a social base that extended beyond the working class, the appeal to artisans and small farmers whose livelihood was being threatened by economic restructuring became more explicit, and, perhaps more significantly, religious affiliation was no longer seen as incompatible with communist party membership. They set out to widen their appeal also by abandoning their attacks on the 'bourgeois democracy' of the societies in which they operated, and by claiming now to accept the rules of the liberal democratic political game, including alternation in office on the basis of electoral results. This change, in which they not unnaturally found it difficult to make people believe, had important implications for the way in which these parties organised their affairs. It meant, for example, that the traditional secrecy that had surrounded their operations had to be abandoned. It meant also that they could no longer be so aggressively militant, in the sense that the mark of success was now to be the marginal vote, in seeking which an abrasive challenge to the basic values of the society around them was hardly productive.

Secondly, they adjusted their ideology to this new image. If the aim was now to win elections in a competitive struggle, and to surrender governmental power if voted out of office, there was little to be gained, and much to be lost, by calling for a 'dictatorship of the proletariat'. The various congresses at which communist parties brought themselves to give up this symbol of the tradition therefore became major landmarks in their respective histories. But the ideological remodelling went much deeper than the disestablishing of that single ideological item. The definitions of the terms in which their new statutes and programmes were couched became much closer to those of the social-democratic rivals from which they had been sundered by the formation of the Comintern.

Thirdly, this new strategy required some adjustment of their organisational norms. There was, perhaps, no obvious reason why a new face to the world should cause them to give up internal practices which were an important part of their identity, and indeed in this realm of internal organisation the changes were at times half-hearted and contradictory. Even the path-breaking Italian party retained an abhorrence of fractional activity in principle, even though it contrived to tolerate in practice quite markedly conflicting *correnti*. But if the traditional militancy of the communist parties was found to be counterproductive in an electoral contest, this was bound, sooner or later, to affect their internal practices. Their critics, too, expected to see some movement away from the traditional norms of democratic centralism, in which debate and open election were eclipsed in the name of revolutionary efficacy.

Organisational change did come, more extensive in some parties than in others, and affecting even the more orthodox parties to some extent. Of particular importance was the decision to accept the organisation of branches (decreasingly frequently referred to as cells) on the territorial principle, rather than in the workplace as in the Leninist tradition. This single reform was seen by McInnes as in itself tantamount to abandoning the communist identity.[4] Certainly it was so seen when it came to dismantling the communist power monopoly in Eastern Europe in 1989. Elections to the party's central organs became more frequently free and open, as opposed to the traditional list system, whereby the leadership handed down a list of candidates, which left members who wished to make their own proposals with the invidious problem of having to strike out other names to make room for new candidates. Control of the electoral process and organisation based upon workplace cells were, of course, central props of the power monopoly in the political life of the ruling parties.

Finally, and in many ways most important of all, Eurocommunism involved taking a distance from the Soviet Union and its Communist Party. This again was often half-hearted, given that the Soviet connection and a reverence for Lenin and the Great October was so much a part of the communist identity, and given also that even the most reformist of communist parties contained strong orthodox elements which had, if possible, to be accommodated. A given party's attitude to the Prague Spring, to the Warsaw Pact's intervention which brought it to a close, to Soviet actions in Afghanistan from 1979, and to the human rights issue in the Soviet Union and Eastern Europe became another highly symbolic touchstone of its position in the division between Eurocommunist reform and Stalinist orthodoxy.

Such were the chief strands of the Eurocommunist position. If they represent what Eurocommunism was about, it might also be asked why such policies came to be espoused in the first place, in parties which in the past had based their strategy on a mistrust of liberal-democratic norms. This is obviously a crucial question, given that it was from within the West European communist parties that arose and developed the most consistent and continuous – if indirect – attack on the communist power monopoly as it had been shaped in the Soviet Union.

Two reasons outweigh all others. The first was local, and concerned the communist power monopoly only tangentially. Social change was not only eroding the communist parties' base in the traditional industries, but it was creating new strands of radical thinking and action. With a thinning worker base the communist parties could not but be responsive to the changing social environment. True, most parties found themselves more willing, and better able, to reach out to the petty-bourgeoisie of artisans and small farmers than to what have come to be termed the 'new social movements'. To that extent Eurocommunism itself did not advance the West European communist parties far down the road of adaptation, but it did at least prepare those parties that had embraced it for the radical upsurge of the 1960s and 1970s, the latter's strong grass-roots elements of youth and feminism reflecting another aspect of post-war social change. This upsurge was to have a severely disruptive, and at times devastating, effect on parties, such as the Communist Party of the Netherlands, that had not earlier taken the Eurocommunist road.

The second major reason for the development of Eurocommunism was the record of the Soviet Union, and this concerned the power monopoly closely. The lifting of the veil on the Stalinist past at the

CPSU's twentieth congress in 1956 was followed later in that same year by the Soviet intervention in Hungary. The two events together caused a severe haemorrhage in communist party ranks in Western Europe, some of the defectors going on to provide initiative and support in the creation of a New Left. Many of those who remained were prepared to read the writing on the wall, and indeed the writing grew longer with the foreclosing on the Prague Spring in a military action in 1968 and with the imaginative use that dissenters in the Soviet Union and Eastern Europe were able to make of their governments' signatures on the Helsinki Final Act in 1975.

This discussion of the what and the why of Eurocommunism now requires illustration from the experience of the parties themselves. This will be provided chronologically, so that some sense can be gained of the sequence of events through which the Western European critique of the communist power monopoly developed. Since the Prague Spring of 1968 constitutes so important a watershed in the story of the collapse of communism in Europe, the account will consider, first, events before that date, and will then go on to examine subsequent developments.

The development of Eurocommunism up to 1968

The Italian party's early departure from orthodoxy in reaching out to the 'middle layers' of society in an attempt to create a 'new party' has already been noted. To establish its credentials in this new role, the party had to show that it had accepted the rules of competitive politics, and that it could offer itself as a party of government on the basis of alternation in office. Already in 1956, at its eighth congress, the PCI had adopted 'Elements for a Programmatic Declaration' which affirmed that

the historic task of proceeding to the establishment of socialism by a new road, other than that by which the dictatorship of the proletariat was realised in other countries, lies before the working class and Italian people.

In this earlier period before 1968 the PCI was given the chance to demonstrate the seriousness of its strategy through the prominent role that it played in local government, particularly in the 'red belt' of Emilia Romagna, where it was strongly implanted. But at national level, too, its activity in parliament came to be that of an integrated participant rather than that of a 'tribune'. Securing the adoption of amendments that it favoured meant doing deals with other parties, whilst its position as the dominant party of the left gave it a major role in committee work.

Further, the extent to which the PCI displayed the organisational practices that lay at the heart of the communist power monopoly as it developed in the Soviet Union diminished significantly. In particular the party set out to break down the walls that separated it from society in the way characteristic of communist parties. As early as the beginning of the 1960s the party decided to abandon an organisational structure based on workplace 'cells' – a structure whose importance in the creation and maintenance of the communist identity was adverted to above. This traditional structure had the deliberate effect of closeting off the communist party, and provided the basis of unity and solidarity from which communists went forth to militate in society. As a result of the move from workplace to territorial organisation, militancy itself lost its edge. This process was to be deepened in a later period by measures such as that passed later at the congress of 1979, when the formal requirement that party members engage in study of Marxism-Leninism was abandoned. Here again an important part of the cement that held together the communist organism was jettisoned.

Next, despite a continuing formal subscription to the 'Leninist principle of democratic centralism', quite distinct currents had begun by 1968 to compete for influence in the party without calls to order in the name of the ban on fractional activity. Finally, the party was prepared to take a critical view of the Soviet Union and of the latter's policies in Eastern Europe. Together with the Yugoslavs, at times the Romanians, and an increasing number of non-ruling communist parties, the PCI refused to endorse automatically the CPSU's positions at international conferences. The refusal of the Italian party to join the CPSU in calling for a universal condemnation of the Chinese Communist Party at a world conference of communist parties convened for that purpose was, in fact, the subject matter of a memorandum written in 1964 by Togliatti, just before he died of a stroke. That memorandum, known to history as Togliatti's Yalta Testament, set out the PCI's position: the Italian party was in basic agreement with the CPSU in the latter's dispute with the Chinese communists, but it would not support the CPSU in striving to excommunicate the Chinese from the communist fold. It proved difficult to convene the conference as more and more parties adopted the Italian position. In the event it was held in 1969, and assembled only 75 of the full 86 parties. Five of these, moreover, refused to sign the final communiqué. It was the CPSU's last attempt to hold a comprehensive international gathering of communist parties.

But in the year before that, the Prague Spring had already brought the CPI into a confrontation with the CPSU. When the intervention occurred in August 1968, it was roundly condemned by the Italians, who never from that point on wavered in that condemnation.

The prominence of the Italian party in the story of Euro-communism has tended to obscure developments of a similar kind in other parties. In Sweden, for example, a change of leadership in 1964 led three years later to a change of the Communist Party's name to 'Left Party Communists' (*Vansterpartiet kommunisterna*), and to a broad 'modernisation' of its structures and thinking. It adopted a policy of independence within the communist movement; it adjusted its ideology by rejecting the formalistic and 'scientific' Soviet definition of democracy in favour of one based on experience and opposed to bureaucracy, overcentralism and manifest injustices; it backed this up in internal organisation by abandoning the principle of democratic centralism in its statutes.

In neighbouring Finland the electoral alliance around the Finnish Communist Party (SKP) formed, in 1958, the largest group in the parliament with 23.2 per cent of the vote, whilst membership of the party itself at that time stood at over 50,000. To be a communist in Finland at that point meant to live one's whole life in an autarkic cultural ambience generated by the party, and it was with a view to breaking down this social and political isolation that reformists within the SKP, having captured the leadership positions at the fourteenth congress in 1966, embarked on a process of de-Stalinisation under Aarne Saarinen. This was to lead to a substantial orthodox minority marching out of a party congress in 1969, to be brought back again later into the party. From 1969 on until the final separation in the 1980s Soviet orthodoxy and Eurocommunist reform coexisted awkwardly side by side in a single party in Finland.

Certain parties – for example the French, the Belgian (after an early shift in strategy in 1954, which had no significant sequel) and the Dutch – stood out against the tide of reform. Of these the French deserves special mention, because of its size (between 300,000 and 400,000 in the period from 1956 to 1968) and the strength of its vote (25.6 per cent in 1956, 22.5 per cent in 1967). One of the strongest communist parties in Europe between the wars, its prestige handsomely boosted by its role in the wartime resistance, well established in local government in certain areas, the French Communist Party was an important part of French political life. It had a leadership deeply imbued with the values of the Stalinist Soviet Union and enjoying, in the person of Maurice Thorez, a continuity from the Stalin days. It was to a great extent the continuing authority of Thorez that prevented the PCF from taking advantage of the weakness of its Socialist rivals to develop a strategy akin to that of the Italian communists in the period between the end of the war in Algeria and the congress of Epinay in 1972, which ushered in Mitterrand's ultimately successful campaign to 're-equilibrate the left' in France in favour of the Socialist Party. Thorez died in 1964, and from the crisis year of 1968 the PCF did begin to make tentative steps in the direction of reform. But in the years from 1956 to 1968 the PCF stood out as a bastion of orthodoxy in a communist world that was experimenting with change.

Thus by the time of the Prague Spring and of the Warsaw Pact's intervention in Czechoslovakia in August 1968, movements for reform within the West European communist parties were becoming entrenched, sufficiently for a significant number of those parties to disassociate themselves from the intervention, and for the Prague Spring to acquire a massive symbolic prominence in European communism across the continent. Before going on to introduce other communist parties and further developments, it would be worth while to pause and take stock of the overall position in European communism at that time.

In the Soviet Union itself Stalinist orthodoxy had survived the initial attempts by Khrushchev between 1955 and 1964 to remedy at least some of the failings of the Stalinist system. None of Khrushchev's many policy innovations within the Soviet Union seriously affected the communist monopoly, and, as will shortly be seen, those that seemed to have been launched with that aim were swiftly undone when Khrushchev fell in 1964. Meanwhile in Eastern Europe the intervention of August 1968 in Czechoslovakia revealed that orthodoxy could still rely on Soviet support should it be threatened.

On the other hand the Prague Spring itself, and the movement of de-Stalinisation that had affected a number of Western European communist parties, had brought the power monopoly more sharply into question than at the earlier turning-point of 1956. Alternatives were now on offer in a diversified communist movement. Whilst the critique of Soviet norms on the part of the Western European parties could only have an oblique effect, the proposals for economic and political change that the Prague Spring had generated cut directly at the roots of the power monopoly in one of the countries where it was in operation – and one, moreover, where its ultimately fatal flaws were particularly clearly revealed.

From Prague Spring to Soviet perestroika

The period from 1968 in Western European communism saw a continuation and a strengthening of the PCI's criticisms of Soviet political behaviour, leading to an explicit condemnation in 1981; the legalisation of the Spanish, Portuguese and Greek communist parties after the return of their countries to the democratic fold; a confirmation of the reformist tendencies associated with Eurocommunism; a move in that direction by the French party, followed after 1977 by an abrupt return to orthodoxy; and an important shift in the CPSU's relations with the various components of the Western European left.

The first and the last of these had a significant effect on the weakening of the communist power monopoly in the Soviet Union, which in turn was to feed back on to the regimes of Eastern Europe. By 1986 Soviet sources themselves were saying that the Italian party had been correct in its criticisms of Soviet communism. It was a confession that necessarily validated the ideas of the Prague Spring.

The fall of Allende in Chile in 1973 led the PCI's leader, Enrico Berlinguer, to develop further the idea of building up a firm bloc of forces on the left of society. It led him also to propose an 'historic compromise' in which the Communist Party, although excluded from power, would support those policies of the ruling Christian Democrats that it could accept as progressive. This policy, in the short run, brought electoral success. With 34.4 per cent of the vote in the national election of 1976 the PCI achieved the highest electoral score of its existence. By then its internal life showed few remnants of the Stalinist style, and accommodated a wide range of views, which, by that date, were being freely defended in *L'Unita* and the party press as a whole by their proponents. On the right, Giorgio Amendola and, after his death, Giorgio Napolitano espoused views that were close to social democracy. On the left, Pietro Ingrao was to play a crucial role in opening the party to the new radical forces of the 1970s. There was also a vocal bloc which kept alive the orthodox tradition. The leadership, steering from somewhere near the party centre, was not in a position to silence any of these *correnti*, but until 1983 it was able to dominate the decision-making process through its control of the party's bureaucracy.

It was Ingrao who was largely responsible for changing this particular prerogative of the leadership by sponsoring the proposal, adopted at the party's 1983 congress, to increase inner-party democracy by removing the policy-making function from executive – and hence co-opted – party organs and giving it to the Central Committee, which is an elected body. Whilst it was not until its seventeenth congress in 1986 that the PCI formally abandoned the principle of democratic centralism, that symbol had in any case by that time been voided of its Stalinist content.

Meanwhile the PCI maintained its criticisms of the Soviet Union's policies in Eastern Europe and of its civil rights record in general. It condemned likewise the Soviet invasion of Afghanistan. But the high point of tension between the CPSU and the PCI came at the end of 1981, when in Poland Wojciech Jaruzelski, under clear Soviet pressure to clamp down on Solidarity's challenge to the leading role of the communist party, declared a state of war and interned Solidarity's leadership. It was at this point that the PCI, as noted, issued the statement in which it said that the 'propulsive force of the October revolution' had 'spent itself'. There appeared to be little now that linked the two parties except a shared history. The arrival in power of Gorbachev, however, was to usher in a new phase in the relations between the two parties. This we must leave to be treated below.

'Eurocommunism and the State'

The end of authoritarian rule in Spain, Portugal and Greece, and the consequent legalisation of the communist parties of those countries, was to add strength to both the reformist and the orthodox strands of Western European communism. Of the three, only in the Spanish case did emergence from clandestinity result in the clear assertion of a Eurocommunist stance. The success of the king in Spain in bringing the post-Franco forces together in the Moncloa Pact, together with the evolution of Santiago Carrillo's views while he was in exile, account to a great extent for the integrationist strategy that the

Spanish party adopted. It was a strategy that had a great initial success, and for a time it seemed that the communists would dominate the left in the transition and beyond. There was every reason for Carrillo to assimilate his party's position to that of the Italian party. Not only did he set out to do this, but he was able to take advantage of the flirtation of the French Communist Party (PCF) with reformist ideas to convene the meeting of the leaders of the Italian, French and Spanish parties in Madrid in March 1977, recorded above. He then, as noted, gave that initiative the stamp of 'Eurocommunism' in the title of a book which he published in the following year.

In that work Carrillo stated his case for regarding the ideas of Leninism as now superseded; they were 'not applicable today because they have been overtaken in the circumstances of the developed capitalist countries of Western Europe'.[5] The communist party

continues to be the vanguard party, in as much as it truly embodies a creative Marxist attitude. But it no longer considers itself the *only* representative of the working class, of the working people and the forces of culture . . . It has no hesitation in accepting, when circumstances warrant, that others may be more accurate than it in analysing a particular situation.[6]

The task of a communist party was now to take advantage of the advances that socialism had made, abandoning claims that its action was based on 'scientific' principles and embracing pluralism. Pluralism for Carrillo meant entering the competitive arena as part of a 'confederation of political parties and other forces' whose aim would be to press back the positions of capitalism in the state. The debt to Gramsci, and the affinity between the views of Carrillo and of the PCI, are evident.

In France, a number of factors – the death of Maurice Thorez, the PCF's decision to support the candidature of Mitterrand in the presidential election of 1965, and the disorientation within the PCF caused by its inability to respond swiftly and coherently to the events of May 1968 in Paris – led to a modification of the party's traditionally orthodox line from the late 1960s until 1977. This showed itself in the party's condemnation of the Warsaw Pact's intervention in Czechoslovakia in 1968, but it was most evident in an opening to society and an end to the secrecy that had enshrouded the party's life hitherto. It was a signal moment when two non-communist journalists were allowed to attend meetings and to interview party functionaries and activists, publishing their conclusions in book form. Marchais' attendance at the Madrid 'Eurocommunist' summit in 1977 therefore followed logically from the PCF's policies of the preceding decade.

Althusser's criticism of the PCF's organisational norms

Ironically it was just at this time that it became clear that the communists' alliance with the Socialists in the Common Programme was enabling the latter to overtake the PCF as the major party on the French left. Late in 1977, with a national legislative election impending in the spring of 1978, the party leadership took the decision to withdraw from the alliance with the Socialists. The extent of discussion and debate in the party permitted by the leadership on this immensely important strategic decision was minimal, the outcry massive. Louis Althusser, one of the party's leading intellectuals, thereupon penned a series of four articles under the title of 'What Cannot Continue in the French Communist Party', which constituted a broadside against the traditional practices of the PCF.[7] The criticisms that Althusser made are of central importance for an understanding of how the power monopoly forged in the Stalinist Soviet Union was continuing to affect the political life of the more orthodox communist parties of Western Europe.

In his critique Althusser drew attention to the way in which the leadership was able to closet itself off from the party by the control that it exercised over the party's organisational life. This included the 'list' system of elections, through which the party could regulate the composition both of the party's congresses and of the leadership group itself, and the various means of closing off opposing opinions in the party's press and at congresses and conferences. Discussion always preceded a congress, so that the congress itself became simply a platform at which the leadership could announce its policies. Any attempt to set up horizontal relationships that would cut across the extreme verticality of the party's organisation 'is still today termed "fractional" '.

Another of Althusser's criticisms that reflects very precisely the practice of the ruling communist parties was the prominent role in party life played by paid officials: '"Popular sovereignty" stops short as soon as you reach the secretariats of the federations directed by paid officials'. That the 'leading role of the party' in carrying through a programme of social and economic development should involve a reliance on a structure of politically reliable 'cadres' made a good deal of sense in the Soviet Union or China at a certain stage of their history, but rather less in the context of Western European liberal democracy. In general, Althusser claimed, the party's functioning recalled that of an army:

Everything that has been said would be incomplete without the addition of the fundamental principle of absolute verticality, which recalls the column of subordination of a military hierarchy . . . In fact there is an astonishing fact which anyone can note for himself: the party is obviously not a state, strictly speaking, but everything happens as if, in its structure and hierarchical functioning, it were closely modelled at one and the same time on the apparatus of the bourgeois state and on [its] military apparatus.[8]

But most important for Althusser was the 'cementing' characteristic of the PCF's procedures. Through these various means of control the leadership was able to project an ideology of unity and solidarity. 'The party is effectively reduced to this caricature: to "cement", at any price, its unity around a leadership which has not only the power to command men but also the power to command the truth, in relation to a "line" which it has fixed all on it own'. To speak against the leadership was therefore to speak against the party and, in view of the 'scientific' value that the party placed on its policies, against history. There was no salvation outside the party and outside the party's line; and it was for the leadership to determine that line. What Althusser was attacking was quite simply democratic centralism as the Stalinist CPSU had defined that concept.

These views of Althusser are one of the most comprehensive critiques of communist patterns of organisation to have been made from within a communist party. Obviously the sense in which the leadership of a non-ruling party can be said to be exercising a monopoly of power must be extremely limited. Yet in the criticisms that Althusser made there was a very strong echo of practices in the Soviet Union which clearly were monopolistic.

By promoting the idea of the party as a self-contained and besieged fortress (an idea that was widely supported by the membership when the CPF was at the height of its strength) the leadership could mark off a territory in which the free flow of ideas could be controlled, whilst the prominent role of paid officials, coupled with the list system of elections and other mechanisms that enabled the leadership to closet itself off from the body of the party, reflected the use of the apparatus structure to secure the monopoly of power that ruling communist parties held.

The French party leadership survived the storm that followed its abrupt rejection of the Common Programme, just as it had withstood many previous assaults on its orthodox positions. But by the late 1970s, in the wake of the signing of the Helsinki Accords, the crisis that confronted communism throughout Europe could be clearly discerned. It has been the burden of this chapter to point out how it was first acutely felt in Western Europe, as it was part of the task of the last chapter to show how important was the Prague Spring as a harbinger of the crisis. All the threads of the impending crisis were to come together when a general secretary of the party which had been responsible for the formation of the communist power monopoly gave the signal for its abolition.

The vindication of the Italian Communist Party and the Prague Spring

The arrival in power in the USSR of Mikhail Gorbachev turned more than one set of assumptions on their heads. From some of Gorbachev's first statements as General Secretary of the CPSU it was clear that it could only be a matter of time before the Soviet verdict on the ideas of the Prague Spring, and therefore on the position of the Italian party which had so strongly supported those ideas, would be revised. The vindication of the PCI's position was in fact to precede that of the Czechoslovak reformers, and it came about in a way that illustrates well one particular weakness of the power monopoly.

It will be recalled that until the policy of glasnost began to do its work in the Soviet Union, the party's monopolistic control of the written and spoken word could screen from Soviet society and from the outside world the tensions to which the system was at any time being subjected, but it could not blot out the expert opinion that was required for the economy to turn and for government and the party to do their work.

The manner in which the Soviet leadership chose to acknowledge the essential correctness of the PCI's analysis over the years reflected this link between the holders of political power and such schools of thought. Readers of the CPSU's theoretical journal *Kommunist* in January 1986 were offered as the lead article a substantial contribution by Vladimir Naumov, an academician, entitled 'The PCI before its Congress'.[9] According to Naumov, the PCI had been 'inspired by innovating ideas that have drawn the attention of communists the world over and have stimulated discussion and theoretical development'. Such innovations included the defence of the idea of different roads to socialism in 1956, and the PCI's later insistence that to campaign against the nuclear danger was not a matter of being 'for' or 'against' the Soviet Union. After examining the PCI's positions on a number of issues, Naumov concluded that, whilst 'differences of opinion continue to exist' between the two parties,

today, the CPSU takes pains to examine every fact and every idea as expressed in a concrete situation, without claiming any monopoly of the truth . . . Today, the fraternal dialogue between the CPSU and the PCI is particularly necessary, just as is, indeed, dialogue between communist parties in general.

Published in a journal with *Kommunist*'s particular standing, this acceptance of the PCI's criticisms could only be regarded as official. Interestingly, however, the argumentation of the rest of the article made it clear that the author had a less obvious aim. He was using this statement concerning an external party to strike a blow in the struggles that were being carried on between reformers and supporters of orthodoxy within the Soviet Union itself. This, of course, did not diminish the significance of the acknowledgement. Far from it; it was clear evidence of the symbolic status and rallying power that the positions of the Italian party, and of the Prague reformers of 1968, had acquired. As such, it was an important ingredient in the mix of ideas and events that were shortly to undermine finally the communist power monopoly. It is to the crucial developments in the monopoly's homeland that we must now turn.

Notes
1 The common features of the two situations are treated by Annie Kriegel in *Les grands procès dans les systèmes communistes* (Paris: Research Project – Crises in Soviet-Type Systems, 1972), pp. 30–1.
2 Joan Barth Urban, *Moscow and the Italian Communist Party* (London: I. B. Tauris, 1986), in particular Chapter 3.
3 Santiago Carrillo, *Eurocommunism and the State* (London: Lawrence and Wishart, 1977), p. 172.
4 Neil McInnes, *The Communist Parties of Western Europe* (London: RIIA and Oxford University Press, 1975), pp. 99–105.
5 Carrillo, *Eurocommunism and the State*, p. 9 *et seq. ibid.*
6 *Ibid.*, pp. 99–100.

7   Louis Althusser, 'Ce qui ne peut plus durer dans le parti communiste', *Le Monde*, 25–28 April 1978.
8   *Ibid.*, 26 April 1978.
9   Vladimir Naumov, 'IKP pered s"ezdom', *Kommunist*, 1 (1989), pp. 102–12.

Further reading

Louis Althuser, *Ce qui ne peut plus durer dans le parti communiste français* (Paris: Maspéro, 1978).
Donald L. M. Blackmer, *Unity in Diversity: Italian Communism and the Communist World* (Cambridge, MA: MIT Press, 1968).
Donald L. M. Blackmer and Sidney Tarrow (eds), *Communism in Italy and France* (Princeton: Princeton University Press, 1975).
Richard Kindersley (ed.), *In Search of Eurocommunism* (London: Macmillan, 1981).
P. Lange and M. Vanicelli (eds), *The Communist Parties of Italy, France and Spain* (London: George Allen and Unwin, 1981).
Howard Machin, *National Communism in Western Europe: A Third Way for Socialism?* (London: Methuen, 1983).
Ronald Tiersky, *Ordinary Stalinism* (London: George Allen and Unwin, 1985).
Michael Waller and Meindert Fennema (eds), *Communist Parties in Western Europe: Decline or Adaptation?* (Oxford: Blackwell, 1988).

Part III

The crisis of the communist power monopoly

8

Reform of the Soviet system

Foreshadowed by developments in the Western European communist parties, by frustrated movements for reform in Eastern Europe, and by a shift in the Soviet Union's relations with the outside world, the signal for the dismantling of the communist power monopoly was finally given by the leader of the CPSU itself shortly after that leader – Mikhail Gorbachev – became General Secretary of the CPSU in March 1985.

Since Stalin died in March 1953, the Soviet Union had seen two surges of reform, separated by a twenty-year-long period of retrenchment. From 1955 Nikita Khrushchev, having asserted his power against his rivals among the other lieutenants of the deceased dictator, embarked on a series of wide-ranging changes. Those who deposed him dubbed his attempts at reform 'hare-brained schemes', only to have their own stewardship labelled 'the period of stagnation' by the incoming reformist leadership around Mikhail Gorbachev from 1985. The Soviet Union, having raised Lenin to a height of veneration above the mêlée, was never able to give credit to past leaders. Indeed, the power monopoly forbade it; monopolising present power has meant rejecting past power-holders, whose contribution necessarily smacked of opposition. It was as 'the anti-party group' that Khrushchev's own opponents lived out their retirement from active politics.

The Khrushchev reforms

Khrushchev had asserted his authority as leader of the CSPU by 1955, and in the period between that date and 1964, when he was removed from power, he introduced a bewildering series of reform measures. Khrushchev's reforms were bold, but they were largely ill-considered. Given the total lack of debate during the Stalin period it is indeed difficult to see how they could have been properly devised, comprehendingly received or sensitively implemented. Nor was it ever Khrushchev's aim, as it eventually became Gorbachev's, to bring the communist party face to face with its own responsibility for the failings of the Soviet economic and political system. Rather it was to revive the party after its long Stalinist atrophy, and those of his reforms that affected the organisation of the party had that aim in view. They could hardly have been expected to undermine the communist power monopoly, although they necessarily revealed where the problems created by the monopoly lay.

The reforms covered a vast range of issues. Some of them would certainly have modified the power monopoly at a number of crucial points. Certain others which had a different intention none the less relied upon the power monopoly for their conception and implementation. A final category served, in fact, to strengthen and consolidate the power monopoly.

The most lasting and historically significant of the reforms in the first category were the dismantling of the terror machine and the easing of the censorship. The gulag was largely emptied and its camps were transferred to the appropriate economic ministries, whilst the publication of Solzhenitsyn's *One Day in the Life of Ivan Denisovich*, a graphic tale of prison camp life, became a symbol of the 'thaw' that was taking place. Although the 'thaw' was balanced by a revival of the propaganda system, the atmosphere in which public life went on was transformed. The thaw did not go so far as to open the channels for public opinion to form, but it did give specialist opinion considerable rein. This was to bear fruit later, and was indeed one of the essential factors preparing the way for the Gorbachev reforms.

The internal thaw was matched by a major shift in foreign policy towards 'peaceful coexistence', and Khrushchev's invocation of this principle at the CPSU's twentieth congress in 1956 was followed by his talks with Eisenhower at Camp David in 1957. Whilst this had no immediate impact on the permeability of the iron curtain and had only a limited effect on the autarky of the Soviet economy, it did mark an important step in the diminishing of the Soviet Union's isolation. As with so many of Khrushchev's policies, it suggested a future without being able to lay a firm track to it.

In the economic sphere, Khrushchev attempted in 1957 to solve the bureaucratic operation and overcentralisation of the planning system by breaking up most of the central ministries and devolving industrial organisation to regional 'economic councils' (*sovnarkhozy*). Opposition to this massive reorganisation was strong, and the reform was undone as soon as its author had been removed from power in 1964. It was, however, during the Khrushchev years that the Kharkov economist Evsei Liberman made the proposals that became, as noted, an important milestone in the economic reform debate in the Soviet Union and Eastern Europe as a whole. Liberman's ideas were not taken up by Khrushchev, but on the other hand some of them were built into the 'Kosygin' reform proposals enacted in 1965. This attempt to modify the power monopoly in the economic sphere must have been prepared during the Khrushchev years, and to that extent represented a rival solution to the problems of central planning to Khrushchev's own. The communist power monopoly was able to see both of them off.

But the Khrushchev reforms that most clearly targeted the party's organisation, and therefore would have gone to the heart of the power monopoly, were his attempt to limit the number of years that a party official could remain in office, and his splitting of the party's territorial apparatus. For the first of these, Rule 25 of the new party statutes adopted at the CPSU's twenty-second congress in 1961 specified fixed terms of office to party committee members and officials. As for the second, in 1962 Khrushchev reorganised the secretariats of the party's apparatus at regional and local level, dividing them into industrial and agricultural sections. Taken together, these reforms undermined Khrushchev's own power base, which lay in the party, and it was a Central Committee composed to the tune of some 30 per cent of the very regional party secretaries whose position Khrushchev had set out to modify that confirmed the Politburo's vote to remove the bold reformer from power. He had sawn off the branch on which he sat.

The extensive legislation of the Khrushchev period included measures to overhaul the educational system and the trade unions. Such reforms in themselves did not affect the power monopoly one way or the other. The actual manner of their introduction, however, did illustrate a feature of it that was to be developed further in the Brezhnev years. The people at large were invited to contribute their ideas on these matters in the press and at meetings, and the party was able to record impressive figures of such participation. But at the same time the mechanisms were in place for filtering the letters and organising the meetings. In fact the party was setting up a bland mechanism that screened the power monopoly and gave a false impression of meaningful participation. Such involvement of the masses was little more than a counterpart of the innumerable incantatory resolutions and enactments of the party which generated a mirage of change and advance towards the socialist goals.

Similarly, the abrupt policy turn to develop the chemical industry with a view to the production of chemical fertilisers, and the massive programmes to plant maize and to open up 'virgin lands', did not in themselves affect the structure of power, and in fact serve as admirable illustrations of it, especially when taken together with the decentralisation of the industrial ministries. They demonstrated the vast extent of the party's power. It could plan over the whole territory of the Union, could switch policies overnight, and could mobilise labour resources (much of it voluntary, through the party-sponsored mass organisations) for gigantic projects.

Finally, however, much of what Khrushchev did actually strengthened the communist power monopoly, and it could be argued that all his reforms were directed expressly to that end. In particular he revived the party after its atrophy during the Stalinist period. With the distinction between the structures of party and state diminished by Stalin's arbitrary power, the communist party had operated as the major transmission belt between the masses and the regime. At the regional level its role was indeed crucial, but at the highest level it had come to lack substance. No congress was held between 1939 and 1952; and it is revealing that after Stalin's death, the head of the party's secretariat and Stalin's apparent heir, Georgi Malenkov, moved to the post of prime minister on the assumption that power lay in the ministerial structure rather than in the party. Taking over the party's leading post Khrushchev was able to set Malenkov aside and to build up his party base. Congresses were regularly held, the Central Committee's role was strengthened and it began to publish a record of its proceedings. It was a strengthened party that Khrushchev's own heirs inherited, and they intended to use it without the limitations that the reformer's other policies clearly aimed to impose.

Somewhat similarly, in reviving the Council for Economic Mutual Assistance (the Comecon), which had been formed to counter the

Marshall Plan in 1949 but had done little since, Khrushchev prolonged, rather than reduced, the autarky associated with the power monopoly. The CMEA gave the Soviet economy a lifeline, based on an internal division of labour within that organisation, which no doubt diluted the autarky of the Soviet economy itself, but ultimately did not abolish it. Here, too, there was work for Gorbachev to do.

From Khrushchev to Gorbachev

Twenty-one years separate Khrushchev's departure from highest office and Gorbachev's assumption of it. They were determinant years, for all the political 'stagnation' that they featured. First of all, they were years of debate – not public debate, which was ruled out, but debate within the institutions of administration and research. Furthermore the debate was informed by experience and experimentation in other countries ruled by communist parties – in China, Yugoslavia and Hungary; indeed positions could be defended within the Soviet Union by proxy, as noted, through comment on these other experiences. To this extent Gorbachev had a 'run up' that was denied to Khrushchev.

Secondly, Soviet society, transformed during the Stalin years, was continuing to mature. In the words of Moshe Lewin, whose book *The Gorbachev Phenomenon* makes clear the central importance of modernisation as a factor in the changes that have been affecting the Soviet Union:

Today well-educated urban citizens, not backward peasants, are the largest demographic group . . . And in ways sometimes overt, sometimes covert, contemporary urban society has become a powerful 'system maker', pressuring both political institutions and the economic model to adapt.[1]

At the governmental and administrative level social change was reflected in the functional differentiation adverted to in the treatment of the monopoly's weaknesses offered above. At the everyday level the songs of Bulat Okudzhava reflected the sophistication of life in an urbanised society whilst the novels of Yuri Trifonov revealed preoccupations and concerns familiar to the citizens of any modern industrialised society. Figure 5 and Table 8 illustrate aspects of social change in Soviet society.

The years between Khrushchev's occupancy of the leadership role and that of Gorbachev were a major turning-point for a third reason. Khrushchev's reforms represented the last attempt to extend and

Table 8   *Increase in schooling in the USSR*

	1914	1928	1940	1959	1975
Primary and secondary schools (millions of pupils)	9.9	12	37.2	36.3	49
of whom students in classes 8–10	0.152	0.170	2.5	2.8	16.3
% of children in these age groups enrolled in school	24.7	31.9	80		
High-school students (millions)	0.127	0.169	0.811	2.15	4.7
No. of students per 1000 inhabitants	8	12	40	102	187

renew the party's monopoly. They were presented as a collective campaign in which all the people were involved and which emphasised the party's right to speak for the collective good of society. This was a politics of idealism. It was followed by a messy pragmatism under Brezhnev, connected to a great extent with an increase in the Soviet Union's world trade and a weakening towards Western consumerism. The contradiction between that and the oppressive Asiatic state became clearer as the Brezhnev period wore on, and it was sharpened by crippling increases in military expenditure incurred with the aim of achieving nuclear parity with the United States. Chiliasm was dead; it remained to grasp the nettle of pragmatism by putting in hand meaningful institutional change.

On the other hand, if Soviet society was ready for change by the time of Brezhnev's death in 1982, it must be asked where were the springs from which change would draw and on what cultural base would it build. The answers to these questions can only indicate the difference between the position of the Soviet Union and, for example, that of the countries of East-Central Europe.

As is frequently pointed out Russia, and then the Soviet Union, despite the aspirations and achievements of the revolution, have never known the rule of law, nor true governmental accountability. In fact, in a convoluted way, the revolution itself, even before the rigours of the Stalinist period developed, operated against the establishment of a machinery of accountability. This arose not only from the pressures of the Civil War, but also from a Bolshevik impatience with constitution-making and the trappings of bourgeois democracy drawn from their reading of Marx. The 'revolutionary consciousness

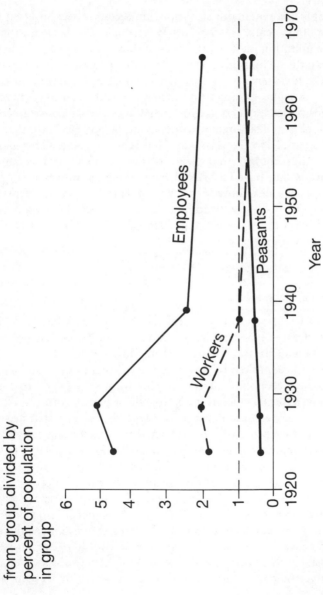

Percent of all students from group divided by percent of population in group

Figure 5 *Relative access to higher education of various social groups 1924–1964*

of right' and class power in the hands of the proletariat provided the only necessary conceptual framework for the setting up of a state which in any case was seen, in the Marxist scheme of things, as temporary.

Probably inherent in this situation, but certainly becoming explicit in the Stalinist years, was an anti-Westernism which meant that in any case imitation of Western ways of doing things was anathema. Nor was it the revolution or Stalin alone that produced this suspicion of the West; it stems from an intellectual current running through Russian thought throughout the nineteenth century. Even a Westernising leader such as Gorbachev was clearly constrained by an awareness of a strong constituency in the Soviet Union that has been antipathetic to Western ways and Western values. This means, among other things, that even if the political and economic mechanisms that have embodied the communist power monopoly have now been dismantled, the way of thinking that underpinned them may not so easily disappear. It may, indeed, be valued as an essential part of the new Russia's identity – that part of it that links the present with the past.

The Gorbachev reforms

When Gorbachev became General Secretary of the CPSU in March 1985 he clearly represented that faction in the party that favoured reform. Leonid Brezhnev had died in March 1982, the end of his period in office marked by a succession of corruption scandals and catastrophic economic decline. He was succeeded by Yuri Andropov, a former chief of the KGB, whose poor health was clearly not likely to allow him to proceed far with the reforms that he set in motion, and even these were restricted to tightening up discipline and a drive against corruption. When he died in March 1983 he was to be succeeded by Konstantin Chernenko, himself also sick, 72 years of age, and a professed opponent of reform.

Gorbachev's accession to the post of general secretary at the unusually young age of 53 was obviously the signal for a programme of reform to be launched. And indeed during the ensuing eight years Gorbachev was to press on with a programme of change against each new obstacle that arose on his path, until the process of change finally overtook him, moving into circumstances that escaped his control and promoting other leaders fashioned by history to assume new tasks. One task, however, he had by then accomplished: he had presided over the demise of the communist power monopoly.

They were eight crowded years. During the first of them, from March 1985 until the Chernobyl disaster in April 1986, Gorbachev's stated policy was one of 'acceleration', and resembled Andropov's attempt to make the existing machinery work more effectively. He, too, undertook a drive against corruption, and added to it one against alcoholism. By the twenty-seventh party congress in March 1986, however, it was becoming clear to him that deeper reforms were required. In the party's response to the Chernobyl disaster in April of that year could be read the first signs that key elements of the structure of power were going to be challenged, and that the impulse was going to come from within the power structure itself.

One of the questions that must be asked is how much of what then happened did Gorbachev actually intend? It is clear that events in the end moved beyond his expectations, and the fact that a Soviet leadership was prepared to take the risk of inviting even the possibility of such change is eloquent evidence of the impasse into which the Soviet Union, particularly the Soviet economy, had arrived. But it is equally clear that Gorbachev was prepared – if not initially, then certainly by 1987 – to strike at the heart of the political and economic problem, which was nothing other than the power monopoly. The question then was where to hold the line, and here events were ultimately to become the master. But if Gorbachev's early statements about glasnost and perestroika are set against the kind of change that Jaruzelski in Poland and the reformist wing of the Hungarian ruling party were attempting to induce, it seems clear that the objective in all these cases was a degree of reform that would preserve a dominant position for the party in society at the cost of abandoning a monopoly of power.

Communism turned out to be unreformable. The processes foreshadowed in the Prague Spring, with their distant echo in Eurocommunist ideas, were given their fateful final impulse by Gorbachev. The pace at which they developed varied, but the dramatic collapse of the Eastern European regimes makes 1989 the historical turning-point. Communist power had already fallen in Slovenia before then, whilst it was not until 1990 that the decisive moment came in the Soviet Union. But it was a general secretary of the party of Lenin who gave the signal that set the process finally in motion, and the early years of Gorbachev's tenure of power therefore have a profound historical significance.

Starting in 1986, the fall of the power monopoly in the Soviet Union cannot be said to have been consummated until the failed putsch of August 1991, and even thereafter it was to prove extraordinarily difficult to rid the economy of certain of its monopolistic features. Since this study has been based on a four-part analysis of the communist power monopoly, its presentation of the fall of the CPSU's monopoly will take each of those elements in turn and trace the manner and rhythm in which each came to be assaulted in the reforms set in train by Gorbachev. In this chapter events up to mid-1988 – the date of the major turning-point constituted by the nineteenth conference of the CPSU – will be presented.

The move away from autarky
Too often ignored in commentary on communism and on the Soviet Union, the autarky characteristic of the communist power monopoly revealed its full significance as the monopoly came under attack. It was the closed frontier that protected the Soviet economy from the effects of changes in world prices, prevented a brain drain during and after the years of rapid economic and social development, and enabled the power monopoly to defend itself by excluding corrosive influences from abroad. To use an image invoked above, it constituted a dam, with carefully controlled sluices, that allowed Soviet life *as a whole* to be lived at a different level – economically, culturally, politically – from outside. The world provides very many examples of inequalities and differences between nations, but in most cases these are marked, precisely, by the emigration of talented and trained personnel, dual cultures, and vulnerability to fluctuations of prices on the world market. The Soviet Union did not fall into that pattern. Through the power monopoly the CPSU attempted, with quite considerable success, to isolate society and the economy from the outside world.

If a single determinant cause is to be sought for the decision of a Soviet leadership to challenge the very workings of the system, it must be the need to end the Soviet Union's isolation from the world economy. It was not surprising, therefore, that the autarky of the Stalin years was one of the first points at which the power monopoly was breached. It will be recalled that Khrushchev's policy of peaceful coexistence was an early move in this direction. The various international agreements that the Soviet Union entered into thereafter, concerning arms control but many other things besides, and the international organisations and conferences to which the Soviet Union was anxious to be party are so many further moves, although in themselves they did little to modify the monopoly at the heart of the Soviet system. We saw, however, that one such convention – the Conference of Security and Cooperation in Europe, which resulted in the Helsinki Accords of 1975 – did play an indirect role in the weakening of the communist party's monopoly of power in Eastern Europe; we saw also that after Helsinki the Soviet authorities themselves were more open to pressure from the West on human rights questions.

These developments, whilst they served to reveal the true nature of the power monopoly, were doing little to remove it. Their significance was two-fold. First they made it clear that the Soviet Union needed to end its isolation; but, secondly, they revealed the conflict between that desired end and the continuation of the power monopoly. They served therefore – continuing the metaphor – to increase the pressure on the dam, whilst raising questions about the dam's value in the first place.

The Gorbachev leadership broke substantial holes in the dam, in the end effectively demolishing it. First, a determined effort was made to change the Soviet Union's image, since on such a change depended the chances of being accepted as a respected partner in the concert of nations. The damage that coercion and isolation had wrought in the past would now be repaired through diplomacy, through an increased integration into the world market and through a controlled accommodation to Western political behaviour. The development of a low-level diplomacy among the forces of the left in Western Europe, and the substitution of contacts with social-democratic parties and the peace movement for unconditional Soviet support for communist parties were noted above. They pre-dated the arrival of Gorbachev in power, as did the awareness among Eastern European leaderships that coercion was giving way to diplomacy.

With the Gorbachev team in power this attempt to alter the Soviet Union's image developed apace, in both large and small ways. For the former, negotiations preparing the way for a withdrawal from military involvement in Afghanistan were set in motion. Restrictions on emigration from the Soviet Union were considerably reduced, the pressure on dissidents at first eased, and then evaporated, as glasnost began to change the very idea of what constituted dissent. At a lesser level Soviet spokesmen appearing on Western television sets began to speak as colleagues and equals of their Western interviewers and abandoned the defensive poses of yesteryear. And whilst Raisa Gorbacheva's Western style offended many sensibilities in the Soviet Union, it won friends abroad.

Secondly, through the summits with US presidents (Geneva in 1985; Reykjavik in 1986; Moscow in 1988; Malta in 1989), through ever increasing participation in international conferences and organisations, through the speeding up of arms reduction negotiations, through the signing in December 1987 of the agreement on Intermediate Nuclear Forces in Europe, and through the intense diplomatic activity of Gorbachev himself and of his Foreign Minister Shevardnadze, the Soviet Union sought to build itself ever more firmly into the international community. In a speech to the United Nations of 7 December 1988, Gorbachev said that the Soviet Union wanted to join the world; and the West responded, the more willingly as the weakening, and then the disintegration, of the Union placed a premium on diplomatic bonds, whilst reducing the likelihood of its posing any substantial military or economic threat. By the time of the Malta summit in 1989 President Bush was inviting the USSR to become observers at the GATT, and approaches were being made for membership of the World Bank and the IMF.

A third element in the Soviet Union's move to end its isolation was to have the most dramatic effects of all. At some point in the rethinking of this strategy the Soviet leadership must have confronted the central question of relations with Eastern Europe. A policy of opening to the world, and of adjusting the Soviet image to this policy, was incompatible with the preservation of coercive domination over the Eastern European countries, or of military support for the communist parties of that region should they come under pressure from restive social forces. And yet a public and across-the-board renunciation of the Soviet guarantee for communist power in the Eastern European countries was unthinkable, in view of the immediate impact it would have at a time when the Soviet Union had problems enough to deal with.

The world was given notice that the Brezhnev doctrine had been abandoned in a manner that was entirely consistent with the Soviet Union's new chosen image. It was the urbane spokesman of the Soviet government, Genadii Gerasimov, who announced, in a wayward (and therefore presumably unpremeditated) reference to the American singer, the 'Sinatra doctrine': 'I had it my way'.[2] On his visits to Eastern European countries from 1987, Gorbachev did not go out of his way to provoke change, but he did make it clear that each country was now master of its own fate.

Reading from the way events fell out, the strategy adopted was, through discreet discussion and pressure, to encourage the Eastern European regimes to follow the Soviet lead of perestroika, whilst making no moves that would hasten the process of change, and doing all possible to avoid a generalised conflagration across the region.

Fourthly, lest these developments seem somewhat remote from the end of autarky in a strict sense, the steps must be recorded that were designed to bring to an end the very concrete monopoly that the Ministry of Foreign Trade held over the movement of goods in and out of the country. This control had been crucial in protecting the Soviet planned economy from an invasion of uncertainties generated by the world market; it was a sluice in the dam that held the economic power monopoly in place. The steps taken to remove it illustrate well the problems that the process of change in the former Soviet Union was to encounter.

As early as August 1986 a Foreign Economic Commission was created to relieve the Ministry of Foreign Trade of its monopoly. But before long it became clear that the liberation of foreign trade was going to be long in coming. In January 1988 the two bodies were fused into a Ministry of Foreign Economic Relations which continued to regulate trade heavily. From 4 January 1989 all registered firms, both public and private, were given the right to export and import; but this simply reorganised the mechanisms of regulation, since registration then became the bar that firms had to overcome. As with so much in the dismantling of the economic element of the power monopoly, the need for deregulation was felt early on, but achieving it did not prove easy.

The move away from autarky had one particularly massive repercussion. Through a chain of cause and effect which is not too difficult to trace, the Soviet Union's opening to the world weakened the internal boundaries between the various republics of the Union. This, however, we must leave to be treated below, when the discussion addresses the political changes that a reform of the party's leading role made inevitable.

In sum, the move away from autarky can be viewed in broad or narrow terms. In the narrowest sense, the monopoly control of foreign trade in the hands of a government department was lifted, but replaced by tight regulation. In the broader sense, the Soviet Union's opening to the world meant loss of control over Eastern Europe as the price of integration into the international forums of Europe and the world. But that increasing permeability of the boundary separating the Soviet Union from the world weakened internal boundaries. This was to lead ultimately to the demise of the Soviet Union itself.

From plan to market
It will be recalled that of the problems that central command planning was generating and that the reformers wished to solve, some stemmed from the pricing system and an absence of equilibrium between supply and demand, some from the connected fact that there was a lack of hard constraints forcing actors in the economy to use resources efficiently, others from lack of choice in acquiring materials and in marketing goods, whilst others again were simply the behavioural responses to the bottlenecks and shortages inherent in the planning system. The failings of the system also showed up in more general terms in poorly produced goods, sloppy or non-existent services and a lack of motivations or, to put it in the very simplest terms, of care.

The measures adopted by the Gorbachev leadership to undo the monopoly in the economy can be viewed under three broad headings. First, steps were taken early on to allow room for initiative at the periphery of the economy, which involved adjustments to the structure of ownership. Secondly, the running debate about how to tackle the core problems of prices and material supplies produced a number of initiatives, which had the effect of destroying monopoly control of the economy but replaced it with what, by the time of the attempted putsch of August 1991 could only be termed confusion. Finally, there were high-sounding but not very effectual moves to generate initiative in the industrial workplace through provisions for self-management.

New forms of ownership to encourage initiative
It was noted above that ownership has counted less than control in the way in which the communist power monopoly operated, and

that it was the extent of control that gave the monopoly its character. The Soviet state has never, in fact, held a monopoly of ownership. State ownership was limited by a small private sector (chiefly comprising the individual plots of collective-farm peasants) but also by a co-operative sector in agriculture. This formal distinction, however, did not prevent the centralised party-state from exercising a determinant control over the agricultural sector. On the other hand, the provision in Soviet jurisprudence for a category of collective use of the means of production made it easier to provide a legal framework for new laws passed with a view to encouraging initiative in the economy.

In November 1986 a Law on Individual Labour Activity was passed, the main effect of which was to legalise small-scale entrepreneurial work which had until then been seen as moonlighting, and had exposed those engaging in it to prosecution. This only enabled individuals and their families to earn an honest rouble (subject to taxation) outside their normal working hours, running a café or effecting electrical repairs and so on. But it was followed by a Law on Co-operatives (26 May 1988) which had a much stronger social impact. This effectively allowed for the establishment of enterprises outside the state sector, and free from the planning mechanism.

The range of application of this major innovation was reduced by an administrative order later in the year, which clawed back publishing, the manufacture and sale of pharmaceutical products, and film and video production from the order's provisions; but the take-up was substantial, and it soon revealed the incompatibility between the existing planning system and private enterprise. The co-operatives relied on state procurement agencies for materials, since there were no other sources. This brought them up against the standard Soviet problems of supply – red tape and shortages – but it also meant that the price was low, and potential profits accordingly high. The less scrupulous co-operators simply bought goods at state prices and sold them on for inflated prices in the market. The scale and type of profit involved also raised entirely new problems of taxation.

The significance of these two laws was that they opened a breach in the state's monopoly of economic activity, encouraging enterprise in an area where initiative had frequently been penalised. They could not affect to any great extent the way in which the wider industrial economy worked. None the less 4.5 million people were working in the new co-operatives (255,000 of them) by June 1991. This amounted to some 8 per cent of the workforce.

The early experience of the co-operatives revealed a resistance in the public mind to the idea of individual gain in the market-place which was very similar to that encountered during the period of the New Economic Policy from 1921 to 1928 – that is, before the economic monopoly fully took shape. But it also illustrated with startling clarity the problems involved in moving from monopoly to a market before an adequate framework of law and regulation had been set up. The end of monopoly could not mean, or ought not to have meant, allowing the market to run riot. The shift that was required, if time and circumstances had allowed it to take place in textbook fashion, would have been from monopoly to a fully articulated law-based system of regulation. This very important conceptual point will be addressed in this book's concluding section. For the moment it is to be noted that one of the early lessons of perestroika – and the co-operatives brought the lesson home with particular force – was that to release economic activity from monopoly without releasing it at the same time into a framework, precisely, of regulation, was to invite socially disastrous consequences.

The Law on Co-operatives was followed a year later by a Law on Leasing, which made the first hesitant and indirect steps towards individual private ownership in the means of production, although here, too, what was chiefly envisaged was autonomous initiatives by 'teams' of workers. The law allowed for workers to buy out a leased enterprise with a guarantee that they would not later be expropriated. It was to agriculture that the law was chiefly directed, teams being leased land, in principle for fifty years, extended to life tenure in March 1989. But it remained unclear to what extent farmers could appropriate land, the arrangements were subject to control by the soviets, and in any case the take-up was slow, farmers fearing a further shift in the political wind.

In fact, as the Gorbachev reforms progressed, it became clear that there were two nettles the leadership was finding particularly hard to grasp, and consequently refrained from doing so. The first was turning the land over to the farmers, giving them real and effective ownership and control. It was, for example, state and *collective* ownership that were put on an equal footing by a further important law on ownership in March 1990. The second was to liberate prices throughout the economy, and it is to the difficulties of disengaging the industrial economy from monopoly that we may now turn.

Central planning resists reform

In an early attempt to deal with the core problems of the planning system, the Central Committee of the CSPU discussed and approved at its June 1987 plenary session the 'Basic Provisions for the Fundamental Restructuring of Economic Management', and these provisions were built into a Law on the State Enterprise. The law aimed to give economic units greater freedom of operation and to loosen their dependence on the plan and on the central supply organisation. It was anticipated that the bulk of sales would take place on the open market that would come into being, and it was projected that state orders would account for only 25 per cent of production in 1989. An enterprises's performance would no longer be judged by fulfilment of targets handed down from above, but by its ability to stay in business and to make profits, which it was then free to reinvest. Those that failed to cover costs would be allowed to go out of business.

Secondly, the role of Gosplan, the state planning commission, was to be correspondingly adjusted. It would concern itself with indicative planning, and would employ regulatory instruments to steer the economy. Investment and credit would largely be given over to independent banks.

Thirdly, the law envisaged a partial reform of the pricing system, although this did not go very far. 'Commercial prices' were to be allowed to reflect demand in retail trade, whilst prices within industry were to be subject to contract. Certain prices, however, were to continue to be centrally set. It was acknowledged that price rises were necessary in order to reduce the distorting effect of subsidies, but the political sensitivity of this issue limited the provisions of the law, and limited even more the chances of its realisation.

Fourthly, a wholesale network was to be set up, which would replace the central supply agency, Gossnab, and would facilitate the movement of finished and semi-finished goods between enterprises, and between enterprise and consumer.

The law remained a blueprint for change, but little more. Its more radical measures – such as the modification of the pricing mechanism – were not radical enough, but even as they stood could not be digested by an economic system habituated to functioning on different principles. The years from 1987 to 1991 were to see a

bewildering series of proposals and counter-proposals put forward
in a duel between radicals and moderates, but this we must leave to
be treated below.

Whilst a start, then, had been made in breaking up the centre's
economic monopoly at the periphery of the economic system, it
proved much harder to make the industrial heart of the economy
move. No such sluggishness was visible in political life, however.
Here the reaction to Gorbachev's policies of glasnost was instant,
and the excitement and uncertainty that consequently invaded
society no doubt played its part in making change in the economy
difficult to achieve.

The leading role of the party

During the period between his accession to power in February 1985
and the disaster at Chernobyl in April 1986 Gorbachev marked out a
position which, taken together with developments that were to occur
in Hungary and elsewhere in Eastern Europe at that time or a little
later, can be termed 'reform communist'. It was in this period that he
made his first appeals, under the term *perestroika*, for serious reform
of the Soviet economic order. At this time, too, he produced and
emphasised a second term that was to mark his reforms – *glasnost*.
Glasnost is translated variously as openness, publicity, or transpar-
ency, but the root meaning of the word has to do with voice. Given
the extensive use of the term in the context of the birth of public
opinion in the last years of the Soviet Union, this etymological
connection with voice is worth noting, although for present purposes
the Russian term glasnost itself will be used.

At the time when Gorbachev first started to call for glasnost in
political life, however, the birth of public opinion still lay in the
future. Then, the chief aim of Gorbachev and of his reforming team
was to put a window in the Soviet administration so as to enable the
centre to reduce inefficiency, corruption and waste. As such, it was a
direct attempt to tackle one of the key problems that the very
working of the power monopoly caused. By blotting out the expression of political demands and the free reporting of events, the party
had a free hand in decision-making, but was starved of the information needed to make intelligent decisions. The term 'glasnost' came,
however, to have a much broader connotation, as a process of
democratisation was fairly rapidly built on the foundations of free
speech.

Gorbachev was calling for glasnost in his first speech as party leader and at the twenty-seventh congress of the CPSU in February–March 1986. But the accident at Chernobyl in April 1986 provided a major test of the sincerity of the new leadership's intentions. True, the blanket of silence that followed the accident could hardly be maintained for very long, given the international repercussions of the affair. None the less, the abrupt turn after 6 May from total silence to a quite novel frankness about what had happened was remarkable. It served to symbolise the new leadership's commitment to the opening up of information flows, and it was to prove a landmark in the developing crisis in Soviet political life.

This first period up to mid-1986 did little to disturb the power monopoly. It was a case of the party leader, with all the authority that the position traditionally conferred, calling the party and the country to order, and taking vigorous steps to correct certain imbalances in the system. In the political sphere the biggest shakeup in this first period was in personnel, as Gorbachev began to dismiss swathes of officials in the ministerial and party structures. But simple dismissals could as well be seen as a move to give the power monopoly a new lease of life and to improve its chances of survival as one to undermine the party's position.

None the less, the prerogatives of the party's apparatus in one of its central areas – that of propaganda and the control of the written and spoken word – was under attack. At this early stage the machinery remained in place, but Gorbachev moved into the key job of Central Committee secretary responsible for propaganda one of his reform-minded lieutenants, Vadim Medvedev. That was in March 1986. In his statements in that role Medvedev often expressly rejected the notion that the party should exercise monopoly control over the circulation of information and ideas, saying that 'the party does not and cannot lay claim to a monopoly in seeking the best paths of social progress: it does not believe that it possesses the ultimate truth',[3] but at this stage the party's apparatus remained in being, if with a modified role.

The changes of the second period, from mid-1986 to mid-1988, took place against the background of expanding glasnost. Once again content and form were evolving hand in hand. Not only did the editors of a number of existing newspapers and magazines, with *Moscow News* and *Ogonek* in the lead at first, begin to take advantage of the new freedom to press for an extension of the reform process; what they were printing itself became part of the pressures for change. Politics had come to life in the Soviet Union. It was during this second period in the crisis of the communist power monopoly, too, that Gorbachev discovered that the party as a whole was not easily to be won over to his positions, and in the autumn of 1986 there developed a first trial of strength between his reforming team and the party's traditionalists. Gorbachev's chief difficulties were to be with the party's apparatus, strongly represented in the Central Committee. That committee was due to meet in plenary session at the close of 1986. In the constant postponing of the plenum until the last date that it could be held in conformity with the party's statutes could be read the tensions that were building up. When it finally met in January 1987 Gorbachev launched an attack on those who were abusing their positions of power in the party, and called for democratic reforms such as would allow the human factor room to develop. Another theme recalled the arguments of the Czech reformers of the Prague Spring, and emphasised yet again the economic underpinnings of the reform process: the way to solving the Soviet Union's economic problems lay through political reform.

The glove thus thrown down, Gorbachev convened a party conference – the nineteenth – which was held from 28 June to 1 July 1988. This was merely a conference, and not a full congress. It was intended to offer an occasion for an exchange of ideas, and not for the taking of decisions. But it was at this conference that the broad lines of a future democratisation of Soviet life were laid down, to be enacted later by various legislative bodies. The conference was remarkable for the openness of the discussion. In a political system that had known only unanimity in public forums, this in itself was a major marker of change. At the same time, the proceedings reflected habits of conducting political affairs built up over the years. Gorbachev was more than a strong chairman, chiding and interrupting speakers directly from the podium, and indeed some of the more radical proposals were adopted with a minimum of debate and with a fair amount of hectoring by Gorbachev himself.

Major changes were proposed in two broad areas, one concerning the representative system, and the other the party. For the first, it was agreed to amend the constitution so as to replace the existing Supreme Soviet, whose members were summoned to Moscow for only a few days in each year, with a parliament of full-time deputies. This new Supreme Soviet would be drawn from a Congress of

People's Deputies, one-third of whose 2,250 members would be elected on a territorial and one-third on a territorial-nationality basis, whilst the remaining third would be proposed and elected by the 'social organisations', which included the party itself and its client mass organisations. A new electoral law was to be drafted which would guarantee competition in election to legislative bodies. There was to be established also a constitutional review commission to oversee the workings of what would in effect be an entirely new order based on formal rules as opposed to a convention of manipulation by the party. The actual passing of these new constitutional provisions, however, and the developments that they gave rise to must be treated below as part of the third period.

But it was in the realm of party organisation that the conference of 1988 made its most specific attack on the power monopoly. Some minor adjustments to the way in which the party was to organise its affairs had been made in the period before the conference of 1988 was held. Debate was to be encouraged in primary organisations, and the reporting-out function of executive bodies was to be strengthened. There had also been wide-ranging discussion in the party's press during early 1988 about how greater democracy might be brought into party life. But at the conference itself Gorbachev went to the roots of the monopoly of power. He attacked the tendency to *podmena* – the tendency for the party to substitute itself for the formal economic and administrative decision-makers – maintaining that this had robbed both state and party of their separate identity and functions. This, however, was a ritual complaint. Much more to the point was Gorbachev's proposal that all posts in the party up to Central Committee level should be filled by open and secret election, and that party officials should be limited to two five-year terms in office. The privileges that the party's monopoly of power had permitted its officials to acquire also came under strong criticism.

In this second period from mid-1986 to mid-1988, then, the party's monopoly of power had been subjected to a convincing assault from above. The control over information and communications vested in the propaganda departments of the party's apparatus was being whittled away – with the reformers' acquiescence – by the development of glasnost, which meant that the party could no longer screen its privileged position from public view. Meanwhile the individuals in whom that privilege was vested were to be subject to

control through an electoral process and through a limit on the time
during which the party's office-holders could hold their position.

At the same time it seems clear that the Gorbachev leadership's
intention to jettison the party's actual monopoly of power was still at
this point seen as a necessary means to preserving its power and the
'socialist choice' in some new form. The new representative institutions, the new element of choice offered in election to them, and their
theoretical integument in the notion of the 'socialist law-based state'
were all to coexist with a communist party that continued to see itself
as fulfilling 'a unifying role' so as 'to integrate into one policy
different, sometimes contradictory, social interests'.[4] Thus, when
freer elections were finally held for a Congress of People's Deputies
in 1989, one-third of the seats was reserved for representatives of the
party and of other 'social organisations'. Such a squaring of the
circle, reminiscent of discussions in Czechoslovakia during the
Prague Spring, was to prove untenable.

It remains to point out that during this period the party's
apparatus as a whole was being severely cut back. This led at times to
perplexed complaints in the countryside at the loss of functionaries
whose job it had been to sort out problems and help cope with
shortages – as was the case in one locality, noted by *Ogonek*, where a
30 per cent cut-back in the forestry department of the party committee was having a disruptive effect on an important local
industry.[5]

Finally, the abandoning of the party's leading role as it had
hitherto been conceived, together with the increasing permeability of
the Union's external frontier, had a massive effect in a crucial area of
Soviet life – relations among the country's constituent nationalities.

Democratisation and the Soviet nationalities

The Soviet Union's decision to withdraw from Eastern Europe
stemmed clearly enough from a policy of seeking integration into the
world economy. But what is sauce for the goose is sauce for the
gander, and it was then open to nationalist leaderships in the
republics to test Moscow's resolve to maintain its grip on what they
perceived as an internal empire. Since the entire policy of perestroika
derived from a position of economic weakness and from an awareness (as Gorbachev lost no opportunity of reminding his critics) that
change must come, they could be forgiven for reasoning in this way.

But there was more to it than that. The component elements of the power monopoly were mutually supporting in a single system. The closed frontier around the 'unbreakable union of Soviet republics'; the organisation of the whole territory in a single economic plan; the vertical structure of the communist party's apparatus; and the ideology of a house which divided against itself must fall – each of these components contributed to the Union's unity for as long as that unity as a whole held. It was, for example, a constant theme in the literature on the Soviet Union that the multinational unit was held together by two key factors: the plan and the party. Through the first the economies of the republics were inextricably linked; whilst it was customary for the second secretary in each of the republican party apparatuses, whose functions included oversight of the *nomenklatura*, to be a Russian, the first secretary being drawn from the republic's majority nationality.

The weakening of one component of the system meant the weakening of the whole. Glasnost destroyed the myth of unity, revealing the strength of separatist feelings; moving away from the plan meant decentralisation of the economy (although this was at first more evident in the aspiration than in the fact); the opening of the political system to rival voices to that of the party made room for nationalist sentiment to invade the already excited new deliberative forums and the electoral process.

Gorbachev and the Soviet leadership were clearly surprised by the strength of movements for national autonomy. Were they captives of their own myth of unity, and of the Leninist belief that simple economic calculation would lead separatist leaderships to rejoin the Union? Neither would be surprising. But nor would another reason, based equally on traditional assumptions. When the policy of change was launched in the mid-1980s, the problems of the Soviet Union appeared to stem from the fact that the state was too strong. It had shown itself capable of coping with all sources of internal dissent through force, and of running a vast economy on the basis of state ownership and state management. But by obliterating opinion and initiative it was preventing society from moving forward; the strength of the state had become counterproductive.

The Gorbachev leadership may not have thought in exactly these terms, but their policies show that their thinking was not far removed from it. The power of the state could continue to be used to control the process of change if things got out of hand. But the state itself turned out not to be immune from the fissiparous forces at work. Even before 1991 it was clear that the Red Army was no longer a cohesive force that could be used to restore order in the national areas; whilst the attempted putsch of August in that year laid bare for all the world to see the impotence of the chief traditional organs of Soviet state power.

National tensions first erupted in Kazakhstan in 1986, as a result of Gorbachev's dismissal of a corrupt party first secretary and his replacement by a Russian. But the full impact of the ethnic response to Gorbachev's policies was to come after this cleaning-up operation, which passed from Kazakhstan to other Central Asian republics. In the Baltic republics of Latvia, Lithuania and Estonia national fronts sprang into existence and demanded the right to enter into direct relations with foreign governments and to issue their own currency. These examples of 'vertical' nationalism, in which units at the periphery were seeking autonomy or separation from the centre, coincided with far more violent cases of 'horizontal' nationalism between and among ethnic groups. In February 1988 a vicious dispute erupted between Armenia and Azerbaidzhan, which led to a wave of reciprocal slaughter on the part of Armenians and Azeris.

These events in Central Asia, on the Baltic and in the Caucasus were but the harbinger of a tide of mobilisation of peoples against each other and against the weakened centre of the Union, which was to put the reform process under extreme pressure in the decisive period from 1988.

Democratic centralism

Gorbachev knew that the greatest obstacles to reform lay in the field of culture. Indeed it could hardly have been otherwise. In Eastern Europe communism was an implant, and it was open to national élites to mobilise support for rejecting it – should the opportunity arise – by appealing to a national culture. But communism was made in the Soviet Union, and effectively by the Russians who were the most numerous and most powerful of the components of the culturally diverse Union. Communism was, and remains, a vital part of the Russian past.

No doubt a dual culture was involved in the party's strenuous attempts to create the 'new socialist man', which has led some analysts of Soviet politics to generate the awkward concept of an 'official political culture' to connote an ideological construct which was certainly never fully internalised by the Soviet population, nor even by the Russians within it. But it is important to bear in mind that this ideological construct was not only created by flesh and blood Soviet men and women, but undoubtedly provided at least a good part of the frame of reference of the Soviet élite. The idea of democratic centralism, with the high value that it put on the unity of the political and social organisms of party, state and society, served a political purpose in maintaining that élite in power, but it also – perhaps because of that very fact – shaped the élite's own thinking. Or rather it shaped the actions and knee-jerk responses of its members to calls for change, since a regional party secretary probably had little time, even if he (never, to my knowledge, she) had the inclination, for reflection.

As for the formal definition of the 'Leninist principle' of democratic centralism in official contexts, the new party statutes adopted at the twenty-seventh congress of 1986 added a further clause to the traditional four. In enjoining a 'collective spirit' and in asserting the importance of 'personal responsibility' it reflected the new leadership's call for discipline and improved performance, but within the traditional organisational framework.

But it was in the views expressed, for example, at sessions of the Central Committee – often perplexed and anxious, though more often indignant – that it could be seen how deeply ingrained was the traditional way of thinking about political relationships and practices. Even the proposals of the reformers remained within the traditional mould. This reflects, in part, the fact that in the early years of perestroika the leadership hoped to save the party's authority by introducing only a controlled dose of reform. But as the process of change snowballed, the question inevitably arose of where the leadership would draw its guiding ideas from. In East-Central Europe this question had a relatively simple answer, given the propensity of the élites of those countries to look westward. But even in the Balkans external patterns of that kind were not so readily available nor universally accepted, whilst Russian society has, for two centuries at least, been torn between a guarded fascination of things Western and an ultimately dominant belief that its salvation lies within itself – that 'there is no measuring of Russia by common standards'.[6]

The upshot, in the period from 1986 to 1988, was the development of a theory of a 'socialist pluralism of opinions'. Nothing could better express both the limits of what the reformers intended to institute and the gulf that separated liberal democratic notions of pluralism from the democratic centralist thinking that the Soviet élite had inherited from the Stalinist era – and, be it said, from the Russian past. The pluralism that Western democracy had developed was based not only on freedom of speech, and thus of opinion, but on organisational autonomy below the level of the state, and on a resulting associative life in which sectional interests could compete for influence, office and material gain. Gorbachev's words on the subject of a 'socialist pluralism of opinions' revealed rather different ideas. It connoted 'the discussion, the scientific search, that is carried out within the boundaries of our socialist choice made by our people once and for all in October 1917'.[7] Freedom to express opinions had to coexist with the party's 'unifying role to integrate into one policy different, sometimes contradictory, social interests'.   This was the voice of orthodox democratic centralism, for which the health of the social organism outweighs the interests of its parts, the communist party's role being to defend the health of the organism, and to express the social interest. It is a collectivist view of political and social relationships that has run through the history of Soviet communism. As Leonid Brezhnev put it two decades earlier, 'The party's policy yields the desired results when it takes into precise account the interests of all the people and the interests of the classes and social groups comprising the people and directs them into one channel'.[8] It was not going to disappear overnight simply because insupportable pressures had forced the party leadership to abandon the more easily jettisoned elements of its monopoly of power.

Yet the same Gorbachev who coined and gave currency to the formula 'socialist pluralism of opinions' was to press on with the process of change, against a perpetual opposition within his party, and who set up an electoral system which, whilst it contained provisions that would effectively guarantee a communist party majority in the Supreme Soviet, none the less made it possible for organised competition in the parliamentary arena to take place. Indeed it was Gorbachev who expressly set out to abandon the party's monopoly of power. There is a conundrum here which will no doubt occupy historians for some time to come. At the time of writing it is extraordinarily difficult to separate out the factors that influenced the shaping of the new Russia during the years which concern us here.

Clearly Gorbachev's thinking evolved with the situation, becoming in a sense more radical whilst remaining always within a tradition of which he was a product. Clearly his early statements concerning socialist pluralism reflected an intention to reform the Soviet system rather than to destroy it, and to preserve a role within the new order for a communist party that was endowed with a role to which other parties that might arise could not aspire. There were moreover political figures, far more radical than Gorbachev, whose aspirations would lead them to make use of the new possibilities that an acceptance of political competition opened up. Yet those possibilities did not lead to the creation of a viable party system, any more than they provided for an orderly succession of power at the apex of the Russian political system. It was not only Gorbachev's hard-headed opponents in the Central Committee who were imbued with the thinking characteristic of democratic centralism. Of all the components of the communist power monopoly, this was the one that was likely, in Russia and indeed elsewhere, to outlive the monopoly and to colour the new social order.

Notes

1   Moshe Lewin, *The Gorbachev Phenomenon* (London: Radius, 1988), pp. 145–6.
2   These were his actual words, the reference presumably being to Sinatra's 'I did it my way'.
3   Ken Jowitt, 'Gorbachev: Bolshevik or Menshevik?', in Stephen White, Alex Pravda and Zvi Gitelman, *Developments in Soviet Politics* (Basingstoke: Macmillan, 1990), p. 285.
4   'K polnovlastiyu sovetov i sozidaniyu pravogo gosudarstva', in M. S. Gorbachev, *Izbrannye Rechi i Stat'i* (Moscow: Politizdat), pp. 165–6.
5   Vitalii Eremin in *Ogonek*, 13 March 1989.
6   F. I. Tyutchev, *Polnoe Sobranie Sochinenii* (St-Petersburg: A. F. Marks, 1913), p. 202.
7   M. S. Gorbachev, 'Politika partii – politika obnovleniya', *Kommunist*, 4 (1988), p. 8. For a full treatment of 'socialist pluralism of opinions' see Niel Robinson, 'Gorbachev and the Place of the Party in Soviet Reform, 1985–91', *Soviet Studies*, Vol. 44, No. 3 (1992), pp. 423–43.
8   Quoted in V. Ayzikovich, 'Vazhnaya sotsiologicheskaya problema', *Voprosy filosofii*, No. 11 (1965), p. 69.

Further reading

Stephen F. Cohen, Alexander Rabinowitch and Robert Sharlet, *The Soviet Union Since Stalin* (Basingstoke: Macmillan, 1980).
David Lane, *Soviet Society under Perestroika* (London: Routledge, revised ed. 1992).

Martin McCauley, *Khruschev and Khruschchevism* (Basingstoke: Macmillan, 1987).

Dev Murarka, *Gorbachov: The Limits of Power* (London: Hutchinson, 1988).

Alec Nove, *Stalinism and After: The Road to Gorbachev* (Boston, MA: Unwin Hyman, 1989).

Richard Sakwa, *Gorbachev and his Reforms* (Hemel Hempstead: Philip Allan, 1990).

Stephen White, *Gorbachev in Power* (Cambridge: Cambridge University Press, 1990).

Stephen White, Alex Pravda and Zvi Gitelman (eds), *Developments in Soviet and Post-Soviet Politics* (Basingstoke: Macmillan, 1992).

9

1989 in Eastern Europe

The crisis of the communist power monopoly came to a head in 1989. The collapse of the communist regimes in Eastern Europe during that year symbolised for an astonished world the malaise that was affecting the whole communist edifice. The path to 1989 had, as noted, been laid by a reforming Soviet leadership under Mikhail Gorbachev who, from the second year of his term in office as General Secretary of the CPSU, had begun to make it clear that the monopoly's day had come, and that the CPSU's future depended upon its being able to guide a process of reform within the system. We have seen that Gorbachev's new policies were the result both of weaknesses within the monopoly and of external pressures, some of the latter stemming from within the communist universe itself. In that universe, made up of ruling and non-ruling communist parties, no change could come until the Soviet Union itself moved from its traditional positions. It was Gorbachev who broke the log-jam, and set in motion a process of change that was to go far beyond Gorbachev's original project, and was to lead to the collapse of the Soviet state itself.

The fuse was lit in 1986. Once lit it threatened detonations of one magnitude or another both in the Soviet Union and Eastern Europe, if Gorbachev remained in power. In the Soviet Union, the reforms progressed step by step, against a strong opposition which suffered from having no alternative policies with which to counter Gorbachev's reforming moves. Five and a half years separated the twenty-seventh CPSU congress in February–March 1986 from the putsch of August 1991, which was the knell of communist party rule in any form in the Soviet Union, although the party's actual monopoly had been signed away before that. In Eastern Europe a period of taking stock of the new situation lasted until only the end of 1988, after which the dominoes tumbled, the Romanian regime collapsing on Christmas Day of 1989 to complete the process within the countries that had once been members of the Soviet bloc. The process came to a head in Yugoslavia in 1990, and was to engulf Albania in 1991.

In this chapter the responses of the Eastern European party leaderships to their alarming new predicament will be examined; the events of the cardinal year of 1989 will be recounted, and some conclusions will be drawn on the events of that epic year, which opened with the Czech dissident Vaclav Havel being put in prison and ended with his installation in the Hradcany castle as president. A final section will be devoted to Yugoslavia, where events followed a different course to arrive, at least in the case of certain of the republics, at a very similar destination.

Reactions to perestroika

For all the leaderships of Eastern Europe, the change of leader and in the Soviet Union was bound to be potentially embarrassing. First of all, their dependence on the Soviet Union meant that they had to make some response to changes in the circumstances of their powerful patron. But the turn to reform in the Soviet Union put their leaderships in a particularly delicate position, since as hold-overs from the earlier period they were implicated in the policies of the Brezhnev period which Gorbachev was so strenuously attacking in the Soviet Union. Thirdly, they obviously had to calculate the risks of failing to follow the lead given by Gorbachev, risks associated to a great extent with the effect that the wind of change would have on the mood of the populace. As noted, their legitimacy was in any case insecure, trapped as they were between the demands of their people and of their Soviet patron, between the role of national leader and of faithful satrap.

Three of the regimes made their opposition to the ideas of perestroika clear from the beginning, and were to maintain this attitude until their fall in 1989 – Romania, the GDR and Czechoslovakia. When Mikhail Gorbachev visited Bucharest in May 1987, the Romanian leader insisted that he was 'against any mechanical and dogmatic imitation of the experience or practice of another country'.[1] Ceausescu had already publicly rejected any notion of introducing market mechanisms into the economy. Nor did Gorbachev appear to be pushing him too hard in the matter. The policies of change proposed in the Soviet Union were likely to pose problems of stability enough at home without inviting instability in Eastern Europe. This must, indeed, have been a difficult corner for the Soviet leadership to turn, and in all his many visits to Eastern Europe between 1985 and 1989 Gorbachev was at pains not to inflame a potentially dangerous situation, whilst at the same time having to make it clear, for diplomatic reasons if for no other, that the Soviet Union would no longer intervene to prop up a beleaguered Eastern European leadership. Thus, during that visit to Bucharest, Gorbachev emphasised the 'right of each country to decide what model of development it wants to follow in accordance with its specific conditions'.

As for the GDR, Gorbachev attended in person the eleventh congress of the GDR's ruling Socialist Unity Party (the SED) in April 1986, where he praised the GDR for its economic performance. But if Gorbachev was looking for an enthusiastic application of the spirit of reform in the GDR he was to be disappointed. The response of the SED's leader, Erich Honecker, was that the GDR's economic performance was indeed exemplary in relation to the other economies of the bloc. The Soviet Union might need a perestroika, but the GDR did not. Nor, in Honecker's view, was it in need of glasnost, though here his views accorded less well with the reality.

It gradually became clear that the new circumstances were breeding discord within the GDR's leadership, but Honecker stuck to his position and succeeded in weathering the challenges to it. His regime was, indeed, especially vulnerable. The proximity of the Federal Republic made East Germans only too aware of what separated the two societies, whilst any manifest signs of discontent would be shown on the FRG's television and beamed back to GDR screens.

Czechoslovakia, like the GDR, was particularly vulnerable as Gorbachev's reforming policies progressed, though for different reasons. Every step of the Soviet perestroika evoked the debates of the Prague Spring and put the Czechoslovak leadership under pressure to reopen that book. Even those who acknowledged the need for change realised that the spectre of 1968 and its aftermath was abroad. One such member of the leadership, the Central Committee secretary Jan Fojtik, claimed that 'the party, in particular its leading

bodies, must retain the initiative in this process . . . Our experience
from the period of crisis proves that this must be the case'.[2]
Gorbachev himself for a long time refrained from endorsing the
policies and ideas of the Prague Spring, saying in May 1987 that 'the
evaluation of the events of 1968 is primarily a matter for the Czech
comrades themselves'. But his very presence in Prague one month
before his making this statement had led to enthusiastic street
demonstrations, with cries of 'Misha, stay with us!'.

At first the leadership was clearly divided, the prime minister
Strougal coming out clearly in January 1987 in favour of reform, the
bulk of the party's apparatus urging orthodoxy and the general
secretary Husak holding the middle ground. But in December 1987
Husak was replaced by Milos Jakes, a known hardliner, and indeed
the party functionary who had been in charge of the 'normalisation'
of 1969 in Czechoslovakia. It was in circumstances of severe police
oppression that the dissident Charter 77 built up, as well as it could,
the movement that was to ease the communist party from power in
1989.

The Hungarians were later to be in the van of political reform in
the region as events reached their denouement at the end of the
decade. At this early point, however, the party was cautious. The
economic reform launched in 1968, and developed since within the
constraints of the party's monopoly, gave the Hungarian regime
reason to claim, with the GDR's leadership, that what was happening in the Soviet Union had still not caught up with what Hungary
had itself achieved. Furthermore, at that early stage, the future was
quite uncertain, and it made some sense to stand pat on present
achievements rather than to put them at risk by venturing into an
open-ended process of political change. The fact that the party
leader, Janos Kadar, was now old and in poor health, acted as a
further brake on change.

Finally, the logic of the power monopoly itself, with its closeting of
the leadership group, contributed to an *immobilisme* that was particularly acutely felt after the thirteenth congress of the Hungarian
Socialist Workers' Party (HSWP) in the spring of 1985. None the
less, there were pressures gestating which, during the following three
years, were to lead to the crucial change of leadership without which
no real change could come. One sign among many was that the
Assembly, though elected in the conventional way and thus
amenable to pressure from the party leadership, began to develop a

life of its own, a tax bill generating an unprecedentedly open debate in the autumn of 1987. With hindsight it can be seen how the process of reform launched in the economic sphere in 1968 had prepared Hungary to adjust to the pressures of perestroika, despite the initial *immobilisme* in the leadership.

At this early stage, two Eastern European regimes showed overt approval of the new Soviet policies – Bulgaria and Poland.

In many areas of economic life the Bulgarians kept pace with, or even anticipated, the Soviet Union in the process of restructuring. Gorbachev's emphasis on self-management, and the 1987 Law on the Enterprise which embodied it, was anticipated in Bulgaria by measures to institute a degree of self-management in 1981 – that is, even before Gorbachev came to power. After 1985, in its language and in its policies, the Bulgarian leadership showed itself a willing disciple of the Soviet Union. The campaign against alcoholism and corruption of Gorbachev's early days was reproduced in Bulgaria. In 1987 the earlier reforms of 1981 in the management of the economy were taken further. Their aim was to give enterprises greater flexibility within the confines of the central planning system. Thus the allocation of supplies would continue to be organised by a central supply organisation, but enterprises that had fulfilled their plan were to be enabled to procure, on a contract basis, supplementary materials in order to manufacture goods for sale on the free market. It was a compromise that left the economic monopoly intact in its essentials. As in the Soviet law of 1987, enterprise directors were to be elected, but the party and the trade unions kept their rights to nominate candidates, which promised little change in the absence of further political reform.

The Bulgarian reform was exceptionally wide in its scope, and was accompanied by a reorganisation of the ministerial structure, a reshuffling of leading personnel (though Todor Zhivkov retained his post at the head of the party), and an administrative reform that recreated a regional structure giving the communes increased powers. The Bulgarian leadership could therefore not be accused of inaction in reponse to the Soviet Union's perestroika. It had little intention, however, of altering the rules of the political game. Nor was it under intense pressure to do so at the time, although Gorbachev did go out of his way to criticise Bulgaria's economic achievements, targeting especially the shoddy quality of Bulgarian goods. Not until 1988 itself, in fact, did a movement of dissent take shape, over the issue of pollution in Ruse, but this is matter for later discussion.

In Timothy Garton Ash's view, the 'beginning of the end' of communist rule in Eastern Europe was the visit of the Pope to Poland in June 1979.[3] Indeed, both the massive impact of Solidarity and the Catholic church's political influence on Polish politics, put the party thereafter permanently on the defensive. Having outlawed Solidarity in 1981, but having also taken note both of the factors that had given rise to it and of the changing situation in the east of Europe, General Jaruzelski moved to shore up the party's authority without having to abandon its leading role in society. The coming of a Soviet perestroika reinforced this policy; indeed the aims of Gorbachev and Jaruzelski coincided closely during the latter half of the 1980s. Well before the coming of Gorbachev, in fact in the direct aftermath of the Solidarity episode, Jaruzelski had launched a Patriotic Movement for National Renewal (the PRON in its Polish acronym) in an attempt to rally society behind this aim. The same goal lay behind the creation of a new set of trade unions, heading up in an umbrella co-ordinating body (the OPZZ), in 1982.

Neither of these initiatives, coming as they did during the period of imposed martial law, can be seen unequivocally as moves to regenerate society, and indeed opinions on Jaruzelski's commitment to real reform are divided. He was, moreover, manoeuvring in a difficult space between hardliners whose apprehensions had been confirmed by the events of 1980–81, and a population conscious of its power at least to frustrate the party's policies. The existence of a palpable reform trend within the PUWP, even if its aims went no further than a loosening of the party's democratic centralist norms, increased his isolation at the head of the party as he set about finding a way of reconciling reform with the retention of the party's authority.

The difficulty of his position was well illustrated in a referendum that was held in November 1987, in the terms of which approval of economic reform was linked to an endorsement of the party's more general approach to the ideas of perestroika. Whilst a majority was secured in support of the leadership's position, the turn-out was so low as to render the victory meaningless, since the stipulated number of voters to validate the referendum had not been achieved. Nobody had won. Society was not easily to be cajoled, as was demonstrated by a wave of strikes – the most serious since the outburst of 1980 – that swept the country in 1988. Those strikes, in the context of an increasingly grave economic situation, led Jaruzelski to take the step that was to lead the Poles to overtake the Hungarians and to put them at the head of the process of change in the region.

Towards the denouement

The communist parties in all six Eastern European bloc countries surrendered their monopoly of power during the course of the single year of 1989. This suggests a uniformity in that process which is in fact belied by the actual course of events. The final denouement was preceded in Hungary by a process of change that reached back into the 1980s. In Poland, too, change was under way even if in both cases the final surrender of the monopoly itself did not take place until the fateful year of 1989. In both Hungary and Poland the effective surrender of monopoly power was negotiated between representatives of the ruling party and of the opposition. In Bulgaria, too, the communist party was brought to negotiate with a consolidated opposition, although the period during which that opposition formed was much shorter than in either Poland or Hungary. Even the latter two cases differed from each other in important respects.

As for the GDR, Czechoslovakia and Romania, the parties clung to their power until, abandoned by their Soviet guarantor of yesteryear, confronted by increasingly insistent demonstrations of popular protest which they now lacked the confidence to put down, and aware of the cumulative effect that the revolutionary snowball was acquiring, they stood down. Only in the Romanian case was bloodshed involved to any great extent, and only one execution, when an escaping Ceausescu was captured, arraigned before a military court and, with his wife Elena, summarily executed.

If one factor is to be selected as of primary importance in the unfolding of this region-wide drama, it is the withdrawing of Soviet support from the regimes. The 'Sinatra doctrine' does go a good way to explaining why the Eastern European regimes fell all together in such a short time, if indeed, as has at times been suggested, the Soviet Union did not itself attempt to guide a landslide that it had itself provoked, but which threatened alarming regional instability. But the worst was avoided; remarkably little instability resulted, and the change of regime in each country was able to proceed according to the rhythm set by the internal developments that preceded the revolutionary events.

The 'negotiated' revolutions

Three cases are of particular interest in terms of their internal development, and of the way in which the communist power mono-poly was, in fact, negotiated away: Hungary, Poland and Bulgaria. It is through their experiences that the complex events leading up to 1989 will here be examined.

In Hungary the *immobilisme* of the early reactions to perestroika was finally broken by the removal from power of Janos Kadar in May 1988. But by that time a number of developments had taken place, most of which brought out aspects of the power monopoly, and marked significant stages in its dismantling. Thus, in the elections held in the summer of 1985, multiple candidacies were allowed. This did not radically affect the electoral system: autonomous organisation for the purpose of fighting the election was still ruled out, and this aspect of the monopoly remained intact. None the less, the party was unable to arrange the election entirely in advance, and the result was that a series of powerful local party figures failed to secure election. As a second example, the mass organisations that underpinned the party's control of strategic sections of society began, in some cases to lose their efficacy as 'transmission belts'. This was especially the case with the party's youth organisation, the KISZ, which became a hollow shell as its membership plummeted, no longer attentive to the party's calls for loyalty. A rather different development, as noted above, had already taken place in another mass organisation, the Peace Council, which took on an independent role in the Europe-wide peace movement of the early 1980s.

Thirdly, the party no longer had the will to enforce compliance consistently as in the past, revealing how control through the mechanisms of placement and manipulation of communications had been but the workaday face of control through coercion and policing. On three occasions – at Monor in 1985, in Lakitelek in 1987, and again at Lakitelek on 3 September 1988 – prominent opponents of the regime met to discuss a strategy of reform. Whilst the party on occasion still broke up street demonstrations by force, it lacked the will to take on a part of the flower of the country's intelligentsia.

But the presence of Imre Pozsgay at the first Lakitelek meeting showed that much more was involved. Pozsgay was at that point general secretary of the Patriotic People's Front, the *apparat* that grouped together the mass organisations under the party's aegis. His presence in the reform camp, on which he was to build as the process of change unfolded, meant not only that the party élite was no longer cohesive, but that a key part of the role of its apparatus was at risk. Indeed, by the time of the first Lakitelek meeting, the gap between reformers inside the party and reformers outside it was smaller than that between the party's reformers and its orthodox leadership.

At the second Lakitelek meeting the Hungarian Democratic Forum (MDF) announced is formation. This was followed two months later by the formation of the Alliance of Free Democrats (SZDSZ), and had in fact been preceded by the creation of an Alliance of Young Democrats (FIDESZ). Soon Hungary had acquired all the major parties that were to dominate political life through the transition period. This was made possible by an Association and Assembly Act, passed in September 1988 – a piece of legislation which, although it was imperfect and was destined to be replaced by a further act in 1989, constituted none the less a major milestone on the road of the power monopoly's demise.

Once Kadar had been deposed in favour of Karoly Grosz at the HSWP's conference in May 1988 a movement developed to force a revision of the party's judgement on the events of 1956. The importance of this movement in the story of the dismantling of the communist power monopoly is that it demonstrated the intensity of certain events as symbols of the monopoly and of its works. Further demands with a high symbolic content were to punctuate the entire record of the events of 1989 in Eastern Europe.

It was not to be until 16 June 1989 that Imre Nagy was re-interred. Three days before this event 'triangular' talks took place between and among the HSWP, the official mass organisations, and the opposition, the last being represented by the political parties that had by then formed.

It is hard to overstate the significance of this constitutional process in which the major forces in Hungarian society worked out a charter for all parties to abide by. It had been, in fact, preceded by a similar event in Poland, and it was to be followed in the next year by 'round-table' negotiations in Bulgaria. In all three cases the talks served to mark the effective end of the party's monopoly of power, although it remained to clear away the many symbolic traces of that power, and to pass the legislation that would attend to the detail of its abolition.

Finally, in October 1989, the HSWP voted to transform itself into the 'Hungarian Socialist Party', thus taking its distance from its past and, no doubt more importantly, attending to its future survival. The party was thereby acknowledging that, whatever new rules were to govern the political game, and whatever chances they might offer of political influence of one kind or another, those rules had radically changed. The party's monopoly of power in Hungary was over.

In Poland the final act started later than in Hungary, but finished earlier. A wave of strikes had swept the country in 1988. These strikes, together with an economic situation of crisis proportions, led Jaruzelski to propose to the Polish United Workers' Party (PUWP) leadership that the opposition forces be brought into dialogue with the party. It was an attempt to save what authority the party still retained, and perhaps even to increase it within changed rules of the political game.

The fateful decision was taken by the party's Central Committee in December 1988 and January 1989, Jaruzelski reportedly only achieving his purpose by threatening to resign. It was the crucial turning-point. On 17 April 1989 Solidarity once again acquired political legitimacy by being re-registered. But February had already seen the opening of round-table talks involving representatives of the PUWP, the official unions (the OPZZ), the Catholic church and Solidarity. These talks thus took place some four months before the Hungarian negotiations, and it is partly this that explains why their results were more limited.

In particular, the right to nominate candidates in elections freely was accorded, but the party reserved for its candidates 65 per cent of the seats in the lower house (the Sejm). This was somewhat similar to the CPSU's reservation of one-third of the seats in the Congress of People's Deputies to representatives of the party itself or of the 'social organisations' that it ultimately controlled. In the newly-created Senate all seats were opened to free election. When the elections were held, Solidarity – which at that point aggregated under one umbrella the various strands of the opposition – won all the 35 per cent of seats open to it in the Sejm, and 99 of the 100 seats in the Senate. It was thus Poland that was the scene of the formation of the first non-communist government in the bloc countries since the 1940s, when in August the Sejm confirmed the appointment of Solidarity's Tadeusz Mazowiecki as prime minister, on a vote of 378 to 4, with 41 abstentions (the government as a whole being approved in September, by 402 votes to nil, with 13 abstentions). Where in this rapid sequence of events the PUWP could be said to have lost its monopoly of political power is a question to which we shall return.

The third case of a negotiated ceding of political power occurred much later in the year, in Bulgaria. Under the communist regime Bulgaria had become an industrial country with an urban culture. It had also, in the 1970s and 1980s, acquired a generational problem, which presented the party with a challenge that was more diffuse than the oppositional currents in East-Central Europe. It was not until 1987, in fact, that an embryonic opposition movement came into being. Meanwhile the generational problem had been contained, and to an extent catered for, by the activities and ideas of Lyudmila Zhivkova, the Western-educated daughter of the party leader, who was appointed to the Politburo as spokeswoman on science, culture and art.

The background to the fall of communist power in Bulgaria lay in the country's treatment of a Turkish minority which comprised approximately one-tenth of the total population. In 1984 the government had required Turks to change their names to Bulgarian forms. The discontent that this naturally created led Zhivkov to adopt a disastrous policy of expulsion. Opposition within the party built up and came to a head in November 1989, when Zhivkov was replaced by Petar Mladenov at the head of the party.

However, within society, too, new developments were taking place. They were triggered initially by an environmental problem on the Danube where a cloud of chlorine gas drifted intermittently across the river to Bulgarian Ruse from a metallurgical plant on the Romanian bank. Although the source of the nuisance lay outside Bulgaria, the pollution of Ruse gave rise to political protest actions, and on 3 March 1988 a Committee for the Defence of Ruse was created, which was the source from which, by a rapid process of aggregation, a united front opposed to the party's rule took shape. A broader formation – Ekoglasnost, formed by members of the Ruse Committee – acquired no little prominence by using a CSCE Conference on the Environment that opened in Sofia at the end of October 1989 to contest the government's policies, but also its power. Ekoglasnost was thus well placed to play a central role within the Union of Democratic Forces (UDF) which came into being on 7 December after Zhivkov had been thrust from power.

The UDF originally comprised ten groups of a remarkably diverse provenance. Apart from Ekoglasnost and other groups formed from the dissidence of the moment, there were revivals of political parties from the pre-communist days (the Radical Party and the Agrarian parties, for example), there were groups formed by former Communist Party dissidents (one of these providing Bulgaria's first president, Zhelyu Zhelev), and, at that stage, there was an independent trade union organisation, Podkrepa. The UDF, therefore, though created late in the day of Eastern European emancipation, played the same aggregating role in the face of communist monopoly power as was played by Charter 77 in Czechoslovakia or Solidarity in Poland.

It was in round-table negotiations between the Communist Party (which in 1990 changed its name to the 'Bulgarian Socialist Party') and the UDF that arrangements were made for the holding of free elections. But the party had astutely already conceded one of the opposition's major demands as soon as it had replaced Todor Zhivkov, and had proclaimed its intention of moving to a multi-party system. As in Poland and Hungary – and indeed in the Soviet Union – the party had signed away its monopoly in the hope of retaining an authority based on new rules of the political game. Free elections were duly held in June 1990. The Socialists won a slender majority in them, and formed a government, but it was forced from office by popular pressure a year later.

The last-ditch cases
The events leading to the collapse of the party's monopoly of power in the GDR, Czechoslovakia and Romania were far more dramatic. It was a single chain of events that brought down the first two of these regimes, both of which resisted pressures for change until change was forced upon them.

On 2 May 1989, in a remote part of the border between Hungary and Austria, the wire fence that constituted the frontier between the two countries was snipped. No one collected snippings of that fence as they did pieces of the Berlin Wall, and yet it was at Hegyshalom that the iron curtain was first breached. Through later gaps made elsewhere in that wire frontier, from August on, holiday-makers from the GDR began to pass. The trickle became a flood, until the haemorrhage of the GDR's citizens reached crisis proportions, putting the Socialist Unity Party under intense pressure. At the same time massive weekly demonstrations took place in Leipzig and in other major cities, increasing the pressure on the embattled SED leadership. On 10 September the forces of the opposition in the GDR created the New Forum, which was to act as their spokesman during the final hectic days of communist power. The beginning of the end came on 18 October, when Erich Honecker, together with a number of other members of the SED's inner leadership, resigned. An attempt by Egon Krenz to present a new leadership with a policy of reform failed miserably. Jens Reich, a founder member of the New Forum, has recorded the decisive moment:

In the afternoon of November 9th, the spokesman Günther Schabowski emerged on to the steps of the Central Committee building to speak to the Press. After various announcements, he glanced at another piece of paper and added that it had been decided that citizens were now free to enter and leave the GDR at will 'with immediate effect'. 'Does that mean today?' asked a journalist. Schabowski shrugged his shoulders and said the fateful words, 'I suppose so'.[4]

It was the signal that all were awaiting, and the destruction of the Berlin Wall began.

In Czechoslovakia, 1989 had started with an act of police repression when a demonstration in Prague in January was broken up, and a number of dissidents, including Vaclav Havel, were arrested. Despite this inauspicious start to the year, the fever of change across the region continued to have its effect. The security police were unable, or unwilling, to prevent visits from Polish and Hungarian ex-dissidents who had by then achieved at least their freedom of movement and at best a government position. Pressure on the beleaguered party leadership mounted as GDR citizens began to arrive in great numbers, abandoning their Trabants and Wartburgs in the streets of Prague as they sought the protection of the FRG's embassy.

On 17 November, the police broke up a student demonstration with great severity. Popular reaction was massive and immediate, and on 24 November the party's leadership resigned *en bloc*. It was with a new party leadership now stripped of its monopoly of power that Civic Forum, created on the evening of 19 November, discussed future arrangements. In the closing days of 1989 Vaclav Havel was elected president.

The last of the regimes to fall was the Romanian. Here the dictatorship of Ceausescu, resting on a formidable political police – the Securitate – had prevented any oppositional movement from forming. He was engaged, during the 1980s, in using his dictatorial powers to destroy the Romanian village by relocating the villagers in industrially-built centres and pulling down their homes. It was in Transylvania, which, having a strong population of Hungarians, represented something of an Achilles heel for the governments of Bucharest, that revulsion against these policies and against Ceausescu's rule in general finally proved stronger than the oppression that the police could muster against it. Demonstrations in Timisoara on 16 December ended in bloodshed, but the spark of a more general protest had been lit. Faced by massive demonstrations in Bucharest itself, Ceausescu chose to flee the country, to be captured and, as noted, summarily tried and shot.

Legislating for change

The point has come to relate these remarkable events to the analysis of the communist power monopoly to which this volume is devoted, bearing in mind that the events of 1989 itself, however sensational, may reveal less about the nature of the monopoly than have other far less sensational developments. The conclusions that will be drawn in what follows will concentrate on those features of the monopoly in its collapse that do in fact help to illustrate its true nature and the way in which it was perceived in the bloc countries.

For the outside world, the events of 1989 and of the immediately preceding period that were mostly prominently reported and most graphically recorded were naturally those that made a visual impact – the ubiquitous demonstrations, the great trek of the East Germans, the murky trial of Ceausescu. But for those who had lived with the monopoly for the past forty and more years, these moments, great as they were, were not the essential milestones. One of them was – the breaching of the Berlin Wall. This for all the world had not only a general dramatic appeal, but a rich symbolic meaning. As concerns the power monopoly, it symbolised, of course, the end of the closed frontier and the isolation of the system. And what really registered in the popular mind in Eastern Europe was precisely such cases of the fall of the major symbols of the monopoly.

Of particular symbolic importance were, first, the rescinding of the article in the constitution that gave the communist party its privileged position; secondly, the abolition of the party's militia (sometimes termed a 'workers' militia'); thirdly, the banning of political organisation in the workplace, which was the basis of the

Leninist 'cell' mode of party operation; and fourthly, an acceptance that the intervention in Czechoslovakia in 1968 had been an error. From outside Eastern Europe some of these demands seem insubstantial when seen against the formation of the first non-communist government (in Poland on 12 September 1989), or the resignation or dismissal of a party chief, or of an entire politburo. But inside the bloc countries they were perceived as the central symbols of the monopoly – the baby, as it were, in the communist bathwater.

The clause in the constitution enshrining the party's leading role was rescinded or amended by the Hungarian Assembly on 18 October 1989, in Czechoslovakia on 29 November, in the GDR on 1 December, in Poland on 29 December and in Bulgaria on 15 January 1990. In Romania the Communist Party was for a brief period outlawed, but the relationship between the party's regional apparatus and the incoming leadership makes Romania a rather special case.

The 'workers' guard' was abolished in Hungary on 20 October and the 'Civic Military Voluntary Reserve' went next in Poland on 23 November. On 25 November the Bulgarian militia dissolved its sections concerned with 'struggle against ideological diversion'. In the GDR the party's militia, the Kampfgruppen, was disbanded in mid-December, although public attention was more drawn to the abolition on 17 December of the hated Stasi, which was strictly speaking a state police force and did not depend on the party. The Romanian Securitate – also a state police force, although it had started life as a party militia – went with the fall of Ceausescu, the Czech party militia having already been disbanded on 21 December.

Condemnation of the crushing of the Prague Spring came in Hungary and Poland on 11 August, in Bulgaria and the GDR in November, with the Czechoslovaks themselves making their statement on 1 December. Two days later the Warsaw Treaty Organisation itself made its collective Canossa.

A second aspect of the revolutionary movements leading up to 1989 in Eastern Europe that has analytical value for an understanding of the communist power monopoly is the way in which in several cases it was almost imperceptibly legislated away. It is here in particular that the momentous events of those years obscure equally, if not more, important developments. In the long battle against the monopoly's positions, a great number of legislative victories were scored which, in hindsight, can be seen as constitutive acts, qualifying the monopoly (and thus in fact marking its impending demise) and adding up, ultimately, to constitutional advances. Some of these victories were in fact own goals scored by the parties – or were at least turned into own goals against the parties by an artful dissidence. Such was the case with the signing of the Helsinki 'third basket', which concerned human rights, in 1975. However cynical or hypocritical the intentions of the ruling parties may have been in taking this step, the world was constantly to be reminded by dissident movements that a constitutional commitment had been given.

But in most cases the victories were direct, if often small, constitutional gains. The first registration of Solidarity in November 1980 was one such moment, and the long battle that it involved testifies to its historical significance. The tide of battle was to recede, and it was not until April 1990 that Solidarity was re-registered. But by that time it was only one item in a string of concessions wrung from the party in the round-table negotiations, each of which was to be legally enacted and to give the changes a constitutional status, even if, as in most cases in the region – including the Polish – it was to be a long time before the change of regime was to be enshrined in a comprehensive constitution endorsed by an elected assembly.

Thus laws acknowledging a freedom of assembly, of association and of speech little by little found their way on to statute books. For example, in January 1989 the Hungarian parliament passed a Law on the Right of Assembly (six against and 24 abstentions), another law enshrining the right to demonstrate peacefully, and a third law making an alternative military service available to conscientious objectors. But it was not only such enabling legislation that marked the advances made against the monopoly. Equally important were 'first times' of another kind, as for example when, on 8 May 1989, the first autonomous newspaper to appear since the 1940s – the *Gazeta Wyborcza*, edited by Adam Michnik – went on sale in Poland.

These piecemeal legislative acts, and the new developments based on them, were each to mark the descent of the communist power monopoly into its grave. They were to be followed, once the regimes had finally fallen, by a stream of new legislation and ordinances that prepared the way for the creation of a multi-party system and for the operation of an economy organised on market principles. Monopoly was gone, and in its place a new organisation of society was in the making, based upon the rule of law.

The Yugoslav case

In all cases where national communities have been given any constitutional acknowledgement by communist governments in Europe,
the fall of the communist power monopoly has led to a tendency for
those communities to demand complete independence. This particular effect of the monopoly's demise has brought with it the
break-up of the state – again in all cases: the Soviet Union itself,
Czechoslovakia and Yugoslavia. But whilst the break-up of
Czechoslovakia occurred in the aftermath of the change of regime, in
Yugoslavia and the Soviet Union the demands for national independence accompanied the change and to a considerable extent
influenced its course.

The extensive and enduring centralisation of the Soviet political
system meant that until Gorbachev's accession to power, the
national components of the Soviet federation had exceedingly little
freedom of action. In Yugoslavia, on the other hand, we have seen
that the League's monopoly of power had itself been federalised in a
process that started in earnest in the mid-1960s. Tito's death in May
1980 removed one of the three factors that held the Yugoslav state
together. Of the others – the LCY and the Yugoslav People's Army –
the first was to prove powerless to stem the pressures for independence that had built up during the 1980s, whilst the latter did not
intervene until the state had effectively been dismantled. By the close
of the cardinal year of 1989 the fate of the communist power
monopoly in Yugoslavia was being determined by struggles within
individual republics, and in particular in Slovenia and Croatia. In
January 1990 the history of the League of Communists of
Yugoslavia effectively came to a close when, on the fourth day of the
League's fourteenth congress, the Slovenian delegation left the hall
after a series of proposals that it favoured had been blocked by the
Serbian party and its allies.

As previous chapters have suggested, Yugoslavia therefore
presents a highly idiosyncratic case in the unravelling of the communist power monopoly in Europe. Having started earlier than in the
bloc countries of Eastern and Central Europe, the process did not
fully mature until the last of the bloc's parties had fallen from power.
After leading in the overall reform process in the region, Yugoslavia
then found itself following in its tail; and the limited nature of the
reforms previously undertaken was thereby revealed. It was the

abandoning of the economic monopoly with the move from central command planning to a 'market socialism', and the attenuated nature of the remaining monopoly in political life that enabled the LCY to establish its credentials as a socialist alternative to Soviet communist norms. An alternative it no doubt was, but such claims as it made to have abandoned entirely the monopoly characteristic of communism were belied by the story of the League's demise.

The starting-point for any account of the final collapse of the communist power monopoly in Yugoslavia must be the election of Slobodan Milosevic as president of the Serbian League of Communists in May 1986, which was followed by Serbia's removal of the party leadership in Kosovo in November 1986 and the imposition of direct rule on that constitutionally autonomous province in March 1989.

The salience of Kosovo in the story of the end of communism in Yugoslavia is quite special. Alone of the six republics that constituted Yugoslavia, Serbia has contained two autonomous provinces, Kosovo and Vojvodina. This constitutional arrangement was made to cater for the two ethnic communities, Albanian and Hungarian respectively, which had a strong presence in those areas. Kosovo, however, had always had a particular place in the Serbian collective memory. Though peripheral to contemporary Serbia, that area was the heartland of the medieval Serbian state under Stefan Dusan, and it was on 'Kosovo field' that the Serbs fell to a Turkish army in 1389. Disturbances with nationalist overtones among the Albanian population in the Kosovo university town of Pristina in 1980 had already aroused Serbian sensitivities. Now, in a Yugoslavia subjected, since Tito's death, to increasing inter-ethnic tensions, and in circumstances of an acute economic crisis, a Serbian leader was playing overtly to Serbian national feeling. The fuse to the powder keg of Yugoslavia had been lighted.

The carnage and human suffering that the break-up of Yugoslavia has caused has obscured the gentler process through which the communists in each of the Yugoslav republics were divested of their monopoly of power. Since the economic monopoly had effectively already been dismantled in the long series of reforms since 1952, what was involved was the political counterpart of those reforms.

It was in Slovenia that the assault was first made on the party's political monopoly. Slovenia was economically the most powerful of the republics. It was also the one geographically closest to the epicentre of change in Eastern Europe in the 1980s, although as long ago as 1966 Slovenia had already earned distinction as the first communist-ruled country in which a prime minister tendered his government's resignation as the result of an adverse vote in the assembly. As in the Soviet Union, but unlike any other country in Eastern Europe, the proposal that free elections be held and a system of competitive politics instituted came from within the Slovene League of Communists' leadership itself, on 11 March 1989. True, forces for reform outside the League were on hand and had been developing ever since a strong emergence in the peace movement at the close of the 1980s. These were to form an electoral coalition – the DEMOS – in opposition to the communists, this time very much in accord with what was happening elsewhere in the region, when the first free elections were held in April 1990.

Before then, however, the fateful fourteenth congress of the LCY had met and had foundered on its inability to accept a number of proposals which reiterated those that the Slovenian leadership had put forward in its own republican context. Some of these proposals concerned political rights. Citizens should no longer be prosecuted for political crimes and those imprisoned on political charges should be released. Torture should be formally abjured. Other proposals, however, went to the heart of the power monopoly, in particular one that would have legalised the formation of political parties. It was proposed also that the LCY itself be restructured and should become an association of independent parties – an 'Alliance of Leagues of Communists'.

There was a degree of support for some or all of these proposals from the delegations of Croatia, Bosnia-Hercegovina and Macedonia – an early indication of the distribution of forces when the final break-up of the Yugoslav federal state occurred, with an embattled Serbia and Montenegro facing four republics claiming, or having already by then achieved, independence. At the time, however, it was precisely on the question of splitting the League into a loose association, which would certainly put the unity of the state itself under stress, that the Slovenians were given least support. The proposals as they stood were not accepted. A watered-down version was passed which could in fact have had the effect of bringing to an end the League's monopoly of political power. But this did not satisfy the Slovenian delegation which, having already committed itself so clearly to reform, and having also, no doubt, weighed up the risks and possibilities involved in its current stance in a Europe which at that moment was in a ferment of change, walked out of the congress. The congress decided to postpone its business rather than to continue without a complete republican delegation.

The Slovenians thereupon proceeded to give effect to their own programmatic statement of 23 December 1989, 'For a European Quality of Life'. They changed the name of the party from 'League of Communists of Slovenia' to 'League of Communists of Slovenia – Party of Democratic Renewal' and adopted a new programme. Business such as the latter requires considerable preparation and the fact that the new programme was adopted at a party conference held but one week after the postponed LCY fourteenth congress is an indication of the extent to which the Slovenes were committed to forcing the pace of change.

The Croatian League shortly followed suit with a name change to 'League of Communists of Croatia – Party of Democratic Change'. Free elections were then held in April and May 1990 in Slovenia and Croatia respectively. The renamed party lost in each case, but in Slovenia the respected communist leader, Milan Kucan, who had played so energetic a role in the struggle for independence – and particularly against Serbian remonstrances and physical reprisals – was elected president. Elections held later in the year in Bosnia and Macedonia likewise brought defeat for the republican Leagues of Communists. Only in Serbia and Montenegro did the communists hold on to power, but it is important to note, first, that the Serbian League followed the example of the Slovenians and Croatians in changing its name, this time to the Socialist Party of Serbia; and, secondly, that whatever form of government emerged in Serbia as it settled into a new role among European nations it would not reproduce the monopoly of the communist days as it has been described in these pages.

It remains to record that at the end of May 1990 the suspended fourteenth congress of the LCY was reconvened and met without the presence of Slovenian, Croatian and Macedonian delegations. It was this rump that, in a brief three-hour meeting, brought down the curtain on the LCY's power monopoly. It endorsed the principle of competitive elections; and it finally renounced the League's leading role. The game of hide and seek which the LCY had been playing since 1952 was over.

Notes

1 *Le Monde*, 27 May 1987; Radio Free Europe: *Background Report* (Eastern Europe)/129, 4 July 1987.
2 RFE: *Czechoslovak Situation Report*/4, 6 April and 26 June 1987.
3 Timothy Garton Ash, 'Eastern Europe: The Year of Truth', *New York Review of Books*, 15 Feb. 1990. Without this, he believes, 'it is doubtful that there would have been a Solidarity'.
4 Jens Reich, 'Reflections on Becoming an East German Dissident, on Losing the Wall and a Country', in Gwyn Prins (ed.) *Spring in Winter* (Manchester University Press, 1990), p. 81.

Further reading

Judy Batt, *East Central Europe from Reform to Transformation* (London: Pinter/RIIA, 1991).
J. F. Brown, *Surges to Freedom* Durham, NC: Duke University Press, 1991).
Karen Dawisha, *Eastern Europe, Gorbachev and Reform* (Cambridge: Cambridge University Press, 2nd ed. 1988).
Mark Frankland, *The Patriots' Revolution* (London: Sinclair-Stevenson, 1990).
Timothy Garton Ash, *We the People: The Revolutions of 1989* (Cambridge: Granta, 1990).
Charles Gati, *The Bloc that Failed: Soviet and East European Relations in Transition* (Bloomington, IN: Indiana University Press, 1990).
Paul G. Lewis (ed.), *Eastern Europe: Political Crisis and Legitimation* (London: Croom Helm, 1984).
Bill Lomax, 'Hungary from Kadarism to Democracy: The Successful Failure of Reform Communism', in D. W. Spring (ed.), *The Impact of Gorbachev: The First Phase, 1985–90* (London: Pinter, 1991).
Jadwiga Staniszkis, *The Dynamics of the Breakthrough in Eastern Europe: The Polish Experience* (Cambridge: Cambridge University Press, 1992).
Vladimir Tismaneanu, *In Search of Civil Society: Independent Peace Movements in the Soviet Bloc* (London: Routledge, 1990).

10

The monopoly's final demise

The overall rhythm of the implosion of the communist power mono-poly should now be clear. The cardinal year in which the process culminated was 1989. In that year the communist parties of Eastern Europe surrendered their monopoly of power, or were effectively driven from it. By then the process that would end with the break-up of Yugoslavia was well engaged. At the end of that year only Albania remained untouched by the storm of change.

Change in the Soviet Union, on which change in the other countries really depended, though cataclysmic in its scale, was much more extended in its incidence. Only gradually did the revolutionary surge develop after Gorbachev's arrival in power in 1985. But here, too, 1989 was to be the cardinal year, and the crucial turning-point was the holding of the first free elections in the USSR since the Constituent Assembly was sent packing by the Bolsheviks in 1917. But whilst the political monopoly was effectively at an end in the USSR by the end of 1989, reform of the economy was to drag on, offering another point of contrast with Eastern Europe where imme-diate moves were taken after the fall of communist power to move towards a market economy. Even in the political sphere, where developments built up to a high point in 1989, that climax has to be seen as spread over the last half of 1988 and into 1990. Indeed it was not until the failed coup of August 1991 that the power monopoly could be said to have been decisively dismantled. What took from 1985 until 1991 to take place in the Soviet Union happened in the space of a few months in, for example, Czechoslovakia and Bulgaria.

By the time of the CPSU's nineteenth conference in June 1988 Gorbachev's anxiety to make his changes irreversible appeared to be bearing fruit. Of those developments that were to take place in the ensuing two years and which concern the power monopoly itself, it is worth selecting for particular attention the moves towards establishing a constitutional order; the holding of contested elections and the inauguration of free and open parliamentary debate; the break-up of the multinational Union; and the continuing difficulties in reforming the industrial economy.

Establishing a constitutional order

The discussions held at the CPSU's nineteenth conference of mid-1988 led, during the remainder of 1988 and 1989, to the passing of a series of laws and constitutional amendments. Given that the Soviet Union was already equipped with a constitution and a fully articulated legal system, this new spurt of legislation calls for comment.

The monopoly of power that the communist party enjoyed meant that a constitution could say what the power-holders wished it to say without it being incumbent on them to abide by the letter of that constitution. Behind all the detailed provisions allowing for the Union's constituent republics to secede, should they wish, lay the raw facts that they would not be permitted to do so, and that an explanation could always be given in terms of the party's ideology and protected against challenge through the party's control of communications. Secession, yes, provided that it did not put the 'gains of socialism' at risk.

What was totally new in the changed circumstances was that the spate of legislation from 1986 onwards was no longer being put out in a void. There was a commitment by public authority – soon to be invested with a legitimacy drawn from an open electoral system – to abide by new rules, whilst the open atmosphere created by glasnost meant that public support for them, and condemnation of enfringements, would be expressed. True, there was no guarantee that the new arrangements would last, although it was Gorbachev's proclaimed intention to make them irreversible. The forces that opposed change were powerful. The political activity that the reforms invited gave no great promise of an orderly transition to a form of democratic politics. But if the future was obscure, the past in certain crucial respects had been left behind. Monopoly hedged about with acknowledged restrictions on its operation is no longer monopoly.

A good illustration of the change that was taking place is provided by the constitutional amendments that were presented to the Supreme Soviet in December 1988, containing the measures that had been discussed at the CPSU's conference of June–July. These measures included a revision of the status of the constituent republics of the Union. Whereas, for example, the 1977 constitution had given the federal centre determination of 'the composition of the USSR [and] the ratification of the constitution of new republics and autonomous republics', the new provisions removed the centre's ratification prerogative and gave it 'unique powers' simply in 'questions of the national and state structure affecting the competence of the Union' (Article 108). This, and other provisions in the proposed amendments, were obviously intended to reduce the powers of the federal centre. They were none the less vigorously contested, in particular by the Baltic republics' representatives. In an earlier day, there was little point in contesting the provisions of a constitution which the ruling party in any case ignored. Now that a real constitutional process was in progress, even a reduction of the centre's powers was worth fighting over.

The constitutional amendments presented to the Supreme Soviet in December 1988 ranged wide and included measures that were to transform the Soviet political system. Resolutions on legal reform brought in a new electoral law and set up the new representative machinery referred to in an earlier chapter – the 2250-member Congress of People's Deputies, which was to form from within itself a new Supreme Soviet composed of full-time parliamentarians. A Constitutional Review Committee was also created. A separation of executive and legislative functions was ensured by forbidding deputies to soviets hold executive positions.

Both before and after this high point in the constitutive process, a flood of legislation was being passed regulating almost every aspect of political and economic life. The passing of laws permitting and regulating co-operatives and the leasing of property was noted above. Further economic legislation catered for joint ventures with foreign firms. The pace of this legislative activity quickened when the new Congress of People's Deputies was in place from the summer of 1989. Of obvious relevance to the destruction of the power monopoly was a press law. It was a mark of the sensitivity of this issue – and also of its importance – that it was not until August 1990 that this law 'On the press and other media of mass information' came into effect. The 1990 law brought to an end the party's monopoly control over information by expressly removing the media from the party's purview. Censorship was legislated away, apart from safeguards for state security and the protection of the rights of individuals. Restrictions on the publication of newspapers or journals with print-runs of less than 1000 copies were eased, and a requirement that publications had to be registered with specified public authorities likewise now did not apply to those with small circulations. Article 33 of the law guaranteed a right of access to 'information from foreign sources, including direct television broadcasting, radio and the press'.

This fell some distance short of full freedom of the press. Moreover those who set out to print independent newspapers had a formidable problem on their hands, given the difficulties of acquiring the newsprint and other materials, let alone printing presses. But the law eliminated important political disabilities, and marked an important turning-point in the dismantling of the power monopoly. The party's supervision of the means of communication and its attempts to isolate Soviet citizens from influences coming from abroad, was formally abandoned. Moreover, its ability to persecute people for political offences was restricted by a new criminal code, the draft of which was presented to the Supreme Soviet in 1989. This brought to an end the application of the two 'anti-dissenter' articles of the 1961 penal code. These two measures between them – the superseding in 1989 of Articles 70 and 190-1 of the 1961 code (which penalised 'anti-Soviet agitation and propaganda' and 'diffusion of anti-Soviet slander' respectively) and the press law of 1990 – had the effect of removing the 'dissenter' from the political scene.

But this is to run ahead. By the time of these last enactments the communist power monopoly in the Soviet Union had been given its terminal blow in the elections to the Congress of People's Deputies in the spring of 1989, and the historic first session of that body in the summer.

The 1989 elections and the first session of the Congress of People's Deputies

The Law on Elections of December 1988 had provided for a nomination process which itself departed significantly from the traditional practice. Then, candidates had to be nominated by a 'social organisation', which meant in effect that the party organised the selection of the single name that would appear on the ballot paper. Now, a meeting of 500 or more residents in a district was competent to nominate candidates, adoption being by a vote of more than 50 per cent of those present. Moreover, no limit was set on the number of candidates to be proposed. Such meetings were duly held between 26 December 1988 and 24 January 1989, and were followed by a round of pre-election meetings during the ensuing month. This reduced the number of candidates, but when the full campaign period started at the end of February 2,895 candidates were left contesting 1,500 seats. Half of these seats, it will be recalled, were allocated on a territorial basis and half on a nationality basis. The distinction had important effects. Moscow, for example, was divided into numerous territorial constituencies; but it was only entitled to one of the 32 national seats allotted to the whole of the Russian Soviet Federated Socialist Republic. The winner of this latter seat would have a special status as Moscow's chosen son or daughter (in the event a son – Boris Yeltsin, who had been dropped from the Politburo the previous year for his radical stance, and now rode back into the limelight endorsed by a popular election in no mean constituency).

Nominations for the remaining 750 of the 2,250 seats – those reserved for the 'social organisations' – were arranged by those bodies, but even here 880 candidates contested the 750 seats.

Election day was 26 March. To be elected, a candidate had to receive 50 per cent or more of the votes. This meant that even an unopposed candidate might fail to be elected – as befell Yuri Solovev, chief of the Leningrad party organisation and a candidate member of the Politburo – and it also led to a complex series of run-off elections, which were completed by 21 May. In the final result, over 30 further party officials who stood unopposed failed to secure election, whilst a number of well-known radicals, including Andrei Sakharov and Tatyana Zaslavskaya, were given mandates.

The result of the party's power monopoly having been banished from the electoral arena was that, when the old Supreme Soviet elected in 1984 was compared with the new Congress, the percentage of women deputies had dropped from 32 to 17, and that of workers from 16 to 11. On the other hand the percentage of party members had risen from 71 to 87. For better or worse, in the selection of their representatives, the people had spoken. Now it was the turn of the elected deputies to speak.

The debates of the Congress, which were televised live, had a clearly cathartic character appropriate to such a dramatic moment.

Soviet citizens watched and listened enthralled as a proposal was made that Lenin be removed from his mausoleum, another that Solzhenitsyn's Soviet nationality be restored to him, yet another that the KGB be reduced in size and moved out of its headquarters of evil memory in the Lubyanka. The fact that most such proposals had no sequel is of less historical importance than the impact created by the possibility of their being made in the parliament of the land. The Congress failed to pass the more structured measures of reform that radical deputies – among them Andrei Sakharov, who had been brought back in 1986 from his exile in Gorky in one of Gorbachev's earliest moves – proposed to the Congress. But an important corner had none the less been turned.

The Congress duly elected a Supreme Soviet, which was to meet for two sessions of three or four months each year. It was equipped with standing committees holding considerable powers. This virtually full-time Supreme Soviet was a key component of the Gorbachev institutional reforms, one of the chief thrusts of which was to transfer power from the communist party to the soviets. It remained, none the less, a bastion of communist power because of the communist party's continuing, if reduced, control of the electoral process. Another important component of the Gorbachev institutional reforms was the creation of an executive presidency, the decision being enacted in 1990 and Gorbachev himself being sworn in as first incumbent of the post on 15 March of that year.

One of the more tense moments in the debates of the first session of the Congress of People's Deputies took place on 8 June, when a substantial number of the representatives from the Baltic states walked out in protest over the election of the Constitutional Review Committee that the constitutional amendments passed in December 1988 had provided for. Their fear was that the Committee, as constituted, would restrict the independence which the reform process was placing within their grasp. This was but one manifestation of national tensions which, visible already in the period to mid-1988, became rampant in this later period.

Towards the dissolution of the union

Chafing under Soviet rule ever since their incorporation into the Soviet Union in 1940, the three Baltic states of Estonia, Latvia and

Lithuania were quick to seize the opportunities apparently offered to them by Gorbachev's policies. During September and October 1988 'popular fronts' were set up in each of these republics, the Estonian newspaper *Voice of the People* publishing at this time the secret protocol of the 1939 treaty between the Soviet Union and Germany, which gave the former *carte blanche* to annex what since the Russian revolution had been three independent states. Estonia and Lithuania followed this up by setting in motion procedures to make Estonian and Lithuanian the national languages in their respective territories. In one sense a simple move to defend national cultures that had been under threat, this proposal had a deeper intent. All three Baltic republics contained sizeable Russian minorities (reaching to some 33 per cent of the total population in the Latvian case), and this early measure was but the first step in a policy of imposing disabilities on non-nationals, the main fruits of which were to ripen long after independence had been won.

In mid-November 1988 the Estonian Supreme Soviet threw down its strongest challenge to date, resolving that its laws had supremacy over laws passed by the federal centre. This was rejected by Moscow, and the struggle began that was to end in separation from the Union. In this test of the sincerity and full intent of the policies of perestroika Moscow could only apply economic sanctions, augmented in early 1991 by covert military operations in Riga and Vilnius. By the end of that year the independence of all three republics had been acknowledged.

By this time the future of the Union was clearly in doubt, with one republic after another declaring its independence. Any attempt to prevent a total degeneration of the position could now only pass through some form of voluntary association. To this task Gorbachev now applied himself, presenting to the Congress of People's Deputies in December 1990 a 'Union Treaty', in the hope (but in some cases, notably in Central Asia, the expectation) that there were sufficient economic and political grounds for the creation of a union of a new kind. The name that he proposed for this – the 'Union of Soviet Sovereign Republics' – retained the familiar initials USSR, but replaced the term 'socialist'.

Events, however, were to continue to evolve. The final act of the drama, coming after the failed coup of 19 August 1991, must be left to be recorded when an epilogue is presented at the close of this chapter. But epilogue it was. The story of the dissolution of the Soviet

Union follows the collapse of the power monopoly and strictly speaking has no place in this record. Once the Baltic states had thrown down the challenge and formed autonomous popular fronts, and once that action had been accepted by the central power-holders, the power monopoly had, as in so many other spheres by that time, been undermined.

It retained enough strength, however, to act out one remarkable scene in which it provided an illustration, in its closing months, of the nature of the power that it had once wielded. At the height of the tension in the Baltic republics, as 1990 turned into 1991, when the Union was faced with the loss of three republics and the risk of further dominoes falling, Gorbachev chose not to use the overt force of the Soviet state in bringing the Lithuanians to order. Limited force was used in an indirect way, and economic sanctions were applied. Whatever applying economic sanctions might mean in other circumstances, here it involved simply turning off the supply of oil, and the economic monopoly was still strong enough to give Moscow control of the supply. The Lithuanians could not turn to an alternative supplier on an internal market, for there was none. True, they had ways and means to survive the measure, but the sight on the world's television screens of a Lithuanian prime minister scouring the outside world for an alternative supply was a graphic testimonial to the force of the communist power monopoly, even in its declining phase.

That same event, however, reveals the wide difference in the rhythms at which the power monopoly unravelled in the political and the economic spheres. If in the area of relations between Moscow and the Union's constituent nationalities it moved at break-neck speed, developments in the economy went at a far more leisurely pace.

Sluggish change in the economy

The contrast between the rapid forward movement of change in political life on the one hand, and the slow rate of reform in the industrial heart of the Soviet economy was striking, and at no point more so than in 1989. Whilst Soviet citizens were missing work in their thousands to watch on television the hitherto unknown spectacle of free and highly critical debate in the Congress of People's Deputies, whilst 'informal' associations with political and a host of other aims were now well entrenched and developing their activities, and whilst very many wide-circulation newspapers and magazines were critically going over Soviet history and equally critically reviewing the political progress of the reform programme, attempts to reform the economic system were in the doldrums. True, rapid progress had been made at the more flexible periphery of economic life, with the policies of encouraging co-operatives and the leasing of land and enterprises. This in itself spelled an effective end of the economic monopoly, and was a direct counterpart of the abandoning of the party's monopoly in political life. But radical change in the industrial system, for a number of reasons, eluded the reformers.

It will be recalled that the initial call for a reconstruction of the economic system, which was what perestroika was claimed to be about, resulted in the drafting and passing of a Law on the State Enterprise. The provisions of that law made clear the path that the reforming leadership intended to tread. It soon became clear, however, not only that the actors within the industrial system were being slow in responding to the new requirements, but also that the central policy-makers were jibbing at the task of applying wholeheartedly some of the reforms that all acknowledged were generally deemed necessary. There developed a trial of strength between reformers and moderates with theoretical economists foremost among the former, and spokesmen of the industrial complex most prominent among the latter.

By the end of 1989 little concrete had been achieved in moving away from what were now acknowledged to be major faults in the system of central command planning – the tendency for deliveries to the state to dominate over contractual or market relations between enterprises; the fact that prices remained to a great extent centrally determined and did not reflect scarcity; and the ability of insolvent firms to stay in business through support from the exchequer. For example, a reform package proposed by Gorbachev's economic adviser Leonid Abalkin in November 1989, which would have abolished central command planning and freed prices, met opposition from the Chairman of the Council of Ministers, Nikolai Ryzhkov, who was speaking clearly for the industrial establishment.

Further proposals by Abalkin in March 1990 were again countered by Ryzhkov, whose own scheme on this occasion conceded that price rises were necessary to end the distortions caused by subsidies, but insisted on the retention, at least during the transitional phase, of the planning mechanisms. The rejection of his proposals by the Supreme Soviet on 14 June 1990 was a severe blow to Ryzhkov, and served to heighten considerably the tensions among all the actors involved in the debate over economic strategy. It was in June 1990 also that Stanlislav Shatalin, who at that point was acting as adviser to the president of the Russian republic, Boris Yeltsin, made his '500-day' proposal, which set out a programme for a resolution of the problem of economic reform through a form of shock therapy.

The confusion by the middle of 1990 was indeed complete. As leader of the Russian republic Yeltsin was by that time locked in personal rivalry with Gorbachev, and that rivalry involved also their respective economic advisers. Meanwhile other republican leaderships, discerning threats to their growing independence in any proposals emanating from the centre, were adopting their own positions. An attempt by Gorbachev and Yeltsin to work together in applying the Shatalin measures met with an uncooperative Ryzhkov, who presented a plan of his own. After a confused summer, in which he had called upon one of his first advisers, Abel Aganbegyan, to draft yet a third scheme, Gorbachev on 16 October produced a compromise programme.

This 'stabilisation programme' pleased no one. It was intended as a gesture towards the anxieties of the industrial establishment, who at least were accorded the benefit of a further delay in the move towards the market. The tensions of the time, however, claimed an important victim when Ryzhkov suffered a heart attack in December. In March 1991 Gorbachev grasped the nettle, raising retail prices by 60 per cent, with compensation of 85 per cent to consumers to cushion the shock. It was a first major step in the direction of ending subsidies, though it fell well short of a liberation of prices (when that came they were to rise 480 per cent in January and February 1992 in Russia).

By mid-1991 the planning system was in full disarray without any clear new pattern having been imposed. The result was a proliferation of organisational forms in the economy, from informal 'associations' – some of them of doubtful legality – to joint stock companies. A law of June 1990 had regulated the latter, the Kama lorry factory making history as the first example. By 1991, too, the institutions were beginning to appear without which the move towards a market economy could not proceed – a commercial banking system, credit institutions and commodity exchanges, for example. But these provisions take us beyond the scope of this book. They are part of the new world that was taking over from a by then defunct monopoly. It remains now to record the final stages of the decomposition of the power monopoly at the heart of the political system – the Communist Party of the Soviet Union.

The crisis in the party

The opposition to his policies from within the structures of the party during the preparation of the January 1987 Central Committee plenum – which, it will be recalled, had been postponed until the latest date allowed by the party statutes because of the mounting tensions – only served to drive Gorbachev towards deeper changes. This had the effect of creating an increasingly anxious *fronde* within the party which for the most part worked behind the scenes, taking advantage of Gorbachev's frequent absences from Moscow to mount provocative actions (as with the campaign against the Baltic separatists in the summer of 1989), or to persuade the editor of some amenable publication to print an attack on Gorbachev and his policies. One such attack appeared on 13 March 1988 in the pages of the conservative *Sovetskaya Rossiya*. The article, entitled 'I Cannot Abandon my Principles' was from the pen of a Leningrad chemistry teacher named Nina Andreeva. In it Andreeva expressed the indignation of those whose world was being undermined by the reforms and by the questioning of the historical role of Lenin and Stalin. It was the voice of Russian nationalism, with scarcely veiled anti-semitic tones.

The immediate sequel to the letter illustrated the sense of Gorbachev's constantly repeated theme that the momentum of the reforms must be kept up so as to make them irreversible. Far from raising a storm of protest, the letter was met with silence on the part of the reform camp. The dark manoeuvring behind the publication of the letter and the suspicion that the more powerful figures of the conservative opposition, such as Yegor Ligachev, had chosen a moment of Gorbachev's absence to reverse him served, at that stage of the reform process, to produce an effect of caution and fear, rather than to stir the champions of change to confrontation with forces whose power they were so accustomed to respecting. Gorbachev had every reason for forcing the issue with an open discussion in the party, which took place, as noted, at the nineteenth conference of the

CPSU, convened for the end of June 1988 – that is, three months after the publication of the Andreeva letter.

In the tradition of the communist power monopoly, unity and cohesion within the party were taken to be the guarantee of the party's ability to influence the life of society as a whole. This was as true for the non-ruling parties as for the ruling. In the former case, the vitality of militancy in society was seen as depending upon a renunciation of militancy within the party, and indeed when the Eurocommunist parties loosened their internal organisational norms, their militancy in society sagged. In the latter case, the party's leading role and its capacity to govern was likewise seen as depending on the monolithic unity of the party at the heart of the political system. The end of the communist power monopoly in the Soviet Union came when that internal unity of the party was undermined.

The turning-point came with the CSPU's conference in mid-1988. The path leading up to it was first laid, as noted, by Gorbachev's determination to press on with his reforms against obdurate opposition within the party which was manifest already at the Central Committee's plenum of January 1987. The 1988 conference did not result immediately in organised divisions within the party, but it opened discussions that were to bury the party's obsession with unity and with a sense of its unique mission. In the record of the conference we find, for example, the economist Abalkin arguing that the single-party system acts as a brake on democratisation; and whilst this was not an express call for the accommodation of differing tendencies within the party, the challenge that it threw down to the party's role in society was bound to feed back on to the party's ability to tolerate competition in its own ranks. This was precisely the course that events were to follow during the following three years.

The conference adopted the measures that were to prove a crucial milestone on the road to the final collapse of the party's monopoly power. It was seen above that in particular it provided for the holding of free elections for the bulk of the seats in the Congress of People's Deputies. Between the conference and the actual holding of the elections in the following year, two major events took place within the party, one carrying forward the drive for change, the other reflecting the impact of change on the party's organisational core – the apparatus.

It was disappointment among radicals in the party at the slow pace of change that led to the creation in January 1989 of the Democratic

Platform, whose spokesmen called expressly for the acceptance of organised tendencies within the party. Its programme went so far as to propose that the party undergo a two-stage process of transformation, and that the first stage should actually comprise the formation of fractions, which would restore the party's internal health. This would pave the way for the second stage, in which the party, attuned now to the exigencies of competitive politics, would enter the lists as one party among many.

In the great trek backwards through history that perestroika involved, calling into question one by one the developments which had set up the monopoly, the reformers had returned to 1921, when the ban on fractions was brought in at the Bolsheviks' tenth congress. The ban was not expressly repealed. But people now acted as if it no longer applied, nor should apply.

The second development took place in December 1988 when a major organisational upheaval saw the abolition of the secretariat at the heart of the party's apparatus and its replacement with six commissions, each with a broad brief covering respectively party affairs and personnel, ideology, social and economic affairs, agricultural affairs, foreign policy, and legal affairs. This was a quite considerable reorganisation. The old secretariat had contained twenty departments; now, under the new umbrella of the commissions, that number was progressively whittled down to nine. The party was responding to the reduction in the role of the apparatus that the policies associated with perestroika required. But at the same time, as long as it remained in being, the party's core could not abandon its interests as an organisation. The reorganisation of December 1988 reflected, in fact, a cautious retrenchment, which was made evident by the nomination of some of the party's more orthodox leaders to the top posts at the head of the various commissions – Ligachev in agriculture, for example, and Viktor Chebrikov, who had headed the KGB from 1982, as head of the commission for legal affairs. Whilst it was as the party's leader that Gorbachev had launched the process of change, whilst he defended it against the conservatives in the party, and whilst he presided, in fact, over the dismantling of the power monopoly as such, it was clear that in his thinking and that of those close to him at that time the organisational heart of the party should not be put at risk.

In the spring of 1989 the elections provided for at the nineteenth conference were held, with the results noted above. The corner had been turned. Unprotected by the party's traditional control over the electoral process, several of the party's leading secretaries in the regions failed to secure election. It was evidence – and evidence was still at that point needed – that the party was vulnerable, and local party leaders found their record being opened for assessment in the press and on the television screen. The protection of the *nomenklatura* process having thus been withdrawn from the party's own officials in the electoral field, it was withdrawn also from state officials at the level of ministers and ambassadors when, on 25 May 1989, Gorbachev announced that commissions of the Supreme Soviet were to examine candidates for such posts. The mechanisms that supported the power monopoly had by now been thoroughly undermined. The scene was set for the final symbolic act to consecrate its demise.

On 9 January 1990, the Supreme Soviet of Lithuania voted to amend the article in the republic's constitution that enshrined the communist party's privileged role in the political system, the Lithuanian Communist Party having split from the CPSU in December 1989. By now the status of Article 6 in the Union's own constitution was under pressure. A plenary session of the CPSU's Central Committee, held on 7 February 1990, voted, on Gorbachev's proposal, to recommend that the article giving the communist party's monopoly of power constitutional status be amended. At an extraordinary session of the Congress of People's Deputies on 13 March 1990 the amendment was passed. The new text stated that

The Communist Party of the Soviet Union and other political parties, as well as trade union, youth and other social organisations and mass movements, participate in the formulation of the policy of the Soviet state and in the administration of the state and social affairs through their representatives elected to the soviets of people's deputies and in other ways.

The mention of 'political parties' in this text lay down the constitutional basis for a multi-party system.

A further highly symbolic moment came in the following year, and in an historical sense completed the amending of Article 6 of the constitution. On 20 July 1991 Boris Yeltsin, as president of the Russian federation, banned political activity in state-owned workplaces. That most characteristic feature of communist organisation had outlived the monopoly itself by a year and four months.

In this way the communist power monopoly in the Soviet Union, after seven decades of existence, was consigned – to use the phrase that Trotsky employed those seventy years earlier with reference to the Mensheviks at the time of the monopoly's creation – to the dustbin of history.

The party went on to hold its twenty-eighth congress in July 1990. In advance of it two 'platforms' independent of the official one had been published. The vigorous debate that had characterised the nineteenth conference marked also what was to be the CPSU's final congress. But already the reports from the congress were relegated to a place in television news coverage after items which often took the party to task for the country's present plight. At the close of the congress a number of radical figures, including Boris Yeltsin, demonstratively left the party.

As yet another sign of the party's increasing weakness, the Politburo was restructured. Greatly increased in size so as to give it wider representation in the Union as a whole, but by that same token losing its character as a cabinet of the key power-holders in the system, its role was clearly reduced to a shadow of what it had been. But it was not destined to live long in that or in any other form.

Epilogue

A period of seventeen months separates the amendment of Article 6 from the failed coup of August 1991, when an attempt to turn back the tide of change was itself checked. On 19 August the world was informed that a State Emergency Committee had been formed under the apparent leadership of Gennadii Yanaev, the USSR's vice-president and involving the prime minister Pavlov, the defence minister Ustinov and the KGB chief Kryuchkov. Political parties that did not support the emergency measures were banned, as were all but a few of the major newspapers.

The inability of the coup's leaders to impose the coercive power with which their various state roles appeared to invest them (or their simple lack of nerve), together with the immediate response of a population that was now prepared to stand up for what it had gained over the past few years, and that found its leader of the hour in Boris Yeltsin, led to the swift disintegration of the Emergency Committee. On 21 August the coup collapsed. The CPSU itself could now no longer survive. On 24 August Gorbachev resigned as General Secretary of the discredited party, recommending that the Central Committee dissolve itself. In November Boris Yeltsin banned the party altogether in the Russian federation, one month before the Soviet Union itself met its end. With the failure of the putsch of August 1991, the bathwater of the communist party was thrown out with the baby of the power monopoly.

The end of the Soviet Union itself was to follow shortly. On 24 August the Ukraine declared its independence, the other non-Russian republics of the Union following suit by the year's end. Before then, however, a series of negotiations between all the republics except Georgia and the three Baltic republics had taken place with a view to finding a generally acceptable form of association to take them into the future. On 8 December, in Minsk, the three Slav republics of Russia, Byelorussia and the Ukraine met and signed an agreement, the preamble of which stated:

We, the Republic of Byelorussia, the Russian Federation (RSFSR), and Ukraine, as founder states of the USSR who signed the Union treaty of 1922, designated below as the High Contracting Parties, state that the USSR as a subject of international law and a geopolitical reality, is ceasing to exist.

Then, on 21 December 1991, in the Kazakhstan capital of Alma Ata, a further agreement was signed by Russia, Ukraine, Byelorussia, Armenia, Azerbaidzhan, Moldavia and the five Central Asian republics, founding a Commonwealth of Independent States with this broadened membership. Mikhail Gorbachev who, as General Secretary of a Communist Party of the Soviet Union, had launched the process of reform which led to these results, resigned as president of the Union on 25 December. The revolution of 1917, carried forward seventy years later into a new phase which had picked up so many of the themes of the early Soviet years, had devoured a latter-day victim. On 26 December the Supreme Soviet formally resolved that the treaty of union of 1922 was no longer valid.

Conclusion

From communal loyalty to sectional interests

This study of the communist power monopoly has included an account of the weaknesses from which it suffered, and has suggested reasons for the abruptness of the collapse of communism at the end of the 1980s. Structural inflexibility and a capacity to conceal its accumulating effects gave the monopoly an air of durability that turned out to be false. To that extent the monopoly's weaknesses and the abruptness of its fall are interconnected. Additionally, in Eastern Europe the monopoly was only likely to last as long as it was supported by Soviet power. Collapse of the monopoly in the Soviet Union therefore meant collapse across the region, and a particularly abrupt change in the Eastern European countries.

In the circumstances, no new form of political and economic organisation could be expected to grow up within the womb of the monopoly. Change, when it came, was ordained from above, but it was not accompanied by a blueprint for the future. Yet the change that was called for was bound to be radical and to involve an overhaul of both economic and political structures and practices. Catering for the new circumstances therefore had the ring of revolutionary change, and inevitably the new arrangements provided a strong contrast with what had gone before. This very contrast threw the contours of what was being replaced into a fresh and sharper relief.

At the same time, as at any moment of significant political and social change, there were bound to be contradictions between the old and the new, and proponents of a new order have had to contend with strong countervailing factors. The move towards the market has been universal, but the speed at which that policy could be pursued has varied extensively. The commitment to greater democracy has been similarly universal, but the extent to which it has yielded a convincing pluralism again has varied considerably. What can be said with as much certainty as human affairs allow is that the monopoly of power characteristic of the communist order has been set aside. In both the Soviet Union and its erstwhile client states, therefore, the analyst is faced with a rupture in political and economic processes created by the monopoly's departure and by a contrast between the monopoly and what has been put in its place, even if the magnitude of that contrast has varied, and however powerful the lingering after-effects of the communist order.

Space does not allow a full treatment of the detail of what has replaced the power monopoly in the former Soviet Union and the various countries of the Soviet bloc, all of which lacked the mechanisms that would facilitate exchange, which are so much part of the furniture of economic life in Western societies, but which were absent from the centrally planned economies. Even where they had existed in parts of Eastern Europe before the communist period, during which the external world had seen revolutionary changes in communications and in business and management techniques, a lacuna of over forty years had to be made good. A banking system, money markets and stock exchanges all had to be brought into being. There was a human problem associated with this; the people who were to run these new institutions – at all levels, and not merely the most exalted – had to be trained: brokers and bankers, accountants, business lawyers, professionals for independent media, for advertising and for marketing, and estate agents.

For an account of such problems – and of the various means that have been adopted for transferring property from the state to the private sector – the reader must look elsewhere. This brief final section will deal with a broader aspect of the change which illustrates retrospectively certain important facets of the communist power monopoly. It concerns the implications of a move from political monopoly to the rule of law, and the associated shift in the basis of social relations from communal values to individual and sectional interests.

The many new ordinances and legislative acts that anticipated or attended the change of regime and hastened its denouement, revealed, for example, the extent to which the communist power monopoly, in its functioning and ideological underpinnings, was incompatible with the rule of law. That is to say, it could not be a matter of introducing the rule of law, or elements of it, into the power monopoly. It was a case of one or the other. This was a severely practical matter. To release market forces without a legal framework to regulate exchange and juridical relations between corporate and individual persons meant courting anarchy in economic life, with dangerous implications for political life as well.

It surprised many that the turn from monopoly and state control to the market involved increased regulation. But in fact it is only non-monopolistic economic activities that require regulation, since they involve multiple autonomous agents whose interactions make up the common good. Those interactions must therefore be given a framework. Regulation, that is, belongs to the market, where it can be applied in severe or weak doses. Monopoly, on the other hand, has no need of regulation; by definition it commands its own field of operation. It can give itself laws, but they will not be laws regulating relations between persons and corporate bodies as autonomous entities.

In this regard, there was always a fundamental difference between Soviet and Western law which was well brought out by Harold Berman in a treatment of *Justice in Russia* dating from as long ago as 1950. Berman devoted an entire section of his book to what he termed 'parental law'. A consideration of this idea reveals that it has much in common with the presentation of the communist power monopoly as 'patrimonial', which was offered in the second chapter of this study.

Berman puts himself in the shoes of an American lawyer visiting Moscow and confronting the Soviet legal system. First, 'our American lawyer in Moscow would be shocked at the extent to which illegal and extralegal activity is still accepted as normal'.[1] Pointing out that the Soviet state was 'not bound by public opinion; it may bow to it, but it is not bound by it', Berman writes that

the subject of law, legal man, is treated less as an independent possessor of rights and duties, who knows what he wants, than as a dependent member of the collective group, a youth, whom the law must not only protect against the consequences of his own ignorance but must also guide and train and discipline.[2]

What, then, in this view, is the relationship between the power monopoly and the law?

The legal system, as the established public order, must compete for sovereignty with the Party. The state rests on the pillar of Party as well as on the pillar of Law – and thirdly, it rests on the pillar of Plan. There has been an attempt to legalise Party and Plan; but Law is still a junior member of this trinity.

That is, the power monopoly, economic and political, used the law for purposes germane to its goals and to its view of its role in society. True, the law provided a stable and regular framework for state action, and the state and its officials were bound by the parent-child relationship, just as the people, too, were bound by it. But the role of the law did not include regulating relationships between groups, organisations and individuals as legal persons, in their social, political and economic dealings with each other. It is in this sense that the removal of the monopoly is to be construed as calling for regulation, rather than constituting a move towards deregulation.

Law, however, as Berman's presentation of Soviet law brings out exceptionally clearly, is a cultural matter, and this in turn suggests that sensitivity must be exercised in analysing the passage from the communist power monopoly to a system of law on the Western European or North American model. The aim in this book has been to show how a single particular pattern of economic and political thought and action operated in a number of countries under the dominant influence of the Soviet Union. Given the diversity of the countries involved, to what extent must the communist power monopoly itself be seen in cultural terms as a set of values to which the populations of these societies had become habituated, rather than simply a set of economic and political mechanisms?

This brief concluding chapter cannot hope to support the burden of a full discussion of this question, to which a considerable discussion has been devoted in the literature on communism.[3] Partial answers have been suggested in this text, prominent among them the resistance in the East European countries to the imposition of what was perceived as an alien model. Certain other considerations may now be added that must contribute to any full answer.

First, the influence of the Soviet Union has been so massive in the story of communism that it is only to be expected that values developed in Soviet society since the Russian revolution should have played a determinant role in shaping the communist power monopoly. The monopoly was at home in the Soviet Union in the sense of deriving from Soviet – ultimately Russian – ways of thinking about social relations and from Soviet reactions to the turbulent events of the revolution and of its sequel, whilst by the same token it has been to varying degrees alien to the cultures of other societies. Obviously this consideration is of crucial importance, since it can be expected to affect the speed and thoroughness with which a given society has rejected the power monopoly. Soviet influence has none the less been sufficiently strong to ensure that the values and attitudes associated with the communist power monopoly were at least to some extent internalised by the citizens of the Soviet Union's client states. Culture cannot, in any case, be detached from political and economic mechanisms; these form part of the amalgam that composes a culture. Albeit the communist power monopoly was wished on the societies of Eastern Europe from without, it could not be expected, departing, to have left no trace. And in fact the traces that it left have been substantial.

A second consideration concerns the economic and social development of the Soviet Union itself. Given the pace of social change in that society – and cultural change, in the sense of the reach of the educational system and of differentiation within it, the development of urban living and the constantly growing access to libraries and other cultural institutions – the moment was bound to come when social development would come into conflict with the norms of yesteryear, urging, and in fact requiring, change in the mechanisms by which society was to be run. Yet equally there was bound to be an effect of cultural drag; people cannot move at the pace that new mechanisms can be devised. The bonds of community, which have been so strong at the foundation of Russian social relations are now required to give way to bonds of secular association.

By bonds of community is meant those suggested by Berman in his treatment of 'parental law', and also by the values that lie behind democratic centralism as they have been described in the foregoing – a view of society as an organism in which the health and well-being of the whole transcend the individual and group interests of its members, and in which the supreme value is loyalty to the social organism. By bonds of association is meant relations formed on a contractual basis between individuals and groups in the furtherance of their interests, involving an acceptance of the legitimacy of such differentiated claims. It is the distinction between *Gemeinschaft* and *Gesellschaft* elaborated by Tonnies – a distinction congenial to a modernisation theory of politics such as has underlain the argument of this study of the communist political monopoly.

The transition from communal loyalty to a fully articulated

associative life cannot be made in a day. This is the sense behind Dahrendorf's celebrated comment that the creation of the rule of law in societies emerging from communism would require six months, the introduction of market six years, whilst sixty years would be required for the formation of civil society.[4] But whatever problems the difficult transition will pose for the Soviet Union, for the purposes of the present analysis it provides useful retrospective insights into the nature of the communist power monopoly, with its strong reliance on bonds of loyalty and its rigorous exclusion of all forms of autonomous association.

As for the other countries that this analysis has treated, the extent to which each will be able to adopt a pluralist form of politics will depend to a great extent, as in the Soviet Union, on the extent to which communal bonds give way to an associative political life. Where an associative life was strong before the communist period, as in the Czech Lands, it may be expected to reassert itself. Where it had not developed to such an extent – as in Hungary – the disappearance of communism will not, or not to the same extent, reveal a society leaning towards associative relations. What it will reveal is simply another version of communality. Loyalty to nation, or loyalty to 'clan' (to borrow an emphasis from the literature on Hungary since 1989),[5] simply replaces the loyalty characteristically required by the communist power monopoly. In such cases, whilst the monopoly will have gone, it will only with difficulty be replaced by a credible pluralism.

It is out of these dissonances – on the one hand that between the communist power monopoly, Russian-born and Russian imposed, and the discrete cultures and pre-communist experiences of the nations that have fallen under Russian influence, and on the other that between communal and associational values – that the fortunes of the various nations of the region will be fashioned. It can be said with certainty that no European society that has known communist rule will remain unmarked by that experience. The question is one of degree, and here variation may be expected to be wide. It is already quite clear, at the time of writing, that a Russia that has sloughed off the power monopoly will retain very substantial elements of the economic structure and political behaviour patterns of the communist period. Rather less obvious, but clear none the less, is the extent to which the overwhelmingly powerful role of the state characteristic of communism will qualify any move towards western models in

East-Central Europe, and in the Balkans.

In sum, if the book is closed on communism in Europe as a system of rule, the book on the heritage of communism remains open. The communist power monopoly has gone, and with it uniformity in the region. The effects of communism remain, however, to influence national fortunes where diversity may be as striking as this uniformity once appeared to be in the day of the communist power monopoly.

Notes
1   Harold J. Berman, *Justice in Russia* (Cambridge, MA: Harvard University Press, 1950), p. 200.
2   *Ibid.*, p. 204.
3   A useful collection of essays on this theme is contained in Archie Brown, *Political Culture and Communist Studies* (London: Macmillan, 1984).
4   Ralf Dahrendorf, *Reflections on the Revolution in Europe* (London: Chatto and Windus, 1990), p. 93.
5   David Stark, 'Privatization in Hungary: From Plan to Market or from Plan to Clan?', *East European Politics and Society*, Vol. 4, No. 3 (1990).

Appendix 1

The *nomenklatura* of the Central Committee of the Polish United Workers' Party

Lists of posts falling under the *nomenklatura* of the Party Central Committee, regional committees and district (town and neighbourhood) committees.

A *Nomenklatura* posts of the Party Central Committee

I Party functions: personnel politically responsible for Party bodies and publications; secretaries of Party committees

1 Heads of Central Committee departments, their deputies, the inspectors, main instructors and political reporters of the Central Committee.
2 The first secretaries and zonal secretaries of regional Party committees.
3 The rector, vice-rectors, institute (group) directors, and scientific workers at the Academy of Social Sciences.
4 The chief and deputy editors of *Trybuna Ludu, Nowe Drogi, Zycie Parti* and *Chlopska Droga*.
5 The directors of the Bydgoszcz and Katowice Party schools.
6 The first secretaries of Party committees in the ministries and central state administration.

II High state functions: the administration of state and economy

1 The president and vice-presidents of the Diet of the People's Republic of Poland.
2 The president and deputy-presidents, the secretary and members of the Council of State.
3 The president and vice-presidents of the Council of Ministers.

4   The president and vice-presidents of the Supreme Chamber of Control.
5   The president and vice-presidents of the Council of Ministers Planning Commission.
6   Ministers, vice-ministers and directors-general.
7   Chairmen to the presidia of regional people's councils.
8   Ambassadors and plenipotentiaries, embassy and legation advisers, consuls-general.
9   The presidents of the Supreme Court and regional tribunals.
10 The public prosecutor of the People's Republic of Poland, his deputies, and regional public prosecutors.
11 The president and vice-presidents of the Polish Academy of Sciences, the administrative secretary and his assistants.
12 The head of the Diet Chancellory and the Council of State Chancellory.
13 The commander-in-chief of the police force, and his deputy.
14 Regional commanders, their first deputies charged with state security, the first deputies charged with the police.
15 The chairman and vice-chairmen of the National Raw Materials Board.
16 The chairman of the National Mining Board.
17 The presidents and vice-presidents of the State Administration.
18 The president and vice-presidents of the National Bank of Poland, and the directors of central banks.
19 Delegates of the government of the People's Republic of Poland.
20 The chairmen and vice-chairmen of the central, regional and sectional boards of the Co-operative Unions.
21 Members of the secretariat of artisan organisations.
22 The directors-general of nationwide industrial unions and of the central management and offices of domestic trade.
23 The regional directors-general of the Polish Railways and of National Telecommunications.
24 The directors-general of the regional unions of Public Works.
25 The commander-in-chief of the Fire Brigade.
26 The directors-general of public institutions (Lot, Orbis, Wars., etc.).
27 The deputy to the permanent Comecon representative of the People's Republic of Poland, the deputy to the Comecon secretary-general nominated by the People's Republic of Poland.
28 Directors of the various Polish offices abroad; the departmental

heads of the Comecon Secretariat and UN Secretariat nominated by the People's Republic of Poland.

III *Functions in social organisations*

1 The president, vice-president and secretary of the Polish Committee of the National Unity Front.
2 The presidents, vice-presidents and secretaries of the Central Trade Union Council; the presidents, vice-presidents and secretaries of the Trade Union Federations.
3 The president, secretary-general and secretaries of the Association of Fighters for Freedom and Democracy.
4 The presidents, vice-presidents and secretaries of the youth organisations.
5 The president of the National Women's Council, and the president of the League of Women.
6 The presidents and secretaries-general of the Higher Technical Organisation and the Polish Economic Society.
7 The chairman of the Higher Council of Co-operatives.
8 The president, *ex officio* vice-presidents and secretaries of the Polish–Soviet Friendship Association.
9 The president and secretary-general of the Society of Polish Journalists.
10 The president and secretary-general of the Union of Polish Writers.
11 The president and secretary-general of the Association of Polish Jurists.
12 The president of the Higher Lawyers Council.
13 The president and vice-presidents of the Union of Agricultural Circles.
14 The president and vice-president of the Union of Agricultural Producer Co-operatives.
15 Full-time presidents, vice-presidents and secretaries of social and cultural associations.
16 The president of the National Defence League.
17 The president and vice-presidents of the Volunteer Firemens Association.

IV *Functions in the Army*

1 The head and deputy-head of the General Staff.
2 The head and deputy-heads of the political directorate of the Army.

3   The inspector-general of Home Defence.
4   The inspector-general of (military) instruction.
5   The Senior Commissariat officer.
6   The inspector-general of the Engineering Corps.
7   The commanders of military regions and their assistants responsible for political matters.
8   Commanders of the Armed Forces and their deputies responsible for political matters in: (a) the air force (b) the navy, (c) aerial defence, and (d) military defence of the frontiers.
9   The head of the Internal Military Corps.
10 The head of the personnel department at the Ministry of National Defence.
11 The head of the (Military) Instruction Inspectorate.
12 The head of the Home Defence Inspectorate.
13 The head of the directorate of the Second General Staff.
14 Persons proposed for the rank of general.

V *Functions in the mass media, publishing houses and scientific institutions*
1   The chairman, deputies and directors-general of the Radio and Television Board.
2   The chairman, vice-chairmen and directors of the 'RSW-Prasa' Board.
3   The chief and deputy editors and the directors of the Polish Press Agency, the Polish 'Interpress' Agency, the Central Photographic Agency, Artistic and Graphic Publications, the Society for Documentary Film Production, and Polish Film News.
4   The director of the publishing co-operative *Ksiazka i Wiedza*.
5   The chief editors of *Ideologia i Polityka* and *Zagadnienia i Materialy*.
6   The directors and chief editors of scientific and literary publishing houses.
7   The chief editors of national circulation dailies, weeklies and monthlies.
8   The directors-general of Polish Radio and Television.
9   The directors of specialised national institutes of scientific research.
10 The directors of the foreign broadcasting service of the Polish Academy of Sciences.

11 Departmental secretaries and assistant secretaries, as well as directors of the Bureau of the Polish Academy of Sciences.

B *Nomenklatura* posts of regional Party committees

I Party functions: personnel politically responsible for Party bodies and publications; the secretaries of Party committees
1 The first secretary and the secretaries of various sections of the district, town and neighbourhood committees.
2 Personnel politically responsible for the regional Party committees.
3 The chief and deputy editors and the secretaries of the regional committee press.
4 The first secretaries of Party committees in higher education; the first secretary of Party committees in the presidia of regional people's councils; the first secretary in the regional police directorate.
5 Full-time secretaries of Party committees in enterprises and combines falling under the regional committee *nomenklatura*, including all those placed under Central Committee management.

II Functions in government bodies, regional administration and the economic apparatus
1 The vice-chairmen and secretaries of the presidia of regional people's councils.
2 The chairman of the Regional Economic Planning Commission, and regional school inspectors.
3 Heads of departments of the regional people's council presidia (as estimated by the executive committees of the regional Party committee).
4 Deputy regional commanders (except the first deputies responsible for State Security and for the Police).
5 Heads of departments of the regional police force (as estimated by the executive committees of the regional Party committee).
6 The vice-presidents of regional tribunals.
7 Deputy regional public prosecutors.
8 The directors of regional penal institutions.
9 The chairmen of (regional) delegations to the Supreme Chamber of Control, the regional inspectors of PIH and OKR.

10   The presidium chairmen of district, town and neighbourhood people's councils.
11   District police commanders and their deputies responsible for State Security.
12   The presidents of district tribunals.
13   District public prosecutors.
14   The presidents of regional administrative tribunals for social insurance.
15   The chairmen of regional arbitration commissions.
16   The directors (presidents) of regional economic organisations, industry unions, regional organs, and regionally administered co-operatives and enterprises (except the chief director of the regional union of Public Works).
17   Regional branch directors of the National Bank of Poland, the Agricultural Bank, the Polish Savings Bank, the State Insurance House, and the Social Insurance Department.
18   The directors-general of key combines and enterprises (and deputy directors if so decided by the regional Party committee).
19   Regional commanders of the Fire Brigade.
20   Directors of medical establishments and of the social services.
21   Leaders of the regional delegations of the General Office for the Supervision of Press, Publications and Public Performances.

III Functions in social organisations
 1   The presidents, vice-presidents and secretaries of regional committees of the National Unity Front.
 2   The presidents, vice-presidents and secretaries of the regional trade-union councils.
 3   The presidents, vice-presidents and secretaries of the regional leaderships of youth organisations.
 4   The president and (full-time) members of the regional leadership of the Association of Fighters for Freedom and Democracy.
 5   The chairmen, vice-chairmen and secretaries of the regional leadership of the Union of Agricultural Circles.
 6   The presidents of the regional women's council and of the regional League of Women leadership.
 7   The presidents, vice-presidents and secretaries of the regional leadership of the Trade Union Federations.
 8   The regional presidents and full-time leaders of artistic, social, cultural, sporting and para-military associations, as well as

professional bodies such as the Higher Technical Organisation and the Association of Polish Jurists.

IV Functions in the mass media, publishing houses and scientific institutions
1 The chief and deputy directors of Polish Radio broadcasting stations and of Polish Television centres.
2 The chief and deputy editors of the main local dailies and cultural and social magazines.
3 The chief and deputy editors of regional press and book publishing houses.
4 The rectors and vice-rectors of higher education establishments.
5 Theatre managers and artistic directors.
6 The directors of (regional) museums.

C *Nomenklatura* posts of district (town and neighbourhood) Party committees

I Functions in the party: personnel politically responsible for Party bodies; secretaries of Party committees
1 Those politically responsible for district (town and neighbourhood) committees.
2 The first secretaries of town committees (not integrated into a district) and of rural communes.
3 The (full-time) secretaries of Party base committees and organisations in enterprises coming under the district *nomenklatura*.

II Functions in government bodies, local administration and the economic apparatus
1 The vice-presidents and secretaries of the presidia of district, town and neighbourhood people's councils.
2 The chairman of the District Economic Planning Commission, and the departmental heads of the district people's council presidia (as estimated by the executive committee of the district Party committee).
3 Primary and secondary school inspectors, the heads of secondary technical colleges.
4 The vice-presidents of district tribunals.
5 Deputy district public prosecutors.

6 Assistant district police commanders (not coming under the regional Party committee *nomenklatura*).
7 The chairmen of people's councils in towns not integrated into a district.
8 The chairmen of commune people's councils, and commune heads.
9 Commune police station chiefs.
10 District commanders of the Citizens' Volunteer Militia.
11 District commanders of the Fire Brigade.
12 The directors of state farms, both integrated and autonomous.
14 The directors (presidents) of district economic organs.
15 Branch directors of the National Bank of Poland, the Agricultural Bank, the Polish Savings Bank, the State Insurance House, SOP, at the level of one or more districts.
16 The directors of industrial-commercial enterprises for public workers and the supply of services (not coming under the regional Party committee *nomenklatura*); the chairman of co-operatives.
17 The directors (heads) of important medical establishments (hospitals, sanitoria).
18 The directors of enterprises forming part of a combine; the directors of factories forming part of a multi-factory enterprise.

III Functions in social organisations
1 The presidents of district committees of the National Unity Front.
2 The presidents of district trade-union commissions.
3 The presidents of the district leaderships of the Association of Fighters for Freedom and Democracy.
4 The presidents of the district leaderships of youth organisations.
5 The presidents of the district leaderships of Agricultural Circles.
6 The presidents of the district women's council and of the district League of Women leadership.
7 The presidents of district physical culture committees.

Warsaw, October 1972

This list was first published in *Revue française de sociologie*, No. 2 (1979), and was translated into English by *Labour Focus on Eastern Europe*, to whom we are grateful for permission to use that translation. Terminology as in that translation.

Appendix 2

The 'Twenty-One Conditions' for Acceptance of a Party into the Third (Communist) International, adopted at the Second Congress of the International in August 1920

The Second Congress of the Communist International rules that the conditions of joining the Communist International shall be as follows:

1 The general propaganda and agitation should bear a really Communist character, and should correspond to the programme and decisions of the Third International. The entire party press should be edited by reliable Communists who have proved their loyalty to the cause of the Proletarian revolution. The dictatorship of the proletariat should not be spoken of simply as a current hackneyed formula, it should be advocated in such a way that its necessity should be apparent to every rank-and-file working man and woman, to each soldier and peasant, and should emanate from everyday facts systematically recorded by our press day by day . . .

2 Every organization desiring to join the Communist International shall be bound systematically and regularly to remove from all the responsible posts in the labour movement (Party organizations, editors, labor unions, parliamentary factions, co-operatives, municipalities, etc.), all reformists and followers of the 'centre', and to have them replaced by Communists, even at the cost of replacing at the beginning 'experienced' men by rank-and-file working men.

3 The class struggle in almost every country of Europe and America is entering the phase of civil war. Under such conditions the Communists can have no confidence in bourgeois laws. They should create everywhere a parallel illegal apparatus, which at the decisive moment should do its duty by the party, and in every way possible assist the revolution. In every country where in consequence of

martial law or of other exceptional laws, the Communists are unable to carry on their work lawfully, a combination of lawful and unlawful work is absolutely necessary.

4 A persistent and systematic propaganda and agitation is necessary in the army, where Communist groups should be formed in every military organization. Wherever, owing to repressive legislation, agitation becomes impossible, it is necessary to carry on such agitation illegally. But refusal to carry on or participate in such work should be considered equal to treason to the revolutionary cause, and incompatible with affiliation with the Third International.

5 A systematic regular propaganda is necessary in the rural districts. The working class can gain no victory unless it possesses the sympathy and support of at least part of the rural workers and of the poor peasants . . .

6 Every party desirous of affiliating with the Third International should renounce not only avowed social patriotism, but also the falsehood and the hypocrisy of social pacifism; it should systematically demonstrate to the workers that without a revolutionary overthrow of capitalism no international arbitration, no talk of disarmament, no democratic reorganization of the League of Nations will be capable of saving mankind from new Imperialist wars.

7 Parties desirous of joining the Communist International must recognize the necessity of a complete and absolute rupture with reformism and the policy of the 'centrists', and must advocate this rupture amongst the widest circles of the party membership, without which condition a consistent Communist policy is impossible . . .

8 In the Colonial question and that of the oppressed nationalities there is necessary an especially distinct and clear line of conduct of the parties of countries where the bourgeoisie possesses such colonies or oppresses other nationalities. Every party desirous of belonging to the Third International should be bound to denounce without any reserve all the methods of 'its own' imperialists in the colonies, supporting not only in words but practically a movement of liberation in the colonies. It should demand the expulsion of its own Imperialists from such colonies, and cultivate among the workingmen of its own country a truly fraternal attitude towards the working population of the colonies and oppressed nationalities, and carry on a systematic agitation in its own army against every kind of oppression of the colonial population.

9 Every party desirous of belonging to the Communist International should be bound to carry on systematic and persistent Communist work in the labour unions, co-operatives and other labor organizations of the masses. It is necessary to form Communist groups with the organizations, which by persistent and lasting work should win over labor unions to Communism. These groups should constantly denounce the treachery of the social patriots and of the fluctuations of the 'centre'. These Communist groups should be completely subordinated to the party in general.

10 Any party belonging to the Communist International is bound to carry on a stubborn struggle against the Amsterdam 'International' of the yellow labor unions. *

11 Parties desirous of joining the Third International shall be bound to inspect the personnel of their parliamentary factions, to remove all unreliable elements therefrom, to control such factions, not only verbally but in reality, to subordinate them to the Central Committee of the party, and to demand from each proletarian Communist that he devote his entire activity to the interests of real revolutionary propaganda.

12 All parties belonging to the Communist International should be formed on the basis of the principle of democratic centralism. At the present time of acute civil war the Communist Party will be able fully to do its duty only when it is organized in a sufficiently thorough way when it possesses an iron discipline, and when its party centre enjoys the confidence of the members of the party, who are to endow this centre with complete power, authority and ample rights.

13 The Communist parties of those countries where the Communist activity is legal, should make a clearance of their members from time to time, as well as those of the party organizations, in order systematically to free the party from the petty bourgeois elements which penetrate into it.

14 Each party desirous of affiliating with the Communist International should be obliged to render every possible assistance to the Soviet Republics in their struggle against all counter-revolutionary forces. The Communist parties should carry on a precise and definite propaganda to induce the workers to refuse to transport any kind of military equipment intended for fighting against the Soviet

---

* i.e., the socialist International Federation of Trade Unions, with headquarters in Amsterdam—ed.

Republics, and should also by legal or illegal means carry on a propaganda amongst the troops sent against the workers' republics, etc.

15   All those parties which up to the present moment have stood upon the old social and democratic programmes should, within the shortest time possible draw up a new Communist programme in conformity with the special conditions of their country, and in accordance with the resolutions of the Communist International . . .

16   All the resolutions of the congresses of the Communist International, as well as the resolutions of the Executive Committee are binding for all parties joining the Communist International. The Communist International, operating under the conditions of most acute civil warfare, should be centralized in a better manner than the Second International. At the same time, the Communist International and the Executive Committee are naturally bound in every form of their activity to consider the variety of conditions under which the different parties have to work and struggle, and generally binding resolutions should be passed only on such questions upon which such resolutions are possible.

17   In connection with the above, all parties desiring to join the Communist International should alter their name. Each party desirous of joining the Communist International should bear the following name: Communist Party of such and such a country, section of the Third Communist International. The question of the renaming of a party is not only a formal one, but is a political question of great importance. The Communist International has declared a decisive war against the entire bourgeois world, and all the yellow Social Democratic parties. It is indispensable that every rank-and-file worker should be able clearly to distinguish between the Communist parties and the old official 'Social Democratic' or 'Socialist' parties, which have betrayed the cause of the working class . . .

21   Those members of the party who reject the conditions and the theses of the Third International, are liable to be excluded from the party.

Source: Robert V. Daniels (ed.), *A Documentary History of World Communism* (London: I. B. Tauris, 1985), Vol. 2 'Communism and the World', pp. 44–7. Punctuation and spelling as in that source.

Chronology

1	Russian Revolution to Second World War
Date	Russia/Soviet Union and international movement *Rest of Europe* Europe in international context
1917	Russian revolution
1918–20	Civil War; 'war communism'
1919	Foundation of Comintern
1920	'21 conditions' for acceptance into Comintern; *European socialists divide over attitude to Russian revolution*
1921	Bolsheviks' tenth congress; ban on fractional activity; New Economic Policy adopted
1920s and '30s	Parliamentary or constitutional democracy cedes to dictatorship in a series of European states
1923–5	Leadership struggle in Soviet Union leads to the defeat of the Trotskyist Opposition
1925	*Bolshevisation of European communist parties*
1928–32	First five-year plan; collectivisation of agriculture; de-kulakisation
1934–38	Stalinist purges

2	Second World War to Gorbachev's accession to power
Date	Soviet Union *Eastern Europe/Yugoslavia* **Western Europe** Europe in the international context
1939–45	Second World War (1941–45 for Soviet Union); final sealing of Soviet frontier

1943	Dissolution of Comintern
1944	'Svolta di Salerno' (PCI)
1945	*End of war brings communist parties to power in Yugoslavia and Albania*
1946	*First nationalisation laws in Yugoslavia*
1947	'Truman Doctrine' presented to US Congress
1946–49	*Communist parties come to power in Poland, Hungary, Czechoslovakia ('Prague coup', 1948) East Germany, Bulgaria and Romania*
1947	Creation of Cominform
1948	*Yugoslavia is expelled from the Cominform*
1949	Creation of CMEA (Comecon)
	Law establishing workers' councils in Yugoslavia
1951	*Yugoslav Federal Planning Commission abolished*
1952	*Yugoslav CP becomes the League of Communists at its sixth congress; end of first Yugoslav reform period*
1953	Death of Stalin
	Disturbances in GDR, Czechoslovakia and Bulgaria.
1955	Khrushchev in power; creation of Warsaw Treaty Organisation
1956	Twentieth Congress of CPSU: 'peaceful coexistence', acceptance of 'parliamentary road to socialism' in Khrushchev's main report; and first de-Stalinisation moves in his 'secret speech'.
	Re-evaluation of Soviet Union leads to defections from CPS and formation of new left in western Europe
	Crises in Poland and Hungary
	Dissolution of Cominform
1957	Khrushchev decentralisation of Soviet economy through creation of *sovnarkhozy*
	Meeting at Camp David between Eisenhower and Khrushchev
1961	*Construction of Berlin Wall*
1962	Khrushchev divides local committees of CPSU into agricultural and industrial secretariats
1963	*New Economic System launched in GDR. Yugoslav constitution extends 'social self-management' to all places of employment*
1964	Khrushchev replaced by Brezhnev as General Secretary of CPSU
	Togliatti's 'Yalta Testament'
1964–5	*Culmination of second major wave of Yugoslav reforms (sixth LCY congress is held end 1964)*

1965	'Kosygin' economic reforms in the Soviet Union
1966	*Rankovic's dismissal marks a victory for reformers in Yugoslavia*
1968	*Prague Spring, followed by 'normalisation'; Hungarian New Economic Mechanism launched*
	Reforms in Swedish CP culminate in change of name; further communist parties move towards 'Eurocommunist' position
1969	World congress of communist parties; disunity makes it the last
1970	*Protest riots in Gdansk force Gomulka's resignation*
1971–2	*'Croatian Spring', followed by normalisation*
1973	Fall of Allende in Chile leads to CPI's 'historical compromise' policy
1974	*Tenth congress of League of Communists of Yugoslavia*
1975	Signing of Helsinki Accords
1976	*Riots in Poland lead to creation of KOR*
1977	*Creation of Charter 77 in Czechoslovakia*
	'Eurocommunist' summit in Madrid; at end of year PCF retreats from this position
1978	*Concordat between GDR's ruling Socialist Unity Party and the Evangelical churches*
	Althusser's broadside against the PCF's norms
1979	*Pope John Paul II visits Poland*
	NATO takes 'dual-track' decision
1979–83	INF missile crisis
	Conflict between Western peace movement and Charter 77 leads to internationalisation of dissent in Eastern Europe
	Series of election results confirms crisis of Western European communist parties
1979	Soviet Union intervenes in Afghanistan
1980	*Disturbances in Pristina mark beginning of terminal series of national tensions in Yugoslavia. Death of Tito. Formation of Solidarity in Poland; first registration of Solidarity in November.*
1981	*December 13: 'state of war' in Poland closes Solidarity period*
	PCI says October revolution has 'lost its propulsive force'
1982	Brezhnev dies; Andropov takes over
1983	Andropov dies; Chernenko becomes General Secretary of the CPSU
1984	*'Szuros article' and Honecker's proposed visit to FRG give hint of independence on part of East European*

	regimes
1985	Chernenko dies

3	The Gorbachev Period

Date	Soviet Union
	Eastern Europe/Yugoslavia
	Western Europe

1985

Mar.	Gorbachev succeeds Chernenko as General Secretary of Central Committee of CPSU
Apr.	Plenum of Central Committee adopts a policy of restructuring and 'acceleration'
Nov.	*Gorbachev meets Reagan at Geneva summit*

1986

Feb./Mar.	Twenty-seventh congress of CPSU
Apr.	Disaster at Chernobyl; *glasnost* is developed in its wake
May	*Milosevic becomes president of the League of Communists of Serbia*
Aug.	Creation of Foreign Economic Commission modifies foreign trade monopoly
Oct.	*Reykjavik summit prepares way for INF treaty*
Nov.	Supreme Soviet passes Law on Individual Labour Activity
Dec.	First disturbances involving non-Russian republics take place in Kazakhstan

1987

Jan.	Gorbachev confronts conservatives at Central Committee plenum; electoral principle to be made real in party and state, and a party conference to be convened
June	Central Committee of CPSU approves economic reform measures, including Law on State Enterprise
Nov.	*Referendum in Poland; result is a set-back for Jaruzelski*
Dec.	*Jakes replaces Husak as Czechoslovak party leader*
	INF treaty signed

1988

Feb.	Acute tension between Armenia and Azerbaidzhan over Nagorno-Karabakh leads to massacres and prolonged hostilities
Mar.	Nina Andreeva letter published
	Committee for the Defence of Ruse set up in Bulgaria
May	Creation of first independent political party since Stalin's accession to power – the Democratic Union. Law on Co-operatives passed.

	Moscow summit
June/July	Nineteenth party conference discusses and approves major political reforms, including electoral competition
Sep.	Reorganisation of Central Committee's central apparatus; creation of six 'commissions' and reduction in number and salience of departments
Sep./Oct.	'Popular fronts' are set up in Baltic republics
Nov.	Estonian Supreme Soviet determines that its laws have precedence over federal laws
Dec.	Constitutional reforms that were approved by nineteenth party conference are passed into law
Dec.'88/ Jan.'89	*Jaruzelski persuades Polish United Workers' Party Central Committee to accept talks with opposition*

1989

Jan.	Democratic Platform created in CPSU
Mar.	Competitive elections are held, in which a number of senior party figures are not elected.
Apr.	*Conclusion of round-table talks in Poland*
May	Gorbachev announces that the Supreme Soviet, through its commissions, is to exercise control over appointments of ministers and ambassadors. Law on Leasing.
	Austria opens its border with Hungary, enabling GDR citizens to pass over to the West. First free newspaper in ex-Soviet bloc goes on sale: 'Gazeta Wyborzca'
May/June	Congress of People's Deputies opens; broadcasted live on TV, it has a major political impact. Radical deputies form the 'interregional group'
June	*Reinterment of Imre Nagy. 'Triangular' talks begin in Hungary.*
Aug.	*Mazowiecki's confirmation in office as leader of first post-communist government in Poland and in the region*
Oct.	*Hungarian Socialist Workers' Party dissolves itself and is reconstituted as the Hungarian Socialist Party; constitutional provision for party's leading role rescinded in Hungary*
Nov.	*Berlin Wall breached. CPCz Party leadership resigns in Prague. Constitutional provision for party's leading role rescinded in Czechoslovakia. Mladenov replaces Zhivkov as Bulgarian party leader*
Dec.	Communist Party of Lithuania splits from CPSU
	Creation of Union of Democratic Forces in Bulgaria. Constitutional provision for party's leading role rescinded in GDR and Poland.

Ceausescu shot in Romania.
Malta summit

1990

Jan.   *Fourteenth congress of Yugoslav League of Communists opens and is adjourned when Slovenian delegates walk out. Constitutional provision for party's leading role rescinded in Bulgaria*

Mar.   **Gorbachev sworn in as executive president. Lithuania declares its independence. Article of constitution guaranteeing party's leading role is rescinded**
Free elections in Hungary

Apr.   *Free elections in Slovenia*

May   **Boris Yeltsin elected president of the Russian republic**
Free elections in Croatia; adjourned congress of LCY, now without the Slovenes, Croats and Macedonians, renounces League's 'leading role', and endorses free elections

June   **Shatalin's '500-day' programme proposed**
Elections in Czechoslovakia and Bulgaria

July   **Twenty-eighth congress of CPSU; Politburo's power is diluted; after the congress a number of prominent leaders leave the party, including Yeltsin**

Aug.   **Press Law comes into effect in USSR**

1991

July   **Political organisation in the workplace banned**
Warsaw Treaty Organisation dissolved

Aug.   **Attempted coup by State Emergency Committee fails**
First fully free elections in Poland. Second elections in Bulgaria bring UDF to power

Dec.   **At a meeting in Minsk Russia, Byelorussia and Ukraine sign an agreement of association; later in month, in Alma Ata, eight further republics join in creation of Commonwealth of Independent States**

Index

Note: Significant references appear in bold type